ALWAYS MANAGING

HARRY REDKNAPP

WITH MARTIN SAMUEL

MY AUTOBIOGRAPHY

EBURY
PRESS

First published in 2013 by Ebury Press, an imprint of Ebury Publishing
A Random House Group company

The image featured on the endpapers of the book is taken from the Tottenham Hotspur
official programme for the Tottenham v West Ham match on 8 April 1966,
where Harry Redknapp scored the first goal of his professional career

The Random House Group Limited Reg. No. 954009

Addresses for companies within the Random House Group can be found at
www.randomhouse.co.uk

A CIP catalogue record for this book is available from the British Library

The Random House Group Limited supports the Forest Stewardship Council® (FSC®),
the leading international forest-certification organisation. Our books carrying the
FSC label are printed on FSC®-certified paper. FSC is the only forest-certification
scheme supported by the leading environmental organisations, including Greenpeace.
Our paper procurement policy can be found at www.randomhouse.co.uk/environment

Designed and set by seagulls.net

Printed and bound in Great Britain by Clays Ltd, St Ives PLC

HB ISBN 9780091917876
TPB ISBN 9780091957575

To buy books by your favourite authors and register for offers visit
www.randomhouse.co.uk

For Sandra,
while I've been managing all these years,
she's the one who's managed me.

CONTENTS

CHAPTER ONE

· ·

THE TRIAL

A feeling of sheer relief. But not like I had ever experienced before. Not the relief of the final whistle on a Saturday afternoon, holding on for three points at Old Trafford. Not the relief of a big Cup win, a title won, or of staying up against the odds. Football's highs and lows were suddenly insignificant. This was a completely different strength of emotion, one I had not felt in all my professional career. I can see her now, the foreman of the jury. Slim girl, nice-looking. Used to come in every day with a newspaper under her arm. I think it was the *Times*. 'Not guilty,' she said, to each charge, very quietly. And this feeling of release swept over me.

The trial lasted fifteen days, but the ordeal overtook five years of my life. That is a lot of thinking time. Many long hours to consider your days as they might be spent. Without Sandra, the love of my life, without my sons Jamie and Mark, without my grandchildren, without my friends, without football. Shut up in prison with … who? Some maniac? I didn't know. Each day in court, I'd look at the twelve people that held my future in their hands. There was a chap wearing a bright white jacket in the middle of January. Another had clothes that were covered in stains. These were the people that would decide my fate? They would never smile; they showed no friendliness at all. Just a blank. What were they thinking? Why did a cheap jacket or a coffee stain even matter to me? Why were the details so important? Some strange thoughts went through my head. What if they were all Arsenal fans? What if they all hated Tottenham Hotspur? You know what some people are like. 'Harry Redknapp? Don't like him, never liked him.' Suppose I got one like that. Each night sleepless, fighting with the pillow. Each morning exhausted, waiting for the taxi to Southwark Crown Court.

The night before the verdict I didn't say goodbye to anybody. No last farewells, just in case it was bad news. My barrister, John Kelsey-Fry QC, always tried to give me confidence. He said the case against me wouldn't stand, that it was outrageous that it had even been brought. But I pushed him to tell me the dark side, the downside. Wouldn't you have done the same, in my position? 'But Kelsey,' I said, 'if it doesn't go right, if they find me guilty, what am I looking at?' I had heard people speculating I might only receive a fine, but he pulled no punches. 'You won't be found guilty,' he said. 'It isn't going to happen. But if it did, it could be two to three years in prison.' Suddenly, I felt very frightened. That was a long sentence, a proper villain's sentence. And his words hung over me, every day, as I prepared for court. I kept telling myself that Kelsey, the cleverest man I had ever met, the best in the business I had been told, was convinced I would be all right. 'This is his job,' I would reassure myself. 'He must know what he's talking about.' And then my mind would come back to the image of that cell, and my cell-mate for two, maybe three, years. How was I going to live? I wasn't sure I could handle it. I knew Sandra couldn't.

I don't think I could have lasted the court case itself without my sons. Jamie came to court with me every day, never left my side, and Mark stayed with Sandra. There was no way I was letting her come to my trial. Being in court would have killed her. It nearly killed me. I simply could not face the thought of her sitting there as well, going through all those emotions, stomach churning in turmoil along with mine.

Life itself was hard enough. I tried to carry on as Tottenham manager, going to our Premier League matches during the case and on one occasion thought it might even be a good distraction to watch our youth team. But those games are smaller, more low key. I couldn't fade into the background, and as I was walking to the stadium I could sense people looking, staring at me. I became convinced they were all talking about me. What were they saying? It was a horrible feeling. I know Sandra found it difficult just going to the shops where she always went. She thought people were gaping, and whispering, too. It felt degrading. Just getting the shopping became a nightmare. Everyone knew where we lived, too, because they'd seen the front of our house on the television news.

One day we went to the supermarket in Bournemouth together and Sandra left her purse at the checkout. I said I would pop back and collect it, but I didn't know the lay-out very well. I saw this door marked 'Exit' and went through it, without realising it was only for use in emergencies. The next think I knew, these huge security guards had my arms up my back, frog-marching me through the underground car park. I was in agony. They were shouting at me, I was shouting back at them – shouting with the pain, too. 'I'm not a thief, I'm the fucking manager of Tottenham,' I told them. At that point, four workmen who were digging up the tarmac spotted me. They all began shouting, too. 'It's Harry Redknapp! All right, Harry? You OK?' 'See?' I told the guards. 'They know who I fucking am!' In the end, we got it resolved, but it only added to fear that I was a marked man. With my name in the papers every week and linked to God knows what, I can imagine what people must have thought when they saw me being led away.

So the idea of having Sandra in that courtroom? I just couldn't. It would have slaughtered me, and slaughtered her, too. I think I would have looked over and cried every time our eyes met and she would have done the same. I decided I couldn't have her anywhere near it. She would be better off out of the way. Her friends were great, Mark was great, the daughter-in-laws were great. They all rallied round and looked after her and she was fine. But the night before the verdict, there was no way I was going to phone up and offer any long goodbyes.

I was struggling with the thought of the consequences myself, but I didn't want to put any doubt in her mind. It would have made her ill, really shaken her to hear that I could go away for many years. So it was difficult, spending that last night alone. And it was a long wait to hear those two little words, I can tell you. The jury went out to make the verdict at around midday, and we were sitting there, in this tiny room that felt like a cupboard. There were the lawyers, my co-defendant Milan Mandaric, Jamie, me ... all afternoon until five o'clock, just looking at each other and waiting to be called back. I felt like I was in another world. Every now and then the tannoy would go and we would hear, 'Smith, court number four.' False alarm, not us. And then back to waiting. By the time it got to late afternoon, we knew we were going to have to return the next day, and that felt even worse.

I went back to the Grosvenor House hotel in Park Lane, where I stayed throughout the trial, with no chance of getting to sleep. I think Kelsey knew that I was scared out of my wits because he offered to come with Jamie and me. 'What a night this is going to be, Kelsey,' I said, because I knew it would be impossible to think of anything but the next morning. When we got there he suggested we go straight to the bar, where he downed a couple of whiskeys then announced we should all go out to dinner. We went up the road, to a steak restaurant called Cuts, owned by Wolfgang Puck, and Kelsey had a few more there as well. I nursed a couple of glasses of red wine in the hope of knocking myself out and getting some rest.

My wine didn't do the trick, unfortunately, and it became another long night. I remember lying in bed wondering about my cellmate again. So many thoughts swirled around my head. What if he's a lunatic? I'm not used to being around people like that. How am I going to cope? And how's Sandra going to get by? Kelsey said between two and three years. He knows, he isn't silly. He's the expert. It's his business. But he said it isn't going to happen. He said it won't happen to me. But it could happen. He admitted that. Two or three years, he said. Round and round like that I went, round in circles until morning came. And those thoughts were not just troubling my mind those fifteen days. I had had nights like that, my mind in turmoil, off and on, for years.

The story began even earlier, in fact, in June 2001, when I agreed to become director of football at Portsmouth. I had left West Ham United and Milan Mandaric, the Portsmouth chairman, offered me a job at Fratton Park, looking after player recruitment. He said he couldn't pay me the wages I was on at West Ham, so he would strike an incentive deal. Each player I brought in, I would receive ten per cent of any profit if we sold him on. Just over a week later, I persuaded Milan to buy Peter Crouch from Queens Park Rangers.

Not that he fancied him. 'Harry,' he said, 'he's the worst footballer I've ever seen in my life. Harry, he's a basketball player. If you think I'm going to pay a million pounds for this player, this useless player, you must be mad.'

I told Milan he was wrong. 'He'll be fantastic,' I said.

In the end, I persuaded him to take a chance. 'OK,' he said, 'but it's your head that's on the block.' I didn't know then how true those words would prove to be. I was right about Crouch, though. He was outstanding for us. We bought him for £1.25 million and sold him to Aston Villa nine months later for £4.5 million – a profit of £3.25 million. As far as I was concerned I was owed ten per cent of that, except by then my job had changed. I wasn't director of football any more; I was Portsmouth's manager.

Instead of ten per cent of the profit on Crouch, I received five per cent. I was probably lucky to get that. Knowing Milan I'm surprised he didn't take his wages, his digs and every other sundry off the commission price. Even so, I wasn't happy. I asked Peter Storrie, the chief executive, where the rest of my bonus was. He said my contract had changed when I became manager and if I had a problem I should talk to Milan about it. So I did. 'You're wrong, Harry,' he said. 'This is a new contract, a manager's contract. You're earning better money now. You get us promoted, you get a big bonus; you win a trophy, you get a big bonus; that bonus from when you were director of football no longer applies. Now you get five per cent of any sale, not ten.'

I was not happy. 'But I bought him and sold him, Milan, and the club made £3.25 million,' I protested.

He wouldn't budge. 'No, that is your new deal: five per cent and no more,' he insisted. I was furious, I really went into one. But the club was doing well, and Milan did not want us to fall out. 'Look,' he said, 'I've got some good investments coming. I'll make some money for you. I'll buy some shares – the stake money is my money, and what we make over the top is yours. I'll look after you, don't worry.'

I said I didn't want that, I wanted my Crouch bonus. I had the hump, but he was adamant.

And that was the plan. But in my mind, that was always my bonus money for Peter Crouch. Milan had his own name for it, but to me it was never anything less than what I was entitled to; only later, when the case was going to court, did I find out that Milan was right all along. I had signed a new contract, a changed contract, and hadn't even noticed. By then, however, that was the least of my problems.

Milan wanted me open an account in Monaco for these investments. He said to use his bank, but I had to go there in person. It sounded like a nice day out. I didn't really know Monaco, and Sandra had never been. We decided to make a weekend of it. Milan gave me directions to the bank. 'Walk up the hill and look for it on the right.' Sandra sat outside in the sun. Milan had told me to ask for the bank's manager by name, David Cusdin. He said he was an Englishman, a big Fulham supporter, and would look after me. Our meeting went like clockwork. I was in there five minutes at most. The last thing Mr Cusdin said was that I would need a security password for the account, if I ever rang up. It could be a name or a number, he explained. I can never remember numbers, so I went for a name. I gave the account the name of my dog, the lovely Rosie, and the year of my birth: Rosie47. I walked out of the bank and back to Sandra and I had nothing: no books, no papers, only what was in my memory. Rosie47. There wasn't even any money in the account at that time. Milan was going to make a deposit and, I'll be honest, I was sceptical it would ever happen. So much so that I forgot about it.

And that's the truth. They tried to make it sound so dodgy in court but I couldn't even remember the name of the bank until it became an issue. I've never been back to Monaco, never saw nor spoke to Mr Cusdin again. The weather was nice, we had a lovely weekend, but the Monaco account wasn't really a part of my life. That was April 2002. I barely gave it another thought until almost two years later.

Portsmouth were in the Premier League by then. It had been a difficult first season, but we were staying up. We put a run together just when it mattered. From March 21 through April we had played six games, won five and drew the other. We beat some decent teams, too: our big rivals Southampton, Blackburn Rovers away, Manchester United, Leeds United at Elland Road. That was the season of the Arsenal Invincibles. They didn't beat us, though, home or away.

Once we were guaranteed to be staying up, I remembered his promise and seized my chance with Milan. It had been a great first season for us. Teddy Sheringham and Yakubu came good at an important time near the end and everyone was delighted, Milan most of all. We had come from miles back. Only a few months previously, everyone thought we were relegation certainties. Now we were getting a second Premier League season. Milan was ecstatic at the end of this match. He was cuddling me in the boardroom. 'I love you, Harry, you are great, Harry.'

No time like the present, I thought. 'Milan, you know those investments you made for me? How did we get on?'

Instantly, his mood changed. 'Ah, disaster,' he said. 'Disaster. Don't worry, let's have a drink.'

'What do you mean, "disaster"?' I pressed.

'I've lost millions, Harry,' he said. 'Millions. The market crashed.'

'So we've got nothing?' I asked.

'There's a little bit left in there,' he said. 'But don't worry, I'll have another go. I'll put some more in and when a good share comes along, we'll see.'

I went back and told Jim Smith, my assistant, about our conversation. 'Harry, are you thick or what?' Jim said. 'I bet he never put anything in there in the first place.' We all started laughing. The main thing was we were staying up. It was time to celebrate. The contents or otherwise of Rosie47 could wait for another day.

In court, the prosecutors tried to depict me as some kind of master criminal, moving money around the banks of Europe to escape tax. Some brain I was, if that was the case, because I volunteered the information about my bank account in Monaco to the investigators. Quest, the company commissioned in 2006 to report on corruption in football, were the first to ask about it. Every manager in the Premier League was interviewed by them. Quest asked me where I banked and I volunteered the information about the extra account in Monaco, as well as my accounts in Britain. It wasn't as if this secret stash had been cleverly unearthed. I told them how it came about, and that they could get further details about what was in there from Milan because I wasn't even sure of the bank's name by then. Now why would I do that, if I had anything to hide? I'd have to be stupid. It would be like a bank robber telling a policeman to search under the floorboards for the loot. I didn't think there was anything wrong with the Rosie47 account. Milan had made an investment for me, the investment was crap, and that's as far as it went. Milan sent a letter confirming this, too. So without me, none of this would have come to light and Quest's man, Nigel Layton, said as much in court. He was fantastic for me, as a witness. He just told the truth. Nobody caught me. I informed them, and without that information they would not have known the account existed. I wasn't bound to disclose everything to Quest – they weren't the police. I could see Mr Layton set the jury thinking. Why would this man reveal all this if he knew it was dishonest?

Quest, and later the police, were on the trail of a specific transfer involving a midfield player at Portsmouth, called Amdy Faye. They wanted to know about a payment of £100,000 made to Faye by his agent Willie McKay. The suspicion was it had been paid to avoid tax. They were asking who at the club authorised this payment: was it me, Peter Storrie, our chief executive, or Milan? I'm the manager, I told them, I don't go into that. Managers don't decide how much the agent gets. That's the job of the chief executive or chairman. I couldn't tell you the wages of my players, and even now I couldn't tell you their arrangements with agents, either. When I was at Tottenham, Daniel Levy, the chairman, dealt with the players over contracts. It was the same at Portsmouth. I wasn't in that meeting. I couldn't have told Quest what Portsmouth paid Amdy, or Willie, that day – or if they paid them anything at all for that matter. I coached the team, I picked the team; I didn't handle the money. Quest accepted I had nothing to do with the £100,000 and Amdy Faye. But when the police picked up on it, all hell let loose.

It was the morning of Wednesday 28 November 2007. I was returning from Germany where I had been watching Stuttgart's match with Glasgow Rangers. I liked the look of Stuttgart's centre-half, a Portuguese player called Fernando Meira. I stayed in the same hotel as Rangers and met up with their manager, Walter Smith, an old friend. Things were going great. My life was good, the Portsmouth team was going fantastic, and I was in a good mood when I arrived back at the airport. I turned on my mobile phone to say good morning to Sandra, and there were so many messages, so many missed calls. I could hear Sandra's voice, in a terrible state, crying down the phone, hysterical. I couldn't understand her. I thought someone had been killed.

So did she. It turned out, that she was in the house alone, it was 6 a.m. and pitch black outside. Suddenly, the buzzer went at the front of our gate, and jammed on. Whoever hit it had pushed it so hard that the thing stuck. So there was a terrible screeching noise and that set off our two dogs barking. Sandra came out of a deep sleep, panicked and in the confusion thought the burglar alarm was going off. She was scared. She was trying to turn the alarm off, but the noise wouldn't stop, and there being no one in the house but her, she immediately thought a burglar was actually inside the property. She didn't know what to do. She looked outside and could see all these lights beyond the gate, so she pressed the buzzer to let them in because she thought it might be someone to help, and suddenly in stormed a crowd of people and cars, policemen, photographers, flashes going off, all piling through our gate.

Sandra's next thought was that there had been a plane crash. She thought the plane had gone down and I was dead – because for what other reason would the police and photographers be there?

It wasn't a burglar, it wasn't a crash – it was a police raid. At dawn, like I was about to go on the run. The photographers were from the *Sun* newspaper, although the police have always denied tipping them off. I still feel angry about it, all these years later. They didn't need to do it like that, as if I were some hardened criminal who might need the heavy mob to subdue him. I wasn't even home. All they did was terrify my poor Sandra. They could have rung me up and asked to interview me. I would have gone down the road to them, or they could have come to me. Search the house, then, do what you want. But instead it was a dozen coppers and my wife, alone and scared to death. Sandra's not an aggressive person. She's not like those women that are married to villains, standing there telling the police to piss off. She's such a gentle person that she ended up making them a cup of tea while they searched our house from top to bottom. Other women would have given them what for, but it's not in her nature.

And do you know what they took away? A computer. A computer that I had bought for Sandra two years earlier at Christmas. She didn't know how to work it; I didn't know how to work it. It was still brand new. I don't think it had even been turned on. That must have been embarrassing down at the station. An unused computer with no material on it. It didn't stop them looking for God knows what, though. They searched everywhere – all to do with Amdy Faye, and I had already convinced Quest that I had no part in that.

So when I came home on the day of the raid, the first thing I had to do was report to the police station in Worthing. I drove down there quite willingly; I didn't even have a solicitor. Peter Storrie was there as well, so I used his man, from Romford. The police asked all the same questions about Amdy Faye's transfer, and received all the same answers. Nothing to do with me; I don't pay the agent's fee. But as it went on, I gave them the same information about my bank details, including the account in Monaco. And their investigation went from there.

That was my first experience of being in a police cell. It's scary. This might sound strange but I kept remembering my mum and dad: good East End people, honest people. What would they think if they could see me here? It seemed so unjust. I brought up a good family, I'm a happily married man, I try to help people if I can. If something needs to be done I turn up. If anything, I'm a soft touch. If the League Managers Association or a charity needs a speaker at a function, they always call me. I know other people have turned it down, but I still go. What have I done to deserve this? If I had been crooked I would have held my hand up, took my punishment like a man. But I knew I hadn't done anything wrong. I thought about all the people that must have been through the courts over the years, knowing they were innocent yet still found guilty. My mum and dad are dead, but I still wondered what they would say if they knew about this. It felt wrong, and very chilling, to be down in those cells for five hours at a time.

It was just me and a policeman most of the time. Bars and no windows. He makes formal announcements on a tape – the time and the date and the name of the person being interviewed – then he would ask questions matter of factly and I would reply. Meanwhile, there were real crooks coming in, some nasty-looking blokes who had been arrested. I just sat there thinking, 'How am I in with this lot? Amdy Faye? What has that got to do with me? What have I done? It's between the agent and the player. Maybe the agent, the player and the club. It's certainly not my business.' I think, after several hours, I managed to convince them that this was not my doing. But I was still furious about the raid on my home, and I took the police to court. My legal advisors said the raid was illegal and a year later a High Court judge agreed. He said the search warrant had been issued unlawfully and there were wholly unacceptable procedural failures in the way the warrant was obtained.

My solicitor, Mark Spragg, called for an inquiry into how the *Sun* newspaper came to be in on the search, too. One officer had made about ten late-night phone calls to the paper on the eve of the raid. The internal police investigation accepted his explanation. He was calling to issue invites to the Christmas party because he'd got a lot of friends there.

At first, I was just being interviewed by police officers. Then the tax men from Her Majesty's Revenue and Customs got involved. And although the investigation started off being about Amdy Faye, the fact I had mentioned the bank account in Monaco to Quest and the police gave HMRC an excuse to go after me. I always wondered whether pursuing the police over that illegal raid counted against me, whether when the police lost that case they became desperate to get their own back because, out of the blue, the bank account in Monaco became important and Amdy's £100,000 was forgotten. Peter and Milan were charged over it, but not me, although the police now wouldn't let their additional case against me go. These were strange times all around, and somebody close to Portsmouth was certainly out to make mischief for me because, in addition to the bad publicity surrounding the HMRC investigation, two stolen letters were being touted around newspapers to place an even greater stain against my character.

I've got my suspicions over who the spiteful informant was, but I will never know for sure. The first stolen letter concerned the Quest investigation. It was Milan's reply to Quest, explaining the story behind the Monaco bank account. The second was a disciplinary letter concerning a row I had with Milan during my time at Portsmouth. It was a fuss about nothing, ancient history – not least because by then I had moved from Portsmouth to Tottenham – but it showed that somebody was trying to blacken my name.

A telephone call from the editor of the *Sun* alerted me to it. He said that the newspaper had been offered a letter sent by Milan during our time at Portsmouth, threatening to sack me if I spoke to him in a disrespectful manner again. The source wanted payment because the letter was detailed and said that I had sworn at Milan a number of times in the course of our argument. It's true, I had. I remember the row very clearly. It was early in the season, 2003–04, one Friday night before a match against Manchester City. We were having dinner and I was telling Milan about a player I had been to watch in Italy, a left-back. He looked fantastic and was coming out of contract. Milan said, 'Harry, he's not a left-back, he's a centre-half.'

I said, 'I went to watch him last week, Milan. He's a left-back. What makes you think he's a centre-half?'

Milan replied that Peter Storrie said he was a centre-half.

I turned to Peter, who was sitting with us. 'How do you know he's a centre-half?' I asked, by now getting quite angry. 'I watched him play left-back. He's a left-back.'

'Well, my stepson checked it online,' Peter explained, 'and they've got him down as centre-half.'

That was it. I went at the pair of them. 'Well, why don't we make your stepson the fucking chief scout?' I raged. I then turned on Milan. 'What fucking chance have I got here with you lot?'

I didn't stop there. I gave him a lot of grief, using some very colourful language, going on and on. It turned into a proper row.

The next day at City, Milan wouldn't even talk to me. I went up to the directors' box to watch the first half, sat next to him, and he moved up one seat he was that upset. Every time I tried to say something he turned his back. We should have won the match, but drew. The mood was tense. Then we got a big win over Bolton Wanderers, 4–0, to go top of the league, with Sheringham on form again. Now Milan wanted us to be friends once more. The problem was, he'd already sent the letter, warning me over the language I used towards him in Manchester. And so a copy of it sat in his drawer, meaningless, until somebody got hold of it and tried to sell it to the *Sun* for £10,000 six years later.

The editor said they had no intention of buying the letter, or publishing it, but he wanted to warn me that someone was trying to trip me up. The next weekend, that person succeeded. I received a call from Rob Beasley, a reporter at the *News of the World*. It was the eve of the 2009 Carling Cup final, Tottenham versus Manchester United, and he had the letter Milan had sent to Quest about the bank account in Monaco.

It had been taken, obviously, from a file at Portsmouth. Beasley admitted paying an informant £1,000. The seller had clearly lowered his price after getting no joy from the *Sun* first time. I cannot think the two calls were a coincidence. It is too far-fetched that a pair of confidential letters go missing, and both end up with newspapers in the same week. Beasley started by asking me questions about the bank account. I'll admit, I just wanted to get rid of him. He was trying to ruin my preparations for a huge match with Tottenham and I certainly didn't think he deserved to hear every last private detail. We ended up arguing and the paper printed the story anyway. Considering the letters were stolen it seems remarkable to me that the *News of the World* investigation would play such a large part in HMRC's prosecution case, and that Beasley would be a key witness. Nobody seemed to worry about the theft, just about my bank account.

And, yes, I know some people think it was all an act, me being a mug with money. I know they see the wealth I have accrued from football, my nice house on the south coast, and assume I must know every trick in the book. But it isn't like that. I'm not smart with money; in fact, I wish half of the things I have read *were* true. I had an account in Monaco, but I couldn't remember the name of the bank. When I came across Mr Cusdin's name in my mobile telephone a year or so later, I couldn't even recall who he was. I didn't even notice that the transfer bonus portion of my contract at Portsmouth had changed. When HMRC were going through my personal finances with a fine-tooth comb, and we needed to account for every penny, I received a call from my accountant.

'What are you doing with your *Sun* money?' he asked. I didn't know what he meant. 'Your money from the *Sun* newspaper, for your column,' he explained. 'Where is it, what have you been doing with it?' I said it would be in the bank. He said it wasn't. So we contacted the *Sun*, and it turned out they hadn't paid me for eighteen months. I didn't know.

Obviously, football managers are well paid, and not having to think about money doesn't really help a man like me. I go to a hole in the wall, I've got a number memorised somewhere, I get £150 out, put it in my pocket and I'm happy. As long as I've got £150, I never worry. As for the rest, I'm hopeless. I'm not proud of that – I'm ashamed, really. Sandra does everything, and she was a hairdresser as a young girl not the head of Barclays Bank. Neither of us are really the smartest, financially. For years, my accountant ran my life. He had complete control and I was totally reliant on him, which was not a healthy situation. Now my old secretary from my days at Bournemouth, Jenny, comes around and helps Sandra pay the bills or sorts out a few letters. As for me, I'm nothing to do with any of it. Sandra hides our bank statements most of the time. We're paying for the grandkids to do this and that, we put some of them through school, and I don't know the half of it. When a bill comes in that I might not like, Sandra probably pays it, then tears it up. What Harry doesn't know won't hurt him – that seems to be the policy.

My dad wouldn't have been any different. I think a lot of people, a lot of old East Enders certainly, didn't go in for anything too complex. My mum kept what she had, which wasn't a lot – a couple of little rings, maybe – in a tin on the balcony of their old block of flats in Stepney. Any money they had between them went in a biscuit barrel. They didn't have a bank account; they didn't go to the bank, they paid their bills in cash and that was how it was. Maybe I haven't moved on enough from that world. Until earlier this year, I still had the same old Nokia phone. I don't send emails, I can't work computers. Every year I insist I'm going to get a smart phone or a laptop. Then another year goes by, and I've done nothing.

The phone call to tell me I would be charged came from my barrister, Mr Kelsey-Fry. 'Bad news, I'm afraid,' he began, and I knew. I felt sick, but he sounded absolutely furious. 'I can't believe it,' he kept repeating. 'I've read it and it's scandalous. This is not right. This should not be going to court.' I was just in a mess. 'I'm going to be dragged through the mud every day,' I told him. 'I don't know if I can handle it. Every day in the papers, on the television, my grandkids seeing this.' He told me I had to handle it, that I had to stay strong, but it definitely had an effect on my health. I don't think it is a coincidence that I needed to have minor heart surgery around the time the case was due to be heard. They called it a procedure, not even an operation, but the stress was clearly taking its toll. We kept thinking the Crown Prosecution Service would pull the case and it wouldn't go the distance, but then the day came and I was walking into Southwark Crown Court. Being on the witness stand was the most traumatic experience of my life.

I tried to remain upbeat, but look back and laugh? It will be a long time before I feel able to do that. The only moment of light relief across the whole fifteen days came before the trial got underway. I'd never been in court before, so I did not know the whole process of picking the jury. A large pool of jurors enters the court and are sworn in; then twelve are picked at random by computer. They all stand as the names are called out. Number one juror takes his seat, then number two. We got to number six and this gentleman was announced as Peter Crouch. He was 6 feet

6 inches and skinny – it could actually have been Crouchy! Everyone in the courtroom started laughing, but there was nothing anyone could do: the computer had spoken and Peter Crouch was on the jury. The rest of the jurors were sworn in and we broke for lunch, ready to start the case that afternoon. You couldn't make it up. But this alternate Peter Crouch never got to play his part in our trial because a reporter from the *Guardian* was so excited with his involvement that he put the news on Twitter. For obvious reasons, jurors cannot be named publicly, but Crouch's details were in the public domain, with the added information that he used to work for Tottenham! So when everyone returned they informed the judge, he had a think about it and concluded the only way forward was for a new jury to be selected. So that was the end of Peter Crouch.

They tried to get me in the back way to court every day, tried to get me down the stairs and away at night without too many people seeing me, but it was still as frightening as hell. I can remember watching Milan on the witness stand, and he was so clever, so confident and quick-witted. The prosecuting QC, John Black, alleged that Milan had only got me to go over to Monaco so that he could pay me offshore and save the tax. 'Yes, Mr Black,' Milan replied. 'I paid £100 million in income tax up to that period but, I remember it now, I woke up that morning and thought, "Milan, your life is boring, have a bit of excitement today, get Harry involved, do something wrong, break the law. You can save £12,000 in income tax. Send Harry to Monaco, open an account, tell him you're going to break the law together and have some fun." I have paid £9 million in income tax this past year, £100 million in my life,

I have employed 40,000 people, but this day, this wonderful day, I decided to break the law over £12,000. And that's what I said to Harry: "If we end up in court, what does it matter?"'

It was brilliant, listening to him. I could see the girls in the jury laughing. They loved him. Milan can be very charming when he wants to be. He came over as a class act and that was fantastic for us.

When it was my turn, I felt totally different. I'm not Milan. I'm not at ease in public situations like that. And I haven't got the brains of the guys asking the questions, either. To make it worse, Detective Inspector David Manley, the policeman who headed up the four-year investigation, came into the court to watch me in the witness box. It was the only time we saw him. He sat directly in front of me, in the line of vision between myself and Mr Black. He was looking at me and through me at the same time, with a glare on his face. It was a scary look and it unnerved me, to be honest. As I was looking over to answer Black, my eyes were drawn to Manley, and then I couldn't even remember what Black had asked me. My mind kept going blank. His presence made it much harder for me.

People think I must hate the police after my experience, but I don't. The desk sergeant at the local station where I went to be interviewed was always as good as gold with me. He was a Newcastle United fan, a big, tall, intimidating man, but he couldn't have been nicer. Manley was different. I felt he was driving the case against me all the time, even when others might have seemed uncertain, and I wouldn't be surprised if he was still seething over my complaint about the raid at our house. It was a strange experience being in court with people who were trying to put you away. I would get in a lift and there would be a couple of the policeman who were lined up against me, and we would rise in silence to the same room on the same floor. Then they would sit thirty yards from me, staring. When I left to go downstairs at the end of the day, they were walking beside me in the same direction. Some people compared it to the two teams in a football match, the opposing sides – but when the final whistle blows on a Saturday you all go off and have a drink together. This was different; it felt very weird. No football manager has ever tried to put me in prison – and that was Manley's aim. Milan went and shook hands with him at the end, but I couldn't. Even now, I try to be very careful about my driving speed.

I can hardly bear to recall how desolate it felt on the witness stand at times. I stood there being questioned over two days by a man who had probably been to Eton, or some wonderful university, and would be a million times more educated than me. I'm sure John Black is a nice guy and I know he had a job to do, but he was questioning me and it felt very intimidating because, obviously, I knew he was on another level intellectually. And I just had to stand up there and do my best, knowing that one wrong word, one lapse of memory or mental blank, could put me away. That is the scariest thing. I had John Kelsey-Fry on my side and he helped, but it was still a hellish, nerve-racking experience.

Right at the end of the first day of questioning, with Manley staring, and the pressure of the constant accusations, I lost my train of thought. Black asked me something and I couldn't answer. I had what I wanted to say in my head, and then it just went, and I got really flustered. I didn't even know how to answer the question; couldn't remember what the question was. I just felt mentally exhausted.

And I think Judge Anthony Leonard simply took pity on me. It was ten to four and we usually wrapped up at four, but he called time earlier that day. I think he knew. He was a fair man. He could see I was mentally out on my feet, he could see that Manley's presence was unsettling me badly, and I think this was his way of playing fair. Black had me on the ropes and was about to hit me on the chin again, when the judge announced that we had heard enough for one day. I felt like a boxer, saved by the bell.

Once I was off the witness stand it all became much clearer. Very patiently and calmly, Mr Kelsey-Fry took me through what I was being asked. I had it completely muddled, all the wrong way round. I wasn't really thinking straight by then. Jamie said it was like that moment when Henry Cooper had Cassius Clay on the ropes, and then he came out a different man in the next round. We came back to the Grosvenor House, went back to my room, changed, went up the road and had a bit of dinner and it all settled down. 'We got you back in the corner, towelled you down, put some smelling salts up your nose, sent you back into the witness box the next morning, and you've knocked him out,' Jamie said. He was right, apart from: for smelling salts read a few glasses of wine.

It was midday when the judge summed up and, as I've said, the next morning before the jury reached its verdict. I just feel lucky to have had Mr Kelsey-Fry on my side. Put simply: he's a genius. Loves Chelsea FC, great golfer, great character – it was my best day's work, engaging him. In fact, if there was one positive from my time in court it was the privilege of watching Kelsey at work. He was razor-sharp, picked up on everything, and the court came alive when he spoke. I even noticed the press gallery getting excited. He had such charisma, a real aura, you felt the jury were with him because they listened so intently. I felt sorry for some of the guys he cross-examined, like Rob Beasley. It was a mismatch.

And yet, for all the confidence and hope he gave me, when the tannoy announced that we were to return to court for the verdict, a feeling of dread swept over me. It was one thing for Mr Kelsey-Fry to believe in me, but twelve jurors had to, as well, and throughout, try as I might, I could detect no helpful vibes from anybody. What did they think of me? I simply did not know. Throughout, Milan had been extremely positive. 'This will be OK, this will be OK,' he kept telling me. Suddenly, he changed his tune. 'What do you think?' he asked, as we stood there. 'I don't know, what do you think?' I replied. 'I don't know,' he said. Then I was scared. We were just waiting. Guilty or not guilty. The head of the jury was Jamie's girl, but what did that matter? If she said 'guilty' I went to prison just the same. I didn't have a washbag on me, I didn't have spare clothes. Where do they take you? Do you go straight there? Suddenly I realised I didn't know the answer to any of these questions.

Not guilty.

I didn't cry during the court case, but I did when I saw Sandra later that day. They had laid food on back at the hotel, and a lot of my friends and supporters were there, but it was too overwhelming for me. I just wanted to get home to her. I jumped in my car and drove south. I needed to be back with Sandra again. People think I must have had a big party that night, but I was in bed by nine o'clock. We had both been left completely exhausted by the ordeal. I hadn't slept for fifteen days, and I wouldn't have thought she had, either. We felt like we had the flu. All we wanted to do was close our eyes and rest easy.

Meanwhile, back in London, imaginations were running wild. Fabio Capello had quit as England manager, and, a free man, honour and reputation intact, I was the runaway favourite to be his replacement.

CHAPTER TWO

....

THREE LIONS

On the steps of Southwark Crown Court, all I could think about was getting back to normality of some kind, but within hours my life and career were turned upside down again, by events completely out of my control. On the morning I was acquitted, Fabio Capello stepped down as England manager, and I was immediately installed as favourite for the job. Everyone said I was the people's choice, the only choice, and I am still asked quite regularly about what went wrong. I wish I knew for certain. Nobody at the Football Association has ever explained why I was overlooked and not even asked for an interview. I have heard all the stories about my fractured relationship with Sir Trevor Brooking, but I cannot bring myself to believe that he would have turned the whole of the FA board against me, even if we have never been best friends.

Sometimes, one face fits and another doesn't. Simple as that. Roy Hodgson, who got the job, was always going to be more the FA's cup of tea than I was. I think with the FA there are certain managers who are considered a little rough around the edges. Indeed, if you look at the people from football that get on at the

FA, men like Sir Trevor or Gareth Southgate, they do all seem a certain type. Don't get me wrong, Gareth's a good lad, a great boy, and I like him a lot. But if you think about that generation of players from the 1990s, why him and not another aspiring manager who might be a little less polished? It doesn't matter who you are on the football field, but the FA offices seem to be the one area of the game where snobbery exists. No disrespect to Roy, but I think we can all see that he is more of an FA man, and that the chairman at the time, David Bernstein, would seem more comfortable in his company. Roy came up through the FA's system and has always been close to the organisers of the game, UEFA and FIFA. He is on their coaching panels at major tournaments. He is just the type that fits the bill.

Roy was one of a generation of players who progressed as a disciple of the coaching principles of Charles Hughes at the FA. There was a bunch of them: Roy, Bob Houghton and Brian Eastick. They came out of non-league football but from an early age were very interested in coaching. They never quite made it as players, but they thought about the game and were always on the FA courses, and once they had got their qualifications these guys went to work all over the world. Bob Houghton has managed everywhere, from Sweden to China, but I always thought of him firstly as an FA man. For that reason, I don't see it is a great coincidence that Roy is now the manager of England, and Brian Eastick takes England's under-20 team. It is as if they were groomed for the job: they were around the FA's senior people from such a young age; they would know exactly how the FA would want an England manager to act.

I'm not knocking Roy. He's got great experience, and he's been around and managed some of the greatest clubs in the world, including Inter Milan and Liverpool. I think he ticks the FA's boxes as England manager just fine. And maybe I don't – well, not in the FA's eyes anyway. Also, at least one of the stories that circulated about the obstacles to my appointment was true: it would have cost the FA an absolute fortune to prise me away from Tottenham.

I have said before that I am useless with contracts but, even by my standards, the one I signed on leaving Portsmouth in 2008 was a cracker. I didn't so much have golden handcuffs at Tottenham, as golden handcuffs, a golden strait-jacket and golden leg irons, locked in a golden box. I don't know about Harry Redknapp, but Harry Houdini would have struggled to get out of White Hart Lane on the terms of my deal.

Don't get me wrong, I was well paid at Tottenham and very thankful for that. But the League Managers Association took one look at my contract and said it was probably the worst one that had ever been signed with regard to release clauses. If the FA put out any feelers at all they would have quickly discovered that it could have cost more than twice Capello's annual salary to compensate Tottenham for my services. I'm sure the FA would deny they were interested anyway, they always like to say they got their number-one choice, but maybe what helped make their minds up was the thought of writing a cheque in the region of £16 million to Tottenham chairman Daniel Levy. He is known for driving a hard bargain at the best of times and, on this one, he had all of us over a barrel.

If we go back to the start of the 2008–09 season, I was manager of Portsmouth and very happy. The tax investigation was rumbling on in the background but, professionally, life was great. I lived twenty-five minutes from our training ground near Southampton Airport, I loved the club and the club seemed to love me. We were in Europe and had just won the FA Cup. We had a good team, and a young Russian owner, Alexandre Gaydamak, whose father, people told me, was as wealthy as Roman Abramovich. Alexandre said he wanted to bring top players in, and we did. We bought Lassana Diarra and Glen Johnson. I took Sylvain Distin on a free from Manchester City. Portsmouth, at that time, had a really strong squad, and I think the success of the players that have moved on proves it. I am very proud of what we achieved in my time there.

So it had not even crossed my mind to leave when I took the phone call to say that Daniel Levy wanted to meet me. I wasn't even that keen, to be frank. It certainly didn't feel like an ambitious move. Portsmouth were playing in the UEFA Cup and I thought the club was going places. Then Peter Storrie, our chief executive, rang to say that Tottenham had asked for permission to speak to me, and it had been granted. I was more than a little surprised. Still, if the club didn't want to keep me, maybe I should hear what Spurs had to say. I arranged to meet Daniel Levy at his house, but was already having misgivings.

All the way on the journey I was mulling it over in my mind. Did I really want to leave my lovely life at Portsmouth? Was this a good move for me? I was about fifteen minutes away when the phone rang again. It was Phil Smith, an agent I knew well and had worked with before. 'I hear you're going to speak to Daniel Levy,' he said. 'Who's doing your deal?' I told him nobody. I didn't have an agent and, besides, there was no deal. In fact, I was just about to call Tottenham and tell them I wasn't interested; I was going to turn the car around and go home. 'Don't do that,' said Phil. 'Just speak to Daniel. I'll come along and we'll all have a talk. I'm sure we can work something out.'

I agreed, but something still didn't feel right. I called Peter Storrie. 'Peter, I'm not going to take it,' I said. 'I don't know whether I want to get into this and I'm happy where I am.'

Peter's attitude surprised me. 'You're mad, Harry,' he said. 'Mad. It's a great opportunity. You've always wanted to manage a big club and this is your chance. You'll do great, you've got to take it.'

Now I really didn't know what to think. I'd felt sure he would be pleased that I was staying. 'I'm just not so keen on it, Pete,' I said. 'Life's good, I'm enjoying the football and even if they pay me more, the extra few quid isn't going to change anything for me. I've done all right.'

'No, you must take it,' he said. He sounded quite insistent. 'Look Harry, as a friend I'll level with you. The truth is that Alexandre wants to sell the club. So he won't be buying any new players in the short term and if he doesn't find a buyer he might start to sell players.'

'What does the owner say about me in all this?' I asked him.

'He said he thinks you should go, too,' Peter replied. 'He wants you to take it, Harry, he thinks it would be good for you.'

I carried on to Daniel's house. Despite what Peter had told me, I still couldn't understand why Portsmouth were so happy to wave me goodbye but, once there, I soon found out. They had already agreed a fee of £5 million in compensation with Tottenham for me. They were obviously thinking, 'Get Harry off the wage bill, get £5 million in, give the job to Tony Adams and we're quids in.' They would have pushed me out the door, if they could. It would have been so easy to keep me. Had they said, 'No, Harry's our manager, he got us into Europe and we want him to stay,' there would have been no quibble from me. But that wasn't going to happen.

So I arrived, Phil arrived, and he and Daniel went away to talk money, while I waited. Phil came back, told me what the deal was – it wasn't that much improvement from my salary at Portsmouth – and said that Daniel wanted me to take charge of a home match against Bolton Wanderers the next day. I accepted, but with more of a deep intake of breath and a resigned sigh than a jump for joy. Tottenham were bottom, with two points from eight matches, and had to win. OK, here we go then. We did the deal. Phil negotiated a good bonus for keeping them up and I felt certain I could do that, but if I ever wanted to leave for another club, Tottenham's compensation package was huge, certainly several times more than it would cost Tottenham to sack me. Phil's lawyer and the League Managers Association looked at it and the consensus was that it would not stand up in law because it was so heavily weighted on Tottenham's side. We asked the club to change it and they refused, but, nonetheless, it was decided to go ahead and sign.

And I am not saying that was why I did not get the England job. For all I know, on the day Capello left, Roy may have been their first choice, but it would have taken one telephone call to find out my contractual situation, after which the FA would know they would have to go to war with Daniel Levy. Did they fancy that? I know I wouldn't. Daniel loves a fight about money: he's a very hard-nosed businessman. Get him on a bad day and I would have ended up far more expensive than Capello – and the FA were already getting a lot of criticism over Capello's £6-million-a-year salary. Of all the reasons doing the rounds for me not becoming England manager, the compensation issue makes most sense. And, in the end, it was probably for the best. The England job suits Roy.

He's a good man, he's their man; they got the guy that fitted and I can only wish him well.

Yet these thoughts come with hindsight. On the day Capello walked away from England, everybody was saying there was only one man for the job and, at that moment, all obstacles seemed surmountable.

The England job had become vacant previously, of course, not least in 2007 when Steve McClaren failed to get the team to the European Championship finals in Austria and Switzerland. I never paid much attention at the time. We all know the qualification level to be our national manager, and no current English-born coach had reached that mark. I wouldn't have put myself in the frame then, and I wouldn't have put many others in, either. English managers were just not getting the big club jobs and therefore weren't experiencing high-level international competition. We weren't the ones competing in the Champions League every other week. Sir Alex Ferguson and Arsène Wenger had been at Manchester United and Arsenal for ever, and the other clubs put their faith in foreign bosses: Rafael Benítez followed Gérard Houllier into Liverpool; Chelsea had appointed José Mourinho and then Avram Grant. No one was giving an Englishman a chance to have a tilt at the Champions League, or even establish a decent winning record in the Premier League. Look at how long David Moyes had to wait at Everton before getting a chance to manage Manchester United.

Yet for me, four years on from McClaren's departure, it felt different. I had won a major trophy, the FA Cup with Portsmouth, I had taken Tottenham to the quarter-finals of the Champions League and established them as a club capable of finishing in the top four. We had beaten Inter Milan, knocked out AC Milan; I had handled good international players and improved others, such as Gareth Bale. There was a groundswell of support for me and I felt it wherever I went. Every time I got in a taxi, every time I went to a football match, the people were for me. The press seemed supportive, too, writing as if my appointment was a foregone conclusion, and I began to think it was almost nailed on, if I wanted it. And I did want it. It would have been a tough call but, had they offered me the job, I probably would have taken it. At the time, I forgot the compensation clause and the other obstacles, and thought only about the positives the job could bring.

I know some of my positive comments about becoming England manager upset Tottenham, but I was only speaking honestly. Daniel wasn't happy that I came out and said that I would like the England job, but I did not intend that statement as a snub to Tottenham. People do not realise how intense the questioning can get when the England position is vacant. For those that are considered candidates, every press conference becomes a bit of an ordeal. You are asked incessantly, 'Are you interested? Would you take it? Are you happy at Spurs?' Every answer is picked over for clues. If I said I was happy with Spurs that was interpreted as a suggestion I might turn down England; if I said I would be honoured to be England manager, I was poised to reject a new contract with Spurs. And I'm not really the sort of bloke to say, 'No comment.' Well, not at the thousandth time of asking, anyway. So I gave the reply I thought was most diplomatic: I am very happy at Tottenham, but it would be difficult for any Englishman to turn down the national job. I still think that's a fair assessment and respectful to all parties. And, let's face it, I was not revealing any state secrets there. It is the pinnacle of your career to manage your country, and if an English manager is offered the job, it would be difficult to turn down.

I think Daniel felt I was being disloyal for saying this, particularly as Tottenham had offered such fantastic support throughout my court case. But that was one of the reasons I didn't see any harm in making an open statement. Everyone at Tottenham knew how I felt about their backing for me in a crisis. I didn't think that bond could be damaged by the honest admission that an English manager is always flattered to be linked with managing England. I still don't see why that came as a slap in the face to them.

Some people think I became distracted once the speculation around England arose, but I don't agree. We still finished fourth, which the club would have been delighted with when the season began, and nobody could have anticipated the set of circumstances by which Chelsea denied us a place in the Champions League. We had injuries and lost momentum, that was why we couldn't hold on to third place. It wasn't as if I was sitting there mapping out starting line-ups for England when I should have been making plans with Tottenham. Professionally, it was always Tottenham first – it was just hard not to feel excited by the potential in that England squad.

All the senior players seemed to be up for me to get the job. I got quite a few text messages at the time from players saying they would love me to manage England: Steven Gerrard, Wayne Rooney, Rio Ferdinand, John Terry.

So there was no time wasted planning for the England job because, as an English manager, I already had my own opinions about the national team. We all do. I'm sure José Mourinho knows what he would do with Portugal right now, if he were asked, and

Arsène Wenger will feel the same about France. I was no different. Even when Capello was in the job and settled, I knew exactly how I wanted the England team to play.

And I knew the man to get them to do it, too. When Tottenham played Swansea on 1 April 2012, I pulled Brendan Rodgers aside after the game and said that if all this speculation about England was true, would he consider coming to the European Championships in the summer, as my part-time coach? I loved what he had done with Swansea, the way he had taken players who had not been encouraged to play adventurous football previously and turned them into outstanding technical, thinking footballers. I thought he would be perfect to develop those ideas with England. I don't think a guy like Brendan would be a gamble for England at all. At Swansea he had Garry Monk, a journeyman professional who used to be with Barnsley, Sheffield Wednesday and Torquay United among others, and Ashley Williams, 159 games for Stockport County, and suddenly they were knocking it about like Franz Beckenbauer and passing the ball into midfield. I thought if Brendan could do that with them, what would he be like with Rio and Terry, or Rooney and Gerrard?

And Brendan was up for it. I told him I wanted England to play with as much technical ambition as Swansea and that he would be ideal for the summer tournament; and he seemed really keen. If I got the job, he said, he would speak to the people at Swansea to get their permission. 'It would be a great experience for you, Brendan,' I told him. 'I want England to play like you play. Pass the ball, play and play and play.' Some people reading this may think it means I was distracted, but I can assure you the conversation took five minutes and the idea was in my head before the job became available. I had been saying it for months previously, that the FA should get a guy like Brendan Rodgers involved with England. I was convinced his way should be England's way, too. So there was never a distraction. I was still totally focused on Tottenham. And we beat Swansea 3–1 that day, by the way.

So on 1 April I was contemplating the way forward for England with Brendan Rodgers – and on 29 April the FA offered the job to Roy Hodgson. I'll admit, I thought it was mine. Everyone seemed so certain, everyone I met from all parts of the game seemed utterly convinced it was my job. I went to a dinner for the London Football Coaches Association, and Gareth Southgate got me up on stage and interviewed me as if I were the next England manager. Sir Trevor Brooking was there that night, too. He was on the FA panel charged with making the appointment. It was not as if he walked out in protest at what Gareth, another FA man, did. I was being made to feel that I was the only show in town.

We had played very well against Blackburn Rovers on the day of Roy's appointment, winning 2–0. I was staying in London that night and I was just pulling into the car park at the hotel when a newsflash came on the radio to say Roy had been offered the England job. It felt strange. After all the speculation it would have been understandable had I been disappointed, but I had a greater feeling of a weight being taken off. Yes, it was a shock, but it meant that, in the end, I didn't have a decision to make. I didn't have to choose between my club and England. The FA had made the call for me. It had been one hell of a year, first with the trial and then this. Now, I thought, it was really back to normal. No more questions, no more dilemmas. I could just get on with managing Tottenham and now, with England gone, I couldn't see myself leaving the club.

The FA's decision came as a surprise, but I wasn't about to lock myself in my room with a bottle of whisky. I think some people were more upset about it than I was. I was at Tottenham for the long haul, definitely now. I wasn't reeling around, thinking, 'Oh my God, what has just happened?' Standing in a dock wondering if you would be going to prison for two years alters your perspective on life. Oh well, that's how it goes. I had a good job at Tottenham before, I thought, and I've got a good job now. No harm done.

Obviously, I've had some time to reflect on it all since and, looking back, perhaps the FA did me a favour. If I'm truthful, I don't know how much I would have enjoyed the job as they now see it. I don't think spending time with the FA people or up at Burton-on-Trent, where the new training centre is based, is my bag. I wouldn't rule out international management, and I thought very seriously about an offer to coach Ukraine twelve months ago, but I'd rather go in every day and see a bunch of footballers than sit around drinking tea with a bloke in a suit. I want to go out on the training ground with players, pick an XI and look forward to Saturday afternoon. I'm at the stage in my career that when I go to Anfield or Old Trafford, I walk around the place reliving the memories and wondering whether I'll ever come back this way again. I'm not ready to give that buzz up just yet – I enjoy it too much, even the difficult times, bottom of the league with Queens Park Rangers. It is a fantastic feeling to walk out at those big grounds, and the older you get the more you appreciate it and want to savour that moment. So to manage England would have been great in its way, but when it didn't happen, I didn't go into deep depression or lose sleep. I phoned Roy to wish him good luck, and I meant it. There are no hard feelings from me.

The way I see it now, though, the moment has passed. I couldn't see myself managing England if the chance arose again. The FA made their decision, they went with Roy, and I cannot see me wanting to work for them in the future. If the job came up again, I wouldn't want to be considered. I've given up on it now, and I think I would rule myself out early in the day, once the questions started flying. I'm happy to lead my life without going through that hassle again. Some people are ambitious, but I've only ever wanted to enjoy my football. I have turned down some interesting opportunities – Tottenham, Newcastle United, Ukraine – because they did not fit where I was at the time. I've managed in the Champions League, I've managed Bournemouth, and I was happy both times.

That doesn't mean to say I do not still have opinions on the way England should play. What Englishman doesn't? We should be better. Doesn't everyone think that? Without doubt we have underachieved. There is nothing more frustrating than getting to a tournament and seeing England outplayed, and then you look at the team-sheet of the opposition and it is full of players that couldn't make it in our Premier League. How often does that happen? You're thinking, 'Hang on, he was at Blackburn – he was useless,' or, 'That bloke couldn't get in West Ham's team.' You see Dirk Kuyt playing for Holland and he looks different class; meanwhile Steven Gerrard – who was better than him at Liverpool, week in, week out – is struggling. It doesn't make sense. The big European nations have not got better individual footballers than us, I'm convinced of it. I look at our team, one to eleven, and I am amazed we have been so poor.

I think it comes down to identity.

We don't have any.

The last England manager I can remember who had a firm idea of how he wanted to play was Glenn Hoddle: three centre-halves, a player coming out from the back to overload midfield; there was a plan to what he wanted to do. Since then we've bumbled along, a hundred different systems: are we kicking it, or are we passing it? That's what I like about Brendan Rodgers: he's not scared to put a weedy little player in midfield if the kid can pass, and then he'll let it all flow through him. There is a shape, there is an idea: the full-backs are high, the centre-halves split; you know how his teams are going to play before you kick off. They are going to pass, they are going to take risks; but England do not have that identity. If you look at England against Italy in the last European Championships, and I know it was difficult for Roy because he had just come in, but when your best pass completion statistic is from Joe Hart to Andy Carroll – goalkeeper to big lump of centre-forward, bypassing nine outfield players – you know you've got a problem. No other major country would record a stat like that.

Don't we all want to see England play the game properly? Well, it is going to take a manager with a clear vision. In 1992–93, when I won promotion to the Premier League with West Ham United, Hoddle finished fifth at Swindon Town and came up through the play-offs. He got them playing some outstanding football with guys that came from nowhere. He had a big centre-half, Shaun Taylor, that Swindon had taken from Bristol City for £200,000 the year before. Everyone thought they knew this kid: solid defender, good header of the ball, couldn't pass. The lower leagues are full of them. Hoddle came in and changed all that. Taylor had spent all his life being told to boot it, lump it, kick it into row Z. We've all heard it said. 'You can't play, son, give it to someone who can.' But Hoddle was telling him he could play – even better, he was showing him how. Next thing, he was dropping off, stepping into midfield – he thought he was at Barcelona. It just shows what can be achieved if someone is prepared to work with players individually, and on a system. There is no reason why England cannot be a much better team than they have been. Before Glenn, Terry Venables was the England manager, and 1996 was a fantastic year for football in this country. The people loved it; they loved how England were playing. Terry had a philosophy; he had a clear idea of how England should play. Next thing, he was gone. Somehow, we always mess it up.

Since then, since Glenn and Terry, there has been no identity in our game. We were nothing under Sven-Göran Eriksson. No identity at all. Roy will keep England organised, for sure, but I just hope he will also be a little bit bold, open up and try to get England playing the type of football we all want to see. If you look at Brendan Rodgers, he's now gone to Liverpool but he still knows how he wants to play, and he made a courageous decision straight off the bat – because Carroll wasn't in that plan. I know a lot of managers who would have thought, 'Keep Andy around, just in case we need to lump it.' But Brendan knows he is never going to play that way, so he can make a clear-headed decision. I think he deserves a lot of praise for that: for having an idea, for sticking to his beliefs. It may seem harsh that Carroll doesn't fit into his philosophy, but that is certainly how Spain operate: this is how we play, and we don't compromise. I just hope England have the confidence to come up with a blueprint of their own before the tournament in Brazil next summer – because the last World Cup was a disaster.

I was so disappointed with the way our standards deteriorated under Capello. In South Africa in 2010 we were just dire. The match against Algeria was a real low. If you were managing the bottom team in the Premier League and you were taken to see the Algerians play and given the pick of their crop – any player you wanted – you'd probably say, 'No thanks.' And there we were, struggling to beat them.

I got off on the wrong foot with Capello, unfortunately. I was managing Portsmouth and was invited into the television studio for one of his early England games. I don't usually do that stuff, but they must have caught me on a good day because I agreed. We didn't play well and I was quite critical of his decision to use Gerrard wide on the left. I wasn't vicious, I just said that it was not his position. The next thing, I heard Fabio had the needle about it. He came down to Portsmouth for a match and he was waiting around upstairs to see me afterwards, with his assistant, Franco Baldini. He definitely had the hump. 'You are a very influential person,' he insisted. 'People listen to you a lot.' What could I do? I told him I was asked on television to give an opinion, and I told them what I thought. What was I supposed to do? Lie? Pretend I thought it was a great decision? I have never gone on television for an England game since – but I always found Fabio difficult after that.

Not that it seemed to make much difference, either way. George Graham told me that he met Capello on holiday in a supermarket in Marbella. George was a huge fan of that disciplined, Italian style of play, so he thought he would go over and introduce himself. He said he was George Graham and that he used to manage Arsenal, and Fabio gave him a complete custard pie. Couldn't have been less interested. George regretted even trying to be friendly.

So I didn't get to know Fabio, and I think that goes for most of the English managers. I don't think he engaged much with our football and, in the end, the FA were probably looking for a way out and were not too disappointed when he quit. I can understand his decision, though, once they had taken the captaincy away from John Terry without consulting him. I would have found that difficult, too, as a manager, because the captain has to be your pick. You've got to work with the players and earn their respect, so should at least be in on the process, even if in exceptional circumstances the FA believed it was not the manager's final call. To treat Capello as they did was highly disrespectful, but the result was probably convenient for all. I suspect they would have got rid of Capello in 2010 if they could – although his qualification record was top class – and his decision suited them. Maybe he was looking for an excuse to go, too. He would have known he would get another top job, as he did in Russia, and he's already a very wealthy man. I just think we ended up underachieving massively under him, as much as with any manager.

It is sad, but England can sometimes be quite painful to watch, and I know from some of the players that it is not an enjoyable experience for them, either. I've heard a great many wonder about carrying on in international football because they get slaughtered if the result isn't right or they don't play well. They leave clubs they love – where everybody is together – go and play for England, and find that this faction doesn't like that lot, and after one off-night everybody gets ripped to pieces. When I was at Tottenham, I had plenty of players who said, 'I don't want to play, pull me out of the squad, I don't want to go.' I'm sure it is different with the older players. I can't imagine Frank Lampard, Steven Gerrard, John

Terry or Ashley Cole not wanting to turn out for their country, but I've known a lot of younger ones that weren't interested. Times have changed. My generation would have given their right arm just to be named in the squad, but the younger ones aren't steeped in that tradition. They can't be bothered. They weren't brought up on England as the pinnacle of a career, as we were.

I think we need to bring this next generation together and get people like Frank Lampard and David Beckham in to talk to them. They haven't always had the easiest times with England, they haven't always been successful, and they've certainly been criticised, but they have always been there for the team, 100 per cent. Maybe it has become too easy to get out: 'I won't play this game, I won't turn up; it's the end of the season, I'd rather go on holiday.' I think they need to be sat down, fifty or sixty of the current elite group across all ages, and told that to play for your country is an honour, and probably the greatest honour. That to want to play is expected, and the way it should be.

Having such strong views on England, I have been asked whether I thought I should have at least got an interview for the job. It's a moot point. Yes, it would have been nice to be considered, but I wouldn't have gone, and I know, in my shoes, Roy wouldn't have, either. We've both been around long enough; they know what we can do. They either want you or they don't. What point is there in auditioning? An interview would smack of an organisation that doesn't know what its plans are – let's see if we can find an England manager out of this lot – and I wouldn't have wanted to be part of that.

In the end, I don't know if there were people at the FA pulling strings for Roy or working against me, and I don't really care either way. I've known Trevor Brooking since he was a kid at West Ham. I can't say we've had a close relationship since I left, but he came to my father's funeral, and I have never had reason to believe he would have done anything to stop me getting the England job. As for Bernstein, the FA chairman at the time, I don't even know the man. A few weeks after Roy was appointed I bumped into him at the League Managers Association dinner, but we didn't talk about England. I certainly wasn't going to start asking awkward questions. These people are strangers to me, anyway. If you look at the people that make the big decisions at the FA, the ones that have the greatest voice, all I would say is: there should be more football people involved. I'd like to see more ex-professionals, more ex-managers, more expertise. It can't be that they have Trevor in as a token figure, and the rest are amateurs.

It's not as if it's going well.

In fact, we've spent fortunes and had some right disasters. The whole set-up needs to change. We need more committees of people who have played or coached football, people who know what is right and wrong in the game. I wouldn't trust the FA to tell me a good manager if their lives depended on it. How would they know? What clubs have they ever run? Who do they speak to that really knows the game? I'm not knocking them because of what happened to me. This isn't about me or Roy Hodgson, but about English football being run by people who really haven't got a clue. And they get to pick the England manager. Then again, it shouldn't surprise us. Look how they treated the greatest English footballer.

CHAPTER THREE

BOBBY (AND GEORGE)

When I go to Upton Park these days, there are two gigantic portraits in the corners at each end. One is of Sir Trevor Brooking, the other of Bobby Moore. Think about that. *Sir* Trevor Brooking; plain old Bobby Moore. No disrespect to Trevor, he was a great footballer and remains a fine ambassador for the game, but it doesn't seem right. How was Trevor knighted and Bobby ignored? How was the greatest footballer and one of the greatest sportsmen this country ever produced reduced to living his final years as a commentator on Capital Radio and a columnist in the downmarket *Sunday Sport* newspaper – rejected by his club, his country, and those who should have placed him at the heart of the game? The hypocrisy that followed his tragically premature death in 1993 sickens me.

Bob's got it all now. The old South Bank named after him at Upton Park, statues outside the ground and at Wembley Stadium. They even use his name to sell West Ham United merchandise these days. 'Moore than a football club' is the slogan. When he was alive they didn't want to know him. I saw him get slung out of there for not having a ticket.

It was the 1979–80 season and I had just returned from four years playing and coaching in America with Seattle Sounders and Phoenix Fire. I went to watch West Ham, who were in the Second Division at the time. I can't remember who they were playing – a team in yellow, I think – but I know I sat next to Frank Lampard's mum. Frank was still playing but West Ham were struggling that season and it was quite a poor gate. They weren't going to get promoted but they were too good to go down. It was a mid-table, middle of the road, nothing match. The players' families and guests used to sit in E block, and Bobby would often come to watch. He didn't want to cause a big commotion walking through the crowd, or hanging around before the game, so he would wait until after kick-off, go up to one of the old turnstiles with the wooden doors, and knock. The bloke would open up and, blimey, it's Bobby Moore. 'Come in, Bob, there's plenty of seats upstairs,' and up he would go. I can see him now. He would sit over in the corner, right out of the way, on these rotten old wooden benches that they used to have, and watch the match on his own.

This day I was sitting in E block next to Frank's mum, Hilda, when from behind me I heard, 'Harry.' I turned around and it was Bobby. We were about fifteen minutes into the game. 'Fancy a cup of tea at half-time?' I said, and he gave me the thumbs-up. Next thing I knew, a steward was marching up the steps towards him. 'Excuse me, Bob' – he looked almost ashamed – 'it's not me, but the secretary wants to know if you've got a ticket.' Bob said he hadn't. 'Then I'm afraid I've been told to ask you to leave.' And he went. Bobby Moore. *The* Bobby Moore. Thrown out of a half-empty stand at West Ham because he didn't have a ticket. Now he's dead you can't move for pictures of him around the place. It disgusts me. I don't think he ever went back after that. Not just to watch a game casually, anyway. If he had a ticket as a press man he would go, obviously, and sit in the press box with the writers, but I don't think he returned to the club seats. What did they want him to do: queue up outside with the punters? Ring the club and ask them to do him a favour? They should have been phoning him to attend their matches. 'Come and be our guest, Bob. Front row in the directors' box every week, Bob.' They should have treated him like he owned the place. Nothing should have been too good for Bobby.

Can you imagine if you were a promising young footballer and Bobby Moore, England's only World Cup-winning captain, came around your house to persuade you to sign for West Ham? Game over. Arsenal and Tottenham wouldn't have stood a chance. Even if the kid was just a baby when England won the World Cup, his dad would have been in awe. In the seventies what man wouldn't have wanted to have a cup of tea, or a beer, and talk football with Bobby Moore? Instead, West Ham were turfing him out of the ground like a hooligan. It still upsets me to think about it.

Bobby was made an OBE after England won the World Cup, but that's not as grand as it sounds. John Motson is an OBE. So is Des Lynam, Garth Crooks and Jimmy Hill. Craig Brown, the former manager of Scotland has a higher award, a CBE, as does Paul Elliott, the old Chelsea defender, and Pelé, who is Brazilian. And don't get me started on those who have received knighthoods for running football. Sir Dave Richards, Sir Bert Millichip. Bobby might not have cared where his name went on any honours list – but I do. To me, it sums up the way he was shunned by the game in the years before his death. Sir Trevor Brooking is the Football

Association's cup of tea. He's their type of person. Bobby was a player's player.

I first really got to know him when I was called up to West Ham's first-team squad in 1965. I had signed for the club two years earlier and played in the team that won the FA Youth Cup in 1963. Bobby was 22 and had been made captain of England that year, but he always had time for the younger players, and I got on well with him. He was the captain of the club, a young captain, and we all looked up to him. To us, he was the governor. Everybody loved him, everybody who came into contact with him wanted Bobby as a friend. You couldn't help it.

What a man. I mean it. What a man. The straightest, most honest bloke you could meet in your life. Not an ounce of aggression in him, not a hint of nastiness. Won the World Cup, and even the opposition loved him. Brazilians idolised him. Not just Pelé, but all of them: Jairzinho, Rivelino. People say the 1970 Brazil team was the greatest of all time, and Bob would have walked into it; in fact, I think he would have made the team of the tournament at any World Cup throughout history. I remember the game England played against Brazil that summer in Mexico. He was the best player on the field. Jairzinho was destroying everybody at the time and there is a moment when he heads downfield from the halfway line, along that right wing where he had been ripping through everybody, and Bobby just pushes him this way, pushes him that way, the pair are one on one but Jairzinho ends up by the corner flag. In slides Bob, nicks the ball off him and he's away up the field with it. You've never seen defending like it.

Bobby played with me at Seattle Sounders, along with Geoff Hurst. We had a great time together. He was one of the best players in the North American Soccer League, obviously, and was picked to represent something called Team America in the Bicentennial Tournament against England and Italy. It was a representative XI, but a real good team of players, and they made Bobby captain. Team America played Brazil in Seattle and I remember there was this lad who used to play for Watford in the line-up. Keith Eddy. He wasn't a big name in England but he'd cracked it in America with New York Cosmos, among all the superstars like Pelé and Carlos Alberto. This friendly against Brazil was the game of his life. He played at the back, did really well, and when the final whistle blew he ran halfway across the pitch to catch up with Rivelino. He was desperate to get his shirt. I was up in the stand with Sandra and Tina, Bobby's wife, and the kids and saw Keith running really hard to catch the king of the stepover. But Rivelino was running, too. He was sprinting like the match was still on, he must have covered ninety yards, and just as Keith was tapping him on the shoulder to ask for his shirt, Rivelino was doing the same to Bobby Moore. Rivelino – the player who invented some of football's greatest tricks and skills. He'd dribble with the ball and just as the defender thought he'd got a tackle in he'd go five yards in the opposite direction and have a shot. One of the greatest strikers of a ball that you'll ever see. And there he was cuddling and swapping shirts with Bobby, having run the length of the pitch for that memento. Poor old Keith Eddy could only look on as they chatted and embraced. Never stood a chance, did he?

Everyone wanted to meet Bobby, everyone wanted a night out with him. And Bobby loved the social side of the game. He captained the England football team, but he would have captained an England drinking team, too, if we had one. (And Frank Lampard

Senior would have been his vice-captain, by the way.) Gin and tonic or lager were Bob's drinks, and he could really put them away. We used to travel to away matches by train a lot in those days, and when we got on board after the game he would make a point of asking how many lagers they had in the buffet car. 'We've got four cases, Mr Moore,' he might be told. 'Right,' Bob would say, 'bring them down here.' And he'd roll off the cash needed for every drop of beer in the place and get stuck in. There was a little group of them – Frank, Brian Dear, Bobby Ferguson – and they'd go through the lot. About ten minutes from Euston, Bob would nip into the toilet, have a shave, change, put a new shirt on and reappear looking immaculate. Not a hair out of place. And then he'd go out drinking again for the rest of the night.

He wasn't an angel – 'win or lose: on the booze', that was Bobby's motto – but they were different times and football was not as professional in its outlook as it is these days. Even so, Bobby was probably the most diligent player in making amends for his sins the next day. He might have been out every Saturday, but he was in every Sunday morning, without fail, to run it off. He would get to the training ground at 9 a.m. in his old tracksuit, put on a plastic bin liner underneath it, and do a dozen laps to get a sweat going. He might have had a dozen lagers chased with ten gin and tonics the night before, but he never missed those Sunday sessions. The rest of us would still be in bed but Bob would be out, pounding around the field at Chadwell Heath, rain, wind or snow.

Sometimes you wondered how he did it. You would leave places barely able to stand up and Bobby would look like he'd just walked in from having his dinner suit fitted. He was like that as a player, too. He used to stand there in the dressing room before a match, everything on bar his shorts, waiting for the bell to go. He'd be wearing his jock strap but holding his shorts by the band with two fingers. When the bell went, he'd slip them on and they would have creases – creases! – along the side. He looked a million dollars as he led the team out. We all started to copy him, but nobody pulled that perfect groomed appearance off quite like Bob.

And he loved football. We all did. We might not have been diligent or looked after ourselves like today's players, but I think we all had real love for playing the game. We would even get together on Sunday, the day after the game, to have a match with our mates. We would either go to our training ground or, if it was a nice day, over to Lambourne End, a patch of land by the forest in Hainault. We would put our coats down and play, just like any other group of mates. Bobby was a regular. There would be England internationals, West Ham players like John Charles or Brian Dear, and some of our friends, like Terry Creasy, who was in business with Frank Lampard. There would be a load of us, we'd play for an hour and then go over the road to a pub called the Retreat. Sometimes, if Tina, Bobby's wife, was away, we'd go back to his house for a party. I loved those days, playing football for fun with Bobby in his prime, weaving away from his big house in Chigwell at eleven o'clock at night. It was great to see Bobby so relaxed and enjoying himself – he was captain of England at the time and he found it hard to let himself go in public.

Even if we didn't play at the weekend, we would find an excuse for a kickabout in midweek. We'd persuade the groundsman to open the gate at Chadwell Heath for us, or even Upton Park, and all pile in. There was a ticket tout that Bobby nicknamed Tostão, because he had a bald head like the great Brazilian. He was always up for a game. The teams would be evenly split up – there were about ten players and ten pals – and off we go. When the real football wasn't going well, that became the highlight of our week. We'd pile in the shower afterwards, get spruced up and go out.

One Sunday, we had played at the main ground and Terry Creasy was relaxing in the bath before we went up to the Black Lion in Plaistow. He was there, soaped up, lying in the bubbles when Ron Greenwood walked in. It took us all by surprise – he never went near the ground on Sunday, and I still don't know why he was there that day. I can see Terry now, tummy sticking out of the bubbles, feet out the end of the bath. Ron took one look at him and turned to us. 'Who's this chappie?' he asked. 'What's he doing here?' We were all left staring at the floor. We couldn't tell him that Terry had a few pubs with Frank and sold tickets for the lads on the side. I think one of us mumbled that he was a friend of ours and we had all been for a run together. I don't think Ron bought it. We were more careful where we played after that.

I think, deep down, Bobby was a shy person and he had to have a drink to let go. Once he'd had a few, he would open up and then he could keep any of the lads company. The boys from Manchester, like George Best and Mike Summerbee, Alan Ball, Norman Hunter, whom he kept out of the England team, they all liked a night out with Mooro. As far as those lads were concerned he was just the best character, a lovely man and great company. I think most of the footballers from around that time wanted to be like Bobby. If he started wearing his clothes a certain way, or going to a certain place up town, everyone followed.

Did we really know him, though? I'm not sure any of us did. Bob wasn't an open personality. Not devious, but private. He'd ask you ten questions before he answered one of yours. You would sit there and suddenly realise that you had done all the talking, and Bobby had barely told you what he thought about any of it. He must have had trouble in his life, and I was as close to him as anybody, but I can never remember Bobby volunteering his problems. Even when he was seriously ill, he kept it to himself. It needed the drink to make him relax but, even then, there were limits. Even as a captain, he was brilliant, but quiet. He led by example, not by shouting and hollering.

Sadly, the more famous he became, the more difficult it was to even switch off as he used to. There was nowhere he wasn't known, and he felt he always had to be on his best behaviour. That was why he relished the days playing football and having a party. He was among mates and he could let his hair down. It was the same for George Best, I think.

I knew George from a distance as a player, a little more when we were together in the States, and I was at Bournemouth as coach when he came to us in the 1982–83 season. We were his last English club. Don Megson was the manager then, and we did a good deal, paying George mostly appearance money – I think Brian Tiler, our managing director, might even have got some of it back by charging our opposition when we played away, because George certainly put a few on the gate. I don't think it would be legal now – and I'm not even sure if it was then – but the news that George was in town saw us playing in front of crowds of 14,000, and the opposition chairman was always up for that. George was a fantastic fellow, really. His teammates loved him. But by then he had a lot of problems. He was probably at his happiest sitting up at the bar in his favourite pub.

We were due to play Bradford City and George didn't turn up. It was Friday and Brian had to go looking for him in London. George was living with Mary Stävin, the former Miss World, and it was Brian's job to persuade him to leave her for Bradford. When he got there, George was already on the loose, out on a bender. She gave him the names of a couple of his favourite haunts and eventually Brian tracked him down. They sat together and had a lager and a chat. 'We need you at Bradford, George,' Brian told him. 'The team needs you, the boys all want you to play.' By the end, George had been persuaded. 'I'm just going for a piss and then we'll go,' he told Brian. So Brian waited. And waited. And eventually he smelt a rat and went into the toilet to check everything was all right. George was gone. He had climbed out of the window. He never made it to Bradford, and then bowled in the next week as if nothing had happened.

Another day he came to see me. 'Harry, where's Salisbury from here?' I told him it was about half an hour away. 'Why?' 'There's racing on – do you fancy it?' he asked. I have never needed much persuading where the horses are concerned, so off we went. I drove – George had no car – and he asked if I could drop Mary off at the station on the way. In got Mary, looking like a film star. She really was a lovely girl. Not just beautiful but friendly, charming – any man would have loved to be with her. After she got out, George turned to me. 'Thank God she's gone,' he said.

'Why, what's the matter?' I asked.

'We went to the pictures last night,' he said – I forget what film he wanted to see – 'and she drove me mad all the way through it. Touching me and kissing me.'

I couldn't stop laughing. 'Really, George? Sounds awful.'

There would have been a queue a million long to go out with Mary, and he was moaning. 'You don't understand, Harry,' he said. 'I was trying to watch the film.' But that was George. Deep down, he wasn't the Jack-the-lad that people thought.

The Salisbury meeting was very popular that day. A lot of the old Southampton boys were there: Mick Channon, Alan Ball, all whooping it up in the champagne bar. I sat having a cup of tea with George, out of the way. That was what he was like. He didn't like being the centre of attention.

There is a long country lane, about three miles, as you drive away from Salisbury and, when the racing was over, we passed two punters walking along it, looking a bit down on their luck. 'Pull over,' said George. 'Look at them. That could be you and me, Harry, couldn't it? We should give them a lift.' George wound down the window. 'You all right, lads? Come on, get in.' They jumped in the back, took one look at George and couldn't believe it. They were both football fans, both had done their money, and now they were getting a lift with George Best. By pure coincidence one even lived in Bournemouth, so we ended up taking both of them all the way home. George chatted to them all the way. They couldn't believe what was happening; they hung on his every word. After they got out, George watched them go. 'There but for the grace of God, eh Harry?' he said. People used to get him wrong. Take his genius with a football away and he was the most down to earth guy you could meet. It was his talent that set him apart. He was a flash footballer, not a flash character.

Bobby was a brilliant player, but he was a defender. George was a forward and the best of all time for me. I've never seen anyone in this country who had his skill with a football. I remember in one of his first seasons, Manchester United beat us 6–1 at Upton Park and he was just unstoppable. There used to be a Salvation Army band that played on the pitch before games at West Ham, and they stood in the same spot, out by the wing, every week. A few months into the season that patch was a quagmire. No grass, just thick mud. It used to drive me mad trying to play through it, but George never had a problem. He would glide over it and do things with the ball that were just incredible. When he went past people, there was nobody in his class. I remember Ron Harris of Chelsea would try to snap him in half every time they played: he would hit him from the side and how George rode those tackles I just don't know. I think he was just so determined to get the last word as a player. He loved scoring against Chelsea, loved getting one over on Ron.

I think they were our first football superstars, Bobby and George, and that had an effect on both of them. Players are used to it now. Every match is on TV all around the world and everyone in football is used to being recognised – stand still for five minutes and a string of people come up to you. It must have been hard for Bobby and George, because celebrity was so new. They wanted to go to the places we had always gone – to the Black Lion in Plaistow or down the road to the local – and that made it difficult. These days, the smart players go to exclusive places where they won't be bothered. They might be drinking £300 bottles of champagne but they are kept apart. They wouldn't be seen dead in an old fashioned boozer like the Blind Beggar in Whitechapel. I know the image they had, but I never thought of George or Bobby as West End people, really. I think Kenny Lynch was as near as Bobby ever got to having a showbiz mate. Maybe it was because Bobby still hung around with his mates from the East End that he never fitted in once he stopped playing.

If I try to piece together why the people at the top in football seemed to reject Bobby, I can only think that it was his reputation for liking a night out that played its part. Ron Greenwood was manager throughout his time at West Ham, but he didn't involve Bobby after his retirement as a player, not even when he went on to manage England. I don't think Ron approved of Bobby's lifestyle, really, the drinking culture that existed in football in those days. He knew Bobby was part of the little group that would be in the Black Lion by 5.30 p.m. after home games, and that we wouldn't leave until we could barely walk home. Ron put up with it, but he didn't like it. I imagine it drove him mad to see the boys get well beat somewhere like Newcastle and then pile on the train and drink all the way home. A lot of clubs had similar sets – even the successful ones, including Liverpool – but we were a real handful at West Ham, and I don't think Ron forgot that. I remember one night away at Stoke City when we were absolutely useless. We were staying up there after the match and Ron was so angry he wouldn't let us out of the hotel. We weren't having that, so a few of us climbed out of the window and went into town to a nightclub. We got back at about 4 a.m. and found the gates around the hotel locked. There was nothing to do but climb. By now, however, we were rather the worse for wear and Bob slipped and caught his foot on a spike. It took ages to get him free. The next day, we made sure he stayed well clear of Ron on the train home, and he came in the next afternoon and claimed he'd had an accident in the garden. He didn't play for two weeks.

Another night, we had played up at Wolverhampton, got back early and ended up in the Blind Beggar, where Ronnie Kray shot

George Cornell. Frank and I were going off to meet our girlfriends and Bobby was going out with Tina, but we thought we'd have a few before we went. We stayed for a while, but it was close to empty, and we were just about to leave when a huge bloke followed me into the toilet. He had a big black overcoat, short black hair and a scar running the length of his face. He might as well have had 'gangster' tattooed on his forehead, you couldn't have drawn one better. 'Tell your mate Bobby Moore that I'm going to cut him from here to here,' he said, indicating a scar like his own.

'What for?' I asked. 'What's he ever done to you?'

'I don't like him,' he said. 'He thinks he's a film star.'

I got out of there as quickly as I could. 'Come on, Bob,' I said, 'I think we'd better leave.' I was looking across to the other little bar, and I could see this bloke waiting in there.

'I'm coming,' said Bob. 'I've just got to go to the toilet.'

'No, don't go to the toilet, Bob,' I said. 'Let's get a move on.' I didn't want to worry him by telling him what I had just heard. 'I'll see you in the morning,' I said, as we left. I hoped that would be true and this bloke was not going to follow us home.

The next day Bob arrived, face intact, and I told him about the threat. 'The bloke looked like a nutter,' I said. 'That's the last time I go there.' But Jimmy Quill, who owned the Blind Beggar with his brother Patsy, was a big pal of Bob's. He was a lovely bloke, Jimmy, but as hard as they come. I've seen a fight start between two giant fellas, and Jimmy come over the bar and knock out the pair of them. He was an ex-boxer, like Patsy, and when he heard about the warning to Bobby he was furious. Jimmy wasn't having it that his mate couldn't use his pub. He said he knew the bloke and would sort it out. I wasn't there when their little pow-wow happened, but

I'm told the next time Scarface came in, Jimmy took him to one side, said they needed to go round the back to have a chat about Bobby Moore – and smashed him to pieces. 'He's a mug,' he told us. 'He won't talk to you like that again.' And he didn't – because we never saw him after that.

Jimmy also had another pub called the Globe that Bobby would use. I remember we were all in there after training one Christmas Eve, and the girls from the local factory were having their holiday drink-up. There was music going and it was quite lively, but the phone rang and it was Tina, Bobby's wife, who had finally tracked him down. He was supposed to be home to take her out and she had been ringing around his favourite pubs. We could all hear Bobby promising Tina that he was about to leave and then he came back and had another one, and the phone went again, and it was Tina. Bob assured her he was getting a cab and would be home in forty-five minutes. Well, that was nonsense, too, and there was a third call, by which time she was fuming. Tina said she was going to phone his mum and she would come and collect him. Bob came back to us laughing about it, but the next thing the doors burst open and there was the formidable Mrs Moore, with the raving hump. She marched over, grabbed his arm like that of a naughty schoolboy, and said, 'Right, Tina's waiting for you, and you're coming with me.' Just as he was getting unsteadily to his feet, she rounded on the rest of us. 'And one of you has mixed his drinks – because he doesn't get drunk like this, you know!' And off Bobby, the World Cup-winning captain of England's football team, went: dragged out of the boozer by his mum. As the doors of the Globe were closing behind him, all we could hear was, 'But, Mu-um, I'm 29.'

They were funny times. It wouldn't happen – it couldn't happen – today; but in the sixties, sessions like that were the norm. It was no different at Chelsea or Arsenal, but maybe Ron Greenwood took against Bobby because of it. He was certainly more likely to talk football with Geoff Hurst, who was a good lad, but not part of any drinking team.

After Ron stepped down, John Lyall succeeded him and I think that was the end of Bobby at West Ham, really. John was a young manager, an unknown, trying to make an impression, and he didn't want a huge presence like Bobby around overshadowing him. I know Bob left West Ham at the end of his career and went to Fulham – and even played against West Ham in the 1975 FA Cup final – but it would have been the easiest thing in the world to get him back. If John had said to him, 'Come over, Bob, come over to the training ground, just drop in, let the kids see you about, watch their training, maybe put on a session for them,' I'm sure he would have done that and the kids would have loved it, too. But John didn't want him anywhere near the place. I think he felt he might be undermined. Maybe John thought that Bobby would be too big, that the players would start looking to him – and maybe some of the other managers around at that time thought the same, too. They probably thought if they brought Bobby in he would be a threat to them. That didn't make any sense to me. Bobby wasn't like that. He didn't have a bad bone in his body.

It's a shame that some people are scared of a big name. How could they not make Bobby Moore welcome at West Ham? It happens, though, doesn't it? You would have thought that Tony Adams would have a job for life at Arsenal, but Arsène Wenger has never given him a chance as a coach, has he? Great character, great leader, great captain of Arsenal, wants to get into coaching: you would have thought it was ideal. But no, Tony ended up in Azerbaijan – and Bob ended up at Oxford, with me.

It was the summer of 1980, not long after I'd seen him get thrown out of Upton Park, that Bobby called me to be his assistant. Not at Oxford United – incredibly Bobby couldn't land a job in professional league football – but Oxford City. They had an owner called Tony Rosser, who had previously been a director at Oxford United. He had a big fall-out and left the club and now it was his ambition to take Oxford City from the Isthmian League to the Football League, and stick it up his old club in the process. It all seemed very bitter and personal. 'Give it a year, Harry,' said Bobby. 'If we do well, we could get picked up somewhere else.' As if the great Bobby Moore should be doing auditions in non-league football.

Getting Bobby in was a big coup for Rosser, and he needed to show he meant business. He was doing the ground up and wanted a coach on site, full-time, even though the players only used to come in to training on Tuesday and Thursday nights. I was paid £120 per week, with a little Ford Fiesta as my company car, to sit in a Portakabin on a building site on my own. Sometimes another bloke, supposedly our chief executive, would sit with me. 'Right,' he'd say, 'let's go and have a look at the new training ground.' And we'd drive up the road and stand in this empty field and say, 'We'll put the dressing rooms there, and pitch number one there,' and then we'd drive back and sit looking at each other for the rest of the day until Bobby and the players turned up at 7 p.m. And because the owner was playing at the fantasy of running a big club I had to be there every morning at 9 a.m. – which meant leaving my home in Bournemouth at 7 a.m. I'd get in very late at night, exhausted, having done precisely nothing for most of the day.

Sometimes we'd be at an away match somewhere like Aveley, in Essex, in the driving rain and I'd think, 'What am I doing here?' And then I'd look at the bloke sat next to me and think, '"What am *I* doing here?" – what is *he* doing here?' It was a hard slog for us, because in that company we were fish out of water. We'd spent all our life in the professional game and we just didn't know the league or what was needed. We got some older ex-professional players in, thinking they would be a class above, but they couldn't hack it. As for the rest, they had already done a day's work by the time they got to training. They were knackered, and we weren't used to that either. We were ordinary, mid-table at best in the league, and then when we played Oxford United in the local Cup final, and we couldn't live with them and lost 5–0. To make matters worse, Tony's business was beginning to struggle and, when the results didn't come straight away as he'd hoped, he began to lose interest. Within a year, the Oxford City project was over.

I enjoyed being with Bobby, but not all the people I met in grassroots football were as charming. We frequently saw a poor side of human nature that year. I think a number of the other coaches were jealous of Bobby for what he had achieved in the game. Beating him became the story they wanted to live off for the rest of their lives – score against us, and they would get completely carried away. I got used to an opposition manager or coach jumping out of his seat and running over to celebrate in front of Bobby. They seemed to delight in sticking it to him and yet, once the final whistle had gone, they would be over wanting his autograph or a picture with an arm around his shoulder like they were best mates. I thought it showed a complete lack of respect and was very distasteful. Yet Bobby let it all wash over him. He never allowed the aggro to get to him, never once took the bait or sunk to their level. He was just above people like that. He posed for all their pictures and signed every autograph, while I stewed in the background, quietly seething. What was it with people? Why were some so spiteful?

I guess Bobby was used to it. I remember when we were at West Ham, we drew Hereford United in the fourth round of the FA Cup, 1972. They had just knocked out Newcastle United in one of the most famous upsets in Cup history. Their players were suddenly big names: Ronnie Radford, who had scored a spectacular winner, and Dudley Tyler, a winger who ended up signing for West Ham for £25,000, which was a record for a non-league player at the time. They had a big centre-forward called Billy Meadows, who used to be at Barnet. He had plenty to say for himself – and plenty to say to Bob. The game got postponed a couple of times, and we ended up playing it in midweek on a really heavy pitch. As soon as the match kicked off, Meadows started abusing Bobby. I'd been around, but this was really beyond the pale. Stuff about Tina: really nasty, personal insults, it was disgraceful. We drew 0–0 and ended up playing the replay at Upton Park on Monday 14 February, with an afternoon kick-off because of the power cuts caused by a miners' strike. The gates were closed two hours before kick-off. There were 42,000 inside and another 10,000 locked out – the tie had caught the public imagination and everyone was up for seeing it. We were in a hotel having our pre-match meal when the entire Hereford team walked in – more master planning from our secretary, as usual – including the lovely Billy Meadows. Up he strolled to Bobby, big as you like, 'All right, Bob – no hard feelings about last week. Sorry if I was a bit out of order.' Bob nodded at him, as if to say forget it, and off Meadows went. Then the game started, and he was at it again – except twice as bad this time. Even then, Bobby wouldn't bite. He should have said to him, 'Piss off, you mug.' In fact, he should have said that in the hotel before the game. But that wasn't his nature. He was too classy to react, too classy to even ask, 'Who the hell are you?' He didn't even crow when Geoff Hurst scored his hat-trick and knocked Hereford out, 3–1.

I helped get Bobby his only job in league management. It was at Southend United in 1984. Anton Johnson, who was my chairman at Bournemouth, confided in me that he was going to buy Southend but didn't know who to put in as manager. I had already turned him down. 'There's only one man for the job,' I told him. 'Bobby Moore.' Anton liked the sound of that and later in the season went for it, but Bobby couldn't stop Southend being relegated and this was another football-club venture that sadly ran out of steam. Anton left quite quickly after the first season relegation fight, and Bobby was on the cusp of building a decent side when he departed, too. He didn't hit it off with the new chairman and was gone at the end of his second season, with Southend finishing ninth. David Webb took the core of Bobby's team up the following year. I hear people say that Bobby failed as a manager, but it is difficult to achieve at that level. You've no money and if you don't make a success of it immediately, people are quick to judge.

It was tougher for Bobby than most managers, too, because all eyes were on him, wherever he went. Bad result at Southend, no surprise there – but bad result at Bobby Moore's Southend and suddenly it was news. And the club wasn't really going anywhere at the time. Frank Lampard went down to Roots Hall, Southend's ground, with Pat, his wife, and they sat in the directors' box as Bobby's guests. Southend were losing and Frank told me that one of the board starting shouting down to the dug-out so that everyone could hear: 'Is this why we're paying you all this money, Moore, to watch a load of crap?' He sounded a complete wrong 'un. I almost regretted helping put Bobby in there, after the way it worked out. It is embarrassing to think of him being treated like that. I've worked at the lower level and unless your club is ambitious and you have a chance to achieve success, it becomes a dead end.

Even so, you'd have thought that someone, somewhere, would have snapped Bobby up and given him a second chance. They only had to see him play to know the way he read and understood the game. And he was Sir Alf Ramsey's captain. That should have meant something, surely? I won't have it that Bob couldn't have become a good manager. His football brain was on a different level when he played, so surely that would have converted to management, over time. To this day I will never know why he could not get a break. I still believe that, with the right support, he could have been the greatest manager in West Ham's history. But we'll never know. I still hear that Bobby was a failed manager, but I tell people that he never got a chance to show otherwise. The year I had with him, even at Oxford City, you could see he knew so much about the game. The results were not always the best, but he always talked sense about football. Everybody that played with him respected his opinion. Having kicked around in non-league football and lower league football, why was he never given a chance to work with players who had an ounce of his incredible ability? Surely, we should have given this man a go at a bigger club? But no one did.

I can remember Alvin Martin asking me about Southend when he had the chance to manage there and, knowing what happened to Bobby, I was a little more cautious with my advice. The first job as a manager is so important. If the club is just drifting and you end up getting the sack it can be the end of you. You must make sure that you've got a chance. Bobby didn't have that at Southend, but after he left nobody thought he could coach, and it was downhill all the way.

I can picture him now, eating fish and chips at the back of the stand at Grimsby Town. I was up there with West Ham and I spotted him out of the corner of my eye. Freezing cold, midweek game, he was doing the summary for Capital Radio for a hundred quid. Big hat on to keep him warm. 'All right, Bob?' I asked. 'All right, H, yeah,' he said. I came away, thinking to myself, 'What are we doing? This is Bobby Moore.' It couldn't happen anywhere else in the world.

I spoke about it with the directors, but there were never any positions for him at West Ham. No one wanted to give him a job. And then he died. That same week Terry Brown, the chairman, started talking about naming a stand after him. I'll admit, I went spare. 'When he was alive, you didn't even give him a ticket, now you want to name a fucking stand after him?' I said. 'He should have been sitting next to you every game. He should have been the figurehead of this fucking club. He would have been the best ambassador any club could ever have.'

I had a few arguments with Terry, but that must rank as one of the biggest. We had murders and fell out, big time, that day. But I meant every word. The greatest footballer this country has ever produced and he ends up sitting at the back of a stand in Grimsby doing radio commentaries? I'm sure Sir Trevor is a great ambassador for West Ham – but he ain't Bobby Moore. And if West Ham couldn't find any use for him, what about the Football Association? How this country didn't make the most of a man like that, I will never know. He could have been fantastic for England and for English football. Germany put Franz Beckenbauer centre stage, France did the same with Michel Platini, so much so that he ended up President of UEFA. Meanwhile, Bobby Moore holds the same rank of honour in this country as Des Lynam. How didn't he get a knighthood? Why didn't he get a knighthood? How did we end up with Sir Dave Richards and Sir Bert Millichip but not Sir Bobby Moore?

We think of scandals in football as a player diving, or high transfer fees, but this, for me, is what scandal really means. The way football treated Bobby changed my attitude, professionally, because seeing him struggle confirmed to me that nobody in this game really gives a monkey's about you once you've served your purpose. Do your best, don't do people a bad turn, but make sure you look after yourself first because, when it comes down to it, nobody cares. Earn as much as you can and don't feel guilty about that, either. Nobody looked out for Bobby – and if they won't look out for him, they certainly won't look out for me or any of the other ex-players. I can name hundreds of footballers now – great players who gave everything – who have to go begging to the Professional Footballers' Association because they need a hip replacement. Some clubs are different. At Everton they are very good at organising dinners and fundraising events for ex-players to be supported medically, but I think that is because Bill Kenwright, their chairman, is a proper Evertonian and runs the club the right way. Dave Whelan at Wigan Athletic is another who seems to have his club's interest at heart, having played the game. Yet if you look at some of the new owners, what do they know of their club's history? They couldn't tell you who played thirty years ago, let alone want to look after them.

When I was manager of West Ham, Ron Greenwood turned up for one of the games, and visited me in my little office. He was talking about walking down Green Street through the crowd, and I asked him why he hadn't driven here. He said he had. 'Then where have you parked?' I asked. 'Up past the station,' said Ron. They couldn't get him a car park ticket, apparently. No room. Ron Greenwood, the greatest manager West Ham ever had, the man that cemented the principles that are at the heart of the club – stuck down a side street past Upton Park station because they couldn't make room for him in the car park. I despaired.

The last time I saw Bobby was the year he died, 1993. He stayed at the Royal Bath Hotel in Bournemouth and we went down to see the racehorses working at David Elsworth's yard. I went to pick him up and when he came out I could have cried. He always had big, tree-trunk legs, but there was nothing of him, he was wasting away; his backside was almost hanging out of his trousers. It killed me. I had to pull myself together. We went out for the day, we went down the stables, had lunch, went to a little fish restaurant, and he never said a word about how ill he was. I knew the problem, we all did, but he never complained, never moaned, never said, why me? So I'll say it instead: why him, for God's sake? And to the people who left him to wither away when his playing career ended, just: why?

CHAPTER FOUR

THE MAKING OF A FOOTBALLER

West Ham United, Tottenham Hotspur, Queens Park Rangers, I've managed quite a few clubs around the capital – but the team I grew up supporting was Arsenal. That was my dad's team, Harry Senior. We were an East End family, so I don't quite know where it came from, but he absolutely loved Arsenal, and so did his brother, Jim. Dad was always over at Highbury, standing behind the goal in the North Bank, and after he stopped playing on Saturdays, he would take me. I would represent East London Schools in the morning, he'd come to watch and then we'd both go off to Arsenal.

We even travelled to the odd away game. I remember just before my twelfth birthday, going up to Sheffield to see Arsenal play in an FA Cup fifth-round replay. Sheffield United had drawn 2–2 at Highbury that weekend, and we were back at Bramall Lane the following Wednesday. It took about six hours on the train and when we got there Dad and Uncle Jimmy disappeared into a pub and I was left standing outside with a packet of crisps. The match was rotten, too. Jack Kelsey, our Welsh international goalkeeper, broke his arm and Dennis Evans, the left-back, had to go in goal – there were no substitutes in those days. Just before the match a thick fog came down and we couldn't see a thing. Bramall Lane was a cricket ground, a huge expanse of land with stands on only three sides, which made it worse. How they played in those conditions I'll never know. We didn't have a clue what was going on, except for the odd cheer from the home crowd, and Arsenal lost 3–0. After that, we had to wait for the first train at seven the next morning, and it was another six hours back to London. I got through the door and grassed the old man up. 'How was it?' my mum asked. 'Well, it was a long wait standing outside the pub, Mum,' I said. 'You what? You left him outside a pub?' Wallop – have that.

Football was a different world back then. The other day I was watching film of the 1957 FA Cup final, Manchester United versus Aston Villa. I would have been ten at the time it was played. Peter McParland, the Villa centre-forward, absolutely nailed Ray Wood, who was in goal for Manchester United, knocked him unconscious and broke his jaw. It was so horrendous, so wrong, that it was almost funny. Wood lay on the floor, unconscious, and the trainer ran on and all he seemed to be worried about was getting his keeper's jumper off so Jackie Blanchflower could go in goal. He pulled and pulled at this thing, a big polo neck and tight, and Wood was just lolling about like a rag doll. He could have had brain damage for all they knew, could have had a broken neck, but they finally got the top off and had him propped, sitting upright. The whole process must have taken about five minutes, and then they picked him up, a dead weight and just slung him on the stretcher. And through it all, the commentator was saying it was a fair challenge and there could be no blame on McParland, and the crowd were booing because they thought Wood had gone soft. It was incredible. About twenty-five minutes later, he came back out of the tunnel, a smelling salts sniffer up his nose, and he could barely stand up. He played outside-right and didn't touch the ball for ages because he was walking around in a daze. Finally, he had a shot and nearly hit the corner flag. 'Ah, Wood, clearly not as good on the wing as he is in goal,' said the commentator. Half-time came, he went off again, and clearly couldn't come back. United went 2–0 behind, scored with seven minutes to go and, suddenly, Wood returned, only this time in goal so United could play eleven against eleven and try for an equaliser. And he still didn't know what planet he was on.

That's how the game was in those days. I remember Lawrie Leslie, a big Scotsman who was the West Ham goalkeeper in the early sixties. He broke an arm against Arsenal in the first half, so they tied it up around his neck and he went out and played 60 minutes on the wing. Hard as nails the players were back then.

And I saw them all from my spot on the left side of the North Bank at Highbury. There was a big raised manhole cover and we'd get there about two hours before kick-off so I could claim my place on it and lean on the barrier. I saw the Busby Babes from there, and Tom Finney, who was my dad's favourite. The old man loved Finney. He reckoned he was the best ever, even better than Stanley Matthews. He thought Matthews was good on the wing, but Finney could play anywhere: through the middle, outside-left, outside-right, he could score goals, do the lot. The crowds weren't segregated in those days, either, so whenever Arsenal played Preston North End there would always be a few away fans in our end, and Dad would get chatting to them about Finney, offer them a cup of tea from his flask; it was a different atmosphere way back.

There was respect, between the fans, and between the fans and the players. It's one of the reasons it makes me sick when you hear people now singing songs about tragedies like the Munich air disaster. I used to watch those boys – Duncan Edwards and the rest of the Manchester United team from that time – I know how fantastic they were. To hear vile songs about them, it makes me ill. Sir Bobby Charlton told me once that when he went to United he thought he was a good player. He'd be working in a factory every day before training, but he still fancied his chances. And he told me that he saw Duncan Edwards and thought, 'No, Bob, you're wrong – you can't play.' That's how good Edwards was.

I saw the Busby Babes' last game in this country: 1 February 1958, they won 5–4 against Arsenal. Everyone played: Edwards, Eddie Colman, Dennis Viollet, Tommy Taylor, David Pegg. Busby sent out another young winger that day, Kenny Morgans, and I remember a kid getting Duncan Edwards' autograph as he came off the pitch. I thought he was so lucky. And then five days later the crash happened. The whole country was in mourning. Everybody was glued to the radio morning, noon and night. What's happening? How's Duncan? I was ten years old and I remember I kept a scrapbook because Duncan was my hero and we were all willing him to come through. Every day I'd cut the latest reports out and it all seemed to be good news. Duncan looked like he was going to pull through. There was even a photograph where he was almost sitting up in bed smiling. When my parents died a few years ago, I cleared out their house and I found that old scrapbook. It brought back a lot of memories. I used to say my prayers for him every night and when he died, well, I was just devastated. We all were. So I don't understand how football has degenerated these days, with those chants about Hillsborough and Munich or gas chambers. They were Manchester United boys, but the whole country was pulling for them. Fans would have felt the same about any group of players. You went to a match and you'd stand and talk football with the away fans, and no one would be shouting abuse or fighting and arguing. Everyone had a rattle and they just went to enjoy the game. If that sounds a rose-tinted or nostalgic memory, I'm sorry, but it's true. Then, for me and my dad, it was a cheese roll at a little café up the road, the 106 bus and then the 277 back to Poplar.

Sometimes we saw Jimmy Logie, one of the Arsenal greats, outside the ground. He would have an old brown mackintosh on, tied up with string, selling newspapers. My dad was an inside-forward like Jimmy and he idolised him. He'd go over and buy a paper even if he already had one, just for an excuse to chat to him. Then we'd be in the queue, trying to get a ticket. My dad was a docker, he never had much money, but sometimes if we couldn't get in the North Bank we'd queue up for seats. Stan Flashman, the famous ticket tout, would walk along the line, flogging his black-market tickets, which we couldn't afford. My dad hated Stan. He used to slaughter him as he went past. I remember we always had to battle to get into games with West Ham, home or away. One season, the old man shot over Upton Park early, got in the queue, then he reached the front before I arrived and had to go in. I couldn't find him, he couldn't find me. We were both panicking. And we got beat about six. Absolutely murdered.

I was a good player, one of the best, as a kid – but I got that from my dad. He could have been a professional, too, but the war intervened. He had it rough as a kid. His dad used to beat his mum, and then they both died when he was 15. He was in the army at 16 and taken prisoner of war, and by the time he came back home the chance had probably gone for him to make a career out of football. He used to play in the Essex Business Houses League with his mates, but he was on a different plane to most of the players there. All the big amateur teams in London from that time, like Walthamstow Avenue and Leyton, wanted him to join them, but he always refused. He just enjoyed playing football for the fun of it with lads he knew from round our way in Poplar. I used to get dragged all over the place to watch him, but I didn't mind. He was usually the best player there by a million miles and I felt really proud of my dad. He could do anything with the ball. Years later I can remember going on holiday to a caravan on the Isle of Sheppey with Frank Lampard and his family, and Dad took Frank to the cleaner's in a kickabout on the green. He was in his fifties by then but he nutmegged Frank, showed one way then went the other – he drove him absolutely mad. Put a ball at his feet twenty years later and he could still do all the tricks.

My football career started when we moved to the Burdett Estate in Poplar. Before that we had one room above my great-grandmother's house in Barchester Street, but the old properties that hadn't been bombed were knocked down soon after the war. The Burdett Estate was great because there were loads of flats, loads of kids, and we were shut away in our own little world. There were no cars on the estate, so we'd come home from school and play football until it was too dark to see. There was a patch of grass at the back of the flats which we called Wembley. I'd come home from Susan Lawrence School – most of my mates went to Stebon, but I didn't want to change – and you'd hear a kid shouting, 'There's a game on at Wembley,' and that was your cue to run over there with your ball. We'd be there all night after that. Cup final day, we would watch the match, and as soon as it was over, bang, it was back to our own twin towers. One team would be Manchester United, the other Aston Villa, and we'd play our version of the game.

There were about four caretakers – we called them porters – on the estate and we nicknamed one Cheyenne, after Cheyenne Bodie, who was this huge cowboy in a western show on television. It was our little joke because the TV Cheyenne was about 6 feet 4 inches and this bloke was about 4 feet 2 inches, and he'd come and try to nick our ball. We hated him. He'd try to sneak up on us but we always spotted him and ran away. He kept threatening to report us to our mums, until one day this hard old docker called Albert Chamberlain frightened him off. Albert had a boy called Alan, who loved football, and after Cheyenne chased us away, Albert rounded on him: 'Why don't you them alone?' he said. 'Ain't you got nothing better to do? What harm are they doing?' I think Cheyenne was scared of Albert because he let us be after that, but it had put an idea in Albert's head. 'Don't worry about him, boys,' he said. 'We'll start our own team up – we'll call it Burdett Boys.' We were all about nine, we were looking at him – we didn't have a clue what he was talking about. But Albert was as good as his word.

There was a little room in the block of flats in the middle of the estate, called the Matchbox. It was about the size of a matchbox, and I don't know what its purpose was, because it had never been used, but Albert got the keys and that became our team room. We had a meeting one Friday to set up our XI, and Albert got us kit and a place in the Regent Boys League, which was over the other side of London, north-west, in Regent's Park. The match was an hour and the journey there was about three. We had to get a bus, then a train, and there was nowhere to change. We were playing teams from Islington, from Camden, and it turned out the only league he could get us into was an under-11. We were all younger, and some of the smallest ones were no more than eight. We were getting chinned every week, but Albert was soon on the lookout for new players. He found a cracker in Terry Reardon. Terry was 11 but he was already on the way to being a man. When he was just 12 he played in the English Schools under-15 Trophy final for East London Boys against Manchester Boys. He could operate three years out of his age group, no problem. Once Terry joined, Albert started nicking a few lads from the other east London clubs and pretty soon we had enough for two teams. By then we had become the best club in the area. We moved leagues and played on Hackney Marshes and won the title year after year. I'd play for East London on the Saturday, Burdett Boys on the Sunday morning, and then wait for our older team to turn up and play for them, too. And that's how it all started – running around with Burdett Boys on a patch of land we called Wembley.

There was nothing for me at school. Susan Lawrence had a fancy new name – it used to be Ricardo Street School but was renamed after a local councillor who became a Labour MP – but the headmaster was the same chap that was in charge when my dad went there. I was lucky, though, because it had two good sports teachers, Mr Enniver and Mr Clark, who were really enthusiastic. Mr Enniver loved his cricket, and they both loved their football. We would meet at nine o'clock Saturday morning and play on a red cinder surface; I don't think I saw a grass pitch until I had left for my senior school. I remember the pair of them going from class to class announcing the trials for the school football team and asking whether anyone was interested. My hand shot straight up. I got picked and my dad came to watch me. I felt ten feet tall.

Mr Enniver absolutely loved me, and Mr Clark was fantastic for me, too. He only died quite recently. He got in touch late in his life and I saw him quite a few times in the decade before he passed away. Unfortunately, though, I left Susan Lawrence only interested in sport. There were three choices in those days: grammar school, central school or secondary modern. If you were clever you went to our local grammar school, George Green on the Isle of Dogs; the average ones ended up at the central schools, St Paul's Way or Millwall; and if you were an idiot like me there were two further choices – Hay Currie School or Sir Humphrey Gilbert School in Stepney. They were the roughest schools in the area by a million miles – a pair of nuthouses, really. You had to be pretty poor in class and have failed the eleven-plus exam to end up at a secondary modern, and I think there was only me and one other boy who went there. I chose Humphrey Gilbert, and I remember Mr Enniver taking me aside before I left. 'Harry, be careful at that school,' he told me. 'If you're not you could get caught up in the wrong things. You'll have to concentrate. I know you love your sport, but you must watch out. Get in with the wrong crowd and you could end up in prison.' People now don't understand what it was like there. They think I exaggerate when I tell them I can't remember having too many proper classes or proper teachers. It was student teachers who got dumped there, mostly. Young women – they would last a day, or a week at most, and run out crying. I can't recall any of the names, because we had so many. They would disappear one afternoon and we'd never see them again.

We did no work, we learned nothing. We'd have assembly at nine, and by ten everyone would be bunking off class and meeting up by the toilets to get up to mischief. The education was non-existent. I think there were probably ten kids in my year who left not being able to read or write. I'm not saying I was much better. If I tried to write a letter, you'd think it was a six-year-old who had got hold of the pen and paper. It's embarrassing, really. My writing is disgusting and my spelling is no better. I might be dyslexic for all I know; it certainly looks like it. I can sign my name or write 'Best wishes, Harry' for autographs, but the rest is a mess. I have never composed a letter in my life because I simply couldn't. If I ever have to put down a proper sentence, I've no idea where to put the full stops and commas, and I start off in capitals, then joined-up letters, then back to capitals. Don't think I'm proud of this. People can't believe it when they see my handwriting – and everyone I've ever met from Sir Humphrey Gilbert or Hay Currie is the same. The education was secondary, but it certainly wasn't modern.

We didn't go to school in the way other kids went to school. We caused havoc and then went home. The only way they could keep order was by using the cane. There was one teacher there, Mr Merton, who was extremely scary. He'd bend you over and beat you with the cane, or give you six across the hand. We dreaded being sent to him because he always made sure it hurt. I got the cane a few times, for not turning up to class or banging the lid of my desk repeatedly. One time we all started singing in class and I got the blame. My favourite trick was playing to an audience in woodwork and metalwork. I didn't have a clue about either of them so I used to act up, get this wiry metal that we used and stuff a load of it down the back of my trousers. Then I would wind up our teacher, Mr Harris, unmercifully until he flew into a temper and ordered me out in front of the class to get the cane. With the wire down my trousers I couldn't feel a thing, but I'd be making all these noises, 'ooh' and 'aargh', as he hit me, all the while winking and grinning at my mates in the room. Everyone would be laughing and Harris wouldn't have a clue what was going on.

Mr Harris was the saving grace for me, though, because he was also our football teacher. I went there at 11 and was straight in the first team with the 15-year-olds. We played in green shirts, but there was no other kit. Most of the boys wore jeans and army boots, even when representing the school. One of our first matches was against our big rivals Hay Currie, and they beat up Mr Harris after the game. He was the referee and he should have gone crooked and given them a couple of goals. They were big, scary boys – a few of them were members of notorious gangster families in the East End, proper villains in the making – and at the end of the match they chased him as he was trying to drive away on his moped. They pushed him off, trod on his wheels and smashed up the spikes. We all just stood there. We didn't fancy fighting them, either. Where I came from you either had to be good at fighting or good at running – and I was always a fast runner. I represented the school at everything: football, cricket and athletics, but our equipment was a joke. I came third in the 400 metres at the London Schools Championships, and I ran in slippers. I was only a yard behind the first two, but they had spikes.

When I first went there the school football team practised in the playground, but after a while we started to get a bus out to

Goresbrook Park in Dagenham. The problem was, by the time they had got all the nutters organised on these old green buses, and then sorted everybody out amid the pandemonium at the other end, it was time to come home. We would waste whole afternoons like that. It was only when I got picked up by Tottenham Hotspur that I saw how important it was to train properly.

I was in the C class, for the lowest academic achievers, which did not help. There was a boy called David Thompson, who had a car that he had nicked, a little Mini that he used to leave parked up the road. He could only have been about 14, but he was already a man. He was useless at football, but we got him in the school team because he used to run at people and frighten the life out of them. Not with the ball. He never had the ball. He'd just run at them, 'Grrr!', they'd get out of the way and we'd score. It wasn't a good team, though. My football career started in earnest when I was picked to play for East London Schools. It was at that moment that any chance I had of leaving with qualifications ended. Each Tuesday and Thursday I would excuse myself from school at about two o'clock, with another boy called Johnny Blake, and we'd go over to Hay Currie for our East London Schools training. It wasn't a long journey but we'd act as if we needed two hours to get there, and then just hang about until all the Hay Currie kids had gone home, and our session began. It was a great thing, and a big thing for me, because East London were a proper team with a proper green-and-gold quartered strip, and Mr Sturridge, the teacher who ran it with Mr Hurley, was also responsible for the England Schoolboys team. It was my first experience of real coaching. We were a unit, we were all mates and good players, and joining up with that group was the highlight of my week.

I think East London Boys kept a lot of kids on the straight and narrow. I don't think I would ever have fallen as far as Mr Enniver feared, but I would definitely have got into a lot more trouble had I not been so busy playing sport. I also played cricket for East London, and ran too, and because I was of a high standard I began coming into contact with professional coaches, like Eddie Baily from Tottenham Hotspur and Dennis Allen, Martin's dad, who played inside-forward for Charlton Athletic. That was probably the best time of my school football years, when Dennis starting coming in once a week to take our team. I think Mr Harris got Dennis in because he knew he had a couple of decent players among the lunatics. School felt like less of a madhouse on those days.

It wasn't as if Dennis could do much. We only had two footballs between all of us, and often he'd only stand there and watch us all play fifteen-a-side in the playground, but I loved the fact that here was a real professional footballer, because I idolised those guys. Dennis used to single me out and talk to me because he knew I had a chance, and all week I would look forward to being with him. I suddenly learned the importance of staying clean, tidy and fit. When Dennis left, his brother Les, Clive's dad, who won the Double with Tottenham, took over the supervision. Footballers had to earn money where they could in those days. He was probably paid £1.

If it hadn't worked out for me in football, I feel sure I would have ended up down the docks. That was where people like me went in those days, and Dad already had my name down. It was all about family connections. You could only get in if you had a dad or an uncle there but, luckily, my whole family were dockers. My dad, his dad, Uncle Jimmy, Uncle Billy. Sandra's family were dockers, too. If you had no education and lived in the East End, the docks opened their gates and in you went. Having failed miserably in exams at Susan Lawrence, I can't even remember taking any at Sir Humphrey Gilbert. I left just before my fifteenth birthday and never looked back. My school wasn't there to provide education.

Yet that East London schools team proved the making of me. We were really good, and started catching the attention of the professional clubs. One by one, our players began to get picked up. Terry Reardon, my friend from Burdett Boys, was the star and every team in England wanted him. Then one night we played at Millwall, in the final of the Criss Shield, against Wandsworth. We won 4–0 and I did really well. I remember we had the Cup and I felt ten feet tall, and as I came off down the tunnel there was a grey-haired man standing there, wearing a lovely big overcoat. He looked like a million dollars. I didn't recognise him, but it was Dickie Walker. He'd been a great centre-half for West Ham and the captain of the club, but I don't think they looked after him very well, and now he was chief scout for Tottenham. 'Is your dad here, son?' he asked. He told me who he was and that he wanted to see Dad before we went home. I went running in. 'Dad, Dad, the Tottenham scout's here – he wants me to go to Tottenham.' Just saying it felt great. Dickie arranged for the pair of us to meet him at White Hart Lane the next day. It was the middle of winter, freezing cold, and I had to wait for Dad to finish work. I had no overcoat, just a plastic mac; and we had no car, so it was an unpleasant walk from the station, but I didn't care. I was going to meet Tottenham. I had never been so excited. When we arrived, Dickie took us straight in to see Bill Nicholson, the manager. Bill was building the Tottenham team that went on to win the Double in 1960–61, the first manager of the twentieth century to do so, but here he was talking to me. I couldn't believe it.

To a young teenager, no more than 13, Bill was a very intimidating figure. He was a man of few words and had an immediate air of authority. He certainly didn't look like the sort of manager who would be up for having a laugh with the lads. 'Hello, son,' said Bill. 'Dickie tells me you've being doing all right, he's seen you play a couple of times. You're a winger, aren't you? Tell me, do you score goals?'

I couldn't lie. 'No, not me, Mr Nicholson,' I told him. 'I don't score many goals.'

He wasn't too happy with this. 'Well,' he said, 'I only know one great winger who didn't score goals and that was Stanley Matthews. Unless you're going to be as good as him, you'd better start scoring.'

And off he went. He was a blunt Yorkshireman and seemed very cold. I can't say I thought I'd have much of a future at Spurs after that brusque encounter.

Yet despite my lack of goals I did start training with Tottenham twice a week after school. Terry Reardon did, too. We got two trains there and two trains back and then made that journey six weeks straight in the school holidays.

There was a small group of us and, in summer, once the professionals were back at training, we all looked forward to the lunch break when the first-team players would come over and entertain us with a few tricks. Those names are legend now: Danny Blanchflower, Dave Mackay, John White. Just wearing the same Tottenham kit as them made us proud. 'Come on, John,' Mackay would say, 'show the lads what you can do.' And White would get the ball, put it on his neck, on his shoulders, let it drop and juggle it. He had possibly the best feet I've ever seen, just unbelievable skill, and we all sat there watching in awe. White was a true great. He had this amazing ability to arrive in the opposition penalty area without being detected, and the Tottenham fans nicknamed him 'the Ghost'. It was such a terrible tragedy that he died so young, struck by lightning on a golf course at the age of 27.

Tottenham were playing the best football in the league at the time and had a fantastic team. Cliff Jones was the fastest winger of his generation, Bobby Smith was a battering-ram striker, and at the back there was Maurice Norman, the first centre-half to go up for corner kicks. Yet White, bought from Falkirk for £22,000, was the pick of them all. Harry Evans, Tottenham's assistant manager, was John's father-in-law, and he used to work with the kids on Tuesdays and Thursdays. Before John died, Harry gave me a pair of his boots and they were the most beautiful black leather, the softest I had ever felt.

What a year that was. I watched a lot of the home matches as Tottenham won the Double – Bobby Smith smashing the ball in the net, the goalkeeper petrified – and even an Arsenal fan could see they were special. But my own career was taking off, too. West Ham, Chelsea, they were all in for me.

One evening on the Burdett Estate, we were playing football near the pram sheds and we spotted two men standing in the shadows. It was too dark to see the football, let alone make out who these shady figures were, but as they stepped into a chink of light I recognised Tommy Docherty, then a young manager at Chelsea. He was there with a scout, Wilf Chitty, to talk about me going to train with them instead. My dad loved the Doc – he was an ex-Arsenal man – and they came up to our flat where my mum made us all a cup of tea and my dad sat around talking football with one of his heroes.

By the time I was ready to sign I had the choice of all the London clubs, even Arsenal. My favourite club, though, was bottom of my list. As much as I loved the Gunners, at that time they had a reputation for buying players rather than developing them, and were by far the biggest London club in the transfer market. Even with Tottenham having such a great team, I still thought I would have more chance with them – but, in truth, the club I had fallen in love with was West Ham. Once they came in, and I got to know the culture there, it was the only choice for me.

I noticed that whenever I went to watch the youth team play, Ron Greenwood, the manager, was present. He really cared about the kids. He didn't just put in the odd appearance to impress you into signing. He knew you, how you were progressing, how far you had to go. The first team was full of home-grown players; Ron wasn't always out buying and West Ham was a place where I felt I would get a chance. They were doing well then, too. Tottenham were obviously the best team in London, but although Arsenal was the biggest club, they weren't streets ahead of West Ham in the league. And Chelsea were relegated in 1962.

Malcolm Allison, a former player, had also made a big impact at Upton Park. He had left by the time I arrived, but his influence could be seen everywhere, not least in the style of West Ham's great young captain Bobby Moore. Bobby swore that Malcolm made him, that without Malcolm he wouldn't have been half as good. Malcolm's career ended prematurely when he fell ill with tuberculosis and had to have a lung removed, but he would coach the kids at West Ham and took Bobby to training twice a week. Bobby said Malcolm was like the boss of the young players, and when he talked they all listened. I think the staff must have listened to him, too, because he stopped them making one of the greatest mistakes in the history of football. When it came to the end of each season, West Ham only had a limited number of new professional contracts on offer and, one summer, were choosing between Bobby Moore and another boy. It looked as if Bobby was going to be unlucky. The report on him said he couldn't run, couldn't head it, had no pace and wasn't big enough to be a centre-half. Malcolm wasn't having that and intervened. 'He's going to be a player,' he insisted forcefully, and, fortunately, the others listened.

Bobby used to tell one story about Malcolm that summed up his philosophy – and West Ham's philosophy at the time. The youth team played Chelsea away at their training ground one Wednesday afternoon. It was muddy, and Bobby was told to mark Barry Bridges. Barry was 17, but he was good enough to have played for Chelsea's first team the previous weekend, and had scored twice. This was an important game, however, so they had brought him back to the youth team as a one off. West Ham drew 0–0 and Bobby thought he did really well against Bridges. He knew Malcolm had been watching and when he came into the dressing room he thought his mentor was going to compliment him on stopping such a good player. Instead, Malcolm was furious. 'If I ever see you play like that, I'll never talk to you again,' he said. 'When our goalkeeper had the ball, what were you doing? You were looking at Barry Bridges. I've told you: drop off, get it from the keeper, and then play. That's your job. Play the ball. Every time the goalie gets it, tell him to give it to you. If he gives it out to the left-back, drop off, make an angle, so you can clip it into the front man's chest. That's how I've told you to play. Instead, you've run around like them all day. You haven't touched the ball. If you ever do that again, it's the last time I'll help you.'

What people thought was Bobby's unique game was actually instilled by Malcolm. Remember Bobby's pass that found Geoff Hurst in the World Cup final? That is what Malcolm had taught him to do. He took time to help Bob, to talk to him, coach him, give him good information. True, Bobby was bright enough to take it in, but he always gave Malcolm credit. He said that Malcolm made him a player. And he helped shape Greenwood's West Ham, too.

Ron was another old-school character, like Bill Nicholson. The manager's door wasn't always open in those days. Even senior players wishing to see Ron had to make an appointment. And you had to be in the first team a good few years before you were on first-name terms. Until that point, he was always Mr Greenwood. As apprentice professionals we had to do the chores. We trained in the morning and then returned to Upton Park to get the first-team kit ready for the next day. The laundry would stink with sweat or be caked in dry mud, but you had to make sure it was washed, dried and rolled up ready for use. After that, we were free, but we were all young and football mad and would often go on to the forecourt for a kickabout. That was the beginning of what would be an outstanding West Ham youth team, although Ernie Gregory, the first-team coach, saw us as more of a nuisance. He came out one day and moved us on, told us he had to get home, and we should go home, too. When Ron found out he gave Ernie the most frightful bollocking. 'As long as they want to stay out there, as long as they are doing something useful, as long as they are playing football, we'll stay here with them as long as they want,' he said. He loved the fact that all his apprentices just wanted to play. We weren't going off down the snooker hall or into the bookmaker's, so what was wrong with that? He was a proper football man, Ron.

In my first full season at West Ham, 1962–63, we won the FA Youth Cup. That was some achievement. Three of the players in that team were first-years, like me, and I was 15 for most of those matches. There is a huge difference in physical presence between the ages of 15 and 18, so it was a very unusual success.

We had a good team. The three youngsters were me, Colin Mackleworth, the goalkeeper, and our left-back, Bill Kitchener. Colin played for Burdett Boys and East London Schools, too, and he and Bill were big strong lads who marched straight into the team. By pure coincidence, when they retired from football, they both became coppers. John Charles, our captain, was the first black player to lead a professional team to a major trophy, and he would later become the first black player to represent West Ham in the top division. John Sissons, probably the most enthusiastic participant in our forecourt games, would be the youngest player to score in an FA Cup final, for West Ham against Preston North End a year later. Our centre-forward was Martin Britt. He was fantastic, another powerful boy who was scoring goals in the first team as a teenager. Martin had some injury problems and lost his place in the team, and the next thing we knew he had gone in to see Mr Greenwood and was off to Blackburn Rovers. Transfers like that didn't happen in those days, players tended to be more patient. But injury got the better of Martin at Blackburn, too, and he was out of the game at 21. A shame; I haven't seen too many who could head the ball like him. Dennis Burnett was our right-back, and he went on to play close to 300 games for Millwall. In fact, almost everyone in that team had reasonable careers. I felt sorry for a lad called Trevor Dawkins, who could have been a fantastic player, but I think Ron held him back too long. Then there was Peter Bennett, who played nearly ten years at Leyton Orient and Bobby Howe, who was with me at Seattle Sounders.

Ron Greenwood was at every game we played and would encourage us by fixing up matches against the first team in training. We'd give them a game, too. Our coach was Jimmy Barrett – Young Jim, as he was known, because his father, also Jim, was a legendary centre-half with West Ham before the war. Young Jim was a midfielder and a hard man, like his dad. He looked after us when we played as West Ham's A-team in the Metropolitan League each Saturday. We'd be up against men's amateur teams like Chelmsford City or Bedford Town, and they didn't like 15-year-olds getting the beating of them. They would try to take lumps out of us, at which point Young Jim would put himself on and settle a few scores. No matter the size of the player, he would sort them out. There were more than a few who thought they had got away with giving some kid a lesson, only to find themselves visited by Jim. He never let a kicking go unpunished.

We were on our own in the Youth Cup, though – on the pitch, at least. Off it, I don't think a group of young players ever had better support. When we got to the semi-final, our opponents, Wolverhampton Wanderers, insisted on playing the game on a Saturday. Mr Greenwood protested, but as it was an away fixture, he had no say. To our amazement, when we arrived to get the coach up to Molineux, there he was, getting on board with us. He chose a youth semi-final over a first-team fixture. Incredible. I've never forgotten that. To see our manager on the bus with us, stopping for tea and toast at a little place outside Wolverhampton, and in our dressing room before the game, gave us such a lift. We got a draw, and when we returned for the replay at Upton Park, the whole team turned out in support: Bobby Moore, John Bond, Alan Sealey – every player was up in the stand, and there must have been 20,000 fans, too. I think that is what made West Ham such a special club for a young player. If we had a big game, the senior players came to watch. You were always made to feel part of it, and that is something we have lost in modern football. I don't think it would be the same at a Premier League club now. I don't think the first team and youth players would have that same bond. Ron showed a lot of imagination in the way he involved the youth and the first team together. We'd play against them, and with them, if he thought you were showing promise. Now the teenagers are kept apart in academy buildings. They have their own pitches – there is distance. When I was 17, I regarded Bobby Moore, our captain, as a mate. West Ham had a completely different atmosphere.

We beat Wolves, and the final was over two legs against Liverpool. Tommy Smith, who went on to be an Anfield legend and notorious hard man, was their captain. We lost the first leg, away, 3–1. There was a big crowd at Anfield, and it was a real disappointment. The return was on the night of the FA Cup final. I can't even tell you who won it that year, I was so wrapped up in our game. It was a full house at Upton Park and by half-time we were 2–1 down, losing 5–2 on aggregate. We came out in the second half and terrorised them. We scored four goals, and won 6–5 on aggregate. It's one of the only times I ever saw Tommy Smith beaten up: Martin Britt bashed him all over the place. Tommy was brave, but at 16 Martin was a man. I was knocking balls into him from one wing, John Sissons was flying down the other – at the end, Ron Greenwood was in tears. You've never seen a man so proud. He loved that his forecourt kids had won the Youth Cup. It meant as much to him as the FA Cup. And that has stuck in my mind ever since. When I took over as manager at West Ham, every Saturday morning, if we were at home and the youth team had a game at our training ground, I would call at Chadwell Heath and watch us play, just as Ron did, before driving on to Upton Park. I knew what it meant to us to have him there, and I hope it meant the same to that generation of youth players.

I would like to think it is not a coincidence that West Ham won the FA Youth Cup in season 1998–99 when I was manager. I'm not trying to take credit, the boys went out and did it and we had a great team that year, but I do think it helped spur them on, thinking the whole club was behind them. Frank Lampard and I followed every game that year, all the way up to Oldham Athletic and against

Coventry City in the final, which we won 9–0 on aggregate. That was Joe Cole's and Michael Carrick's group. In 1995–96 we got beat 4–1 on aggregate by Liverpool in the final, when Rio Ferdinand and Frank Lampard played for us, and Liverpool had Jamie Carragher, and Michael Owen killed us coming off the bench.

I played my first senior game for West Ham on 23 August 1965, against Sunderland at Upton Park. We'd lost our first game of the season 3–0 at West Bromwich Albion, and Ron probably thought drastic action was needed. It was a night match under floodlights, Martin Peters scored from my corner and we drew 1–1. I'd had a taste of a big Upton Park crowd in the FA Youth Cup, but this was a step up again. Night matches always felt special there, and it was a great atmosphere. The following Saturday we beat a top Leeds United side, with Billy Bremner and Johnny Giles, all the greats, 2–1. I was on my way.

Football felt very different then. We were all boys from the same area, with the same backgrounds. Nobody thought they were a big star; we all mucked in together and had a laugh. I didn't feel at all intimidated coming from the youth team. Ron Greenwood had cleverly integrated the groups so there was never awkwardness. When we'd finished training, we'd all go round the Central Café, with our four-bob dinner vouchers, enough for steak and kidney pie, chips, beans, sticky roly-poly pudding with custard, two Coca-Colas and change. Sometimes, we'd hide the Coke bottles under the table, so when Peggy came round to settle up we'd do even better out of it.

Pre-season was rather different in those days, too. In Ron Greenwood we had the best, most forward-thinking coach in the country. We all had great respect for him and our training was always interesting – yet when compared to some of today's sports science ideas, it was prehistoric. First morning, we got weighed. Then everybody would board a Lacey's coach, nearly fifty of us – first team, youth team, three to a seat, some standing up in the aisles, Ron Greenwood at the front – and off we'd go, to Epping Forest. There, Ron would lead us on a little walk and then off we'd trot up a hill, running to where Ernie Gregory, the first-team coach, would give us our next directions. We'd have a little jog and then back down Epping New Road, the whole team in single file, lorries flying past us, until we reached the next point in the forest. After about half an hour of this, we would be strung out like washing. Bobby Moore was already steady near the back, Brian Dear last, and on we'd go for another three miles, ending up at a point called Mott Hill. By then, it wasn't unusual to see Brian riding a milk float, drinking a pint and wearing the milkie's hat, shouting, 'Come on, you lot.' He'd jump off about a hundred yards from the end of the run, and join the rest of us staggering to the finish. Then it was back on the coach and west towards our training ground. If the coach stopped at Grange Farm that meant Ron thought we hadn't worked hard enough the first time and another run was scheduled. For this one, we'd race across the field and over the little bridge, Bobby and Brian still bringing up the rear, until it was time for the coach to meet us again. One year, John Bond hid in the boot of the coach to get out of it and Peter Brabrook shut it for a joke and scared the life out of him. By the time we finished we had run and run and run in the boiling heat of a summer morning. And then it would be time to get back to Chadwell Heath for the afternoon session.

Next up, lunch. Steak and kidney pie, boiled potatoes; it was amazing we could play at all given the amount of food we ate each day. The kids like me would then go out to play cricket or football, while we waited for the afternoon session to begin. The old pros used to look at us as if we were mad. 'Give it a few years,' John 'Budgie' Byrne would warn us darkly, 'you won't want to be doing that then.' Our running session over, in the afternoon we would work on ball skills. By then our legs had seized up from the morning exercise, our calves were cramping and like concrete, and we could barely walk, let alone control the ball. And that's how it used to be. That was the most progressive training in the country.

Those games of cricket were fun, but also dangerous. Real cricket balls, and some real cricketers, too. Jim Standen, our goalkeeper, won the County Championship with Worcestershire in 1964 and topped their bowling averages with 52 wickets; Ron Tindall also played for Surrey; Eddie Presland and Geoff Hurst played for Essex. But most of the boys were useful. Frank Lampard and Roger Cross represented South of England Schools, and Martin Peters was a talented player.

Alan Sealey, who scored both goals for West Ham in the European Cup-Winners' Cup final in 1965, had his career as good as ended by a game of training-ground cricket. It was press day at the start of the 1965–66 season, our first day back for pre-season training. We'd had our run, had our lunch and were playing a game of cricket before going out to work again in the afternoon. One of the guys hit a high ball, and 'Sammy', as we called him, set off after it. We'd been having our team photographs taken and the benches had been left out on the edge of the pitches. We could all see Sammy heading towards them. We were shouting to warn him, but he probably thought we were just messing about. He only had eyes for the catch and then – bang – straight over the bench. Poor fella, he didn't just break his leg, he smashed it to pieces. In those days a player could not recover from an injury like that. He came back, limped, couldn't get rid of it, and played four more games for West Ham before retiring. A terrible shame.

Back then there was no equivalent of modern physiotherapy and medical science. Our physio, Bill Jenkins, was one of the most terrifying men I have ever met. And it wasn't just to me – the whole team was petrified of Bill. He was a Welshman, one of the first into the Auschwitz concentration camp as a medic, and had clearly seen some terrible sights. Not that this gave him a more enlightened or caring attitude towards humanity. He would torture you by turning the machines up to full, or punch you in the chest. He would regularly have Budgie Byrne in tears or screaming in pain. I can hear him now. 'You fucking lump of shit, you pile of shit,' he'd say. He would put all of the sucker pads on you and then run an electric current through to make the muscles tense then relax; and then he'd start to get angrier and angrier and turn them up so high it felt like the inside of your leg was being ripped out. That's why West Ham had so many injury problems – the last place anyone wanted to go was the physio's office. Unless you were desperate and had broken your leg in half, you didn't go near Bill.

He would come in on Sunday to treat any injuries from the match the previous day, but unless the patient brought him a bottle of Liebfraumilch or half a dozen lagers he'd tell you to fuck off. Bobby Moore, captain of England, would come in needing help, and be told to fuck off over the off licence or just fuck off home. We would end up paying Paddy O'Leary, our little Irish groundsman and the poorest ha'porth you've ever seen, to come back with Bill's beers, and only then could you climb on to the treatment table. The problem was, Bill then got quite intoxicated – and when he was in that state it made him even worse. Bill died quite early on in my West Ham career, but his son Rob carried on some of the traditions. Rob was much kinder than his dad, and very laid back – but he still liked the odd beer to get him going on a Sunday.

He was our mate, though, Rob. If you went to see him on Monday, he'd come round taking orders for breakfast. 'What do you want, Harry?' 'I'll have an egg and bacon sandwich, please, Rob; white bread.' Then he would phone down to the other groundsman at the Chadwell Heath training ground. 'Hello, Bert, is the manager there? Oh, gone out training, has he? When? Just now? Right you are. No, no message. It's not important, I'll speak to him later.' And then, having got the all clear that there was no way Ron Greenwood would be paying us a surprise visit, he'd send out to Doug's Café for sandwiches and tea. Players these days wouldn't believe how it was back then. Charlie Mitten, up at Newcastle United, used to love greyhound racing, and the players often couldn't get on the treatment table because one of his dogs was getting a rub down instead. When I went to Bournemouth as a player, one of the staff was Arthur Cunliffe, a pre-war England international who had a fine career as a winger with Blackburn Rovers and Aston Villa. Arthur was a nice old boy with a pipe, who originally used to help the groundsman out, preparing the pitch. Suddenly, he was our physio. He'd never been on a course, had no formal training, but our manager, John Bond, liked him. I tore a thigh muscle in pre-season training and limped off. 'What's the matter?' asked Arthur. I told him about the tear. He felt my leg. 'Don't worry, that's fine,' he said. 'You can go back on now.' Like an idiot I did, kicked a ball and then the muscle tore properly. I was in agony. I hobbled off and went to Arthur's office where he had one of the new ultrasound machines. I had four days of treatment but it got no better. Each morning Arthur would spend an hour or more, rubbing this transducer probe on my thigh area. Nothing ever happened. No improvement, no real sensation. I wasn't sure Arthur knew how to work it. After about a week of this I began studying the machine more closely. 'Arthur,' I said, 'we had one of these at West Ham. Isn't there supposed to be a little green light that comes on?' He hadn't plugged it in. He'd never plugged it in. He had been treating the entire first team with this since the start of pre-season and not once had it been switched on. No wonder we couldn't get fit.

Back to West Ham, and after training, we'd do what any group of workmates did. We'd go to the pub. We started off in the East End, where we all came from but, after a little while, as people moved out, so did the haunts. The Retreat in Chigwell was a favourite. Football teams were boys' clubs back then. There were not so many nationalities, language barriers and divisions. The West Ham players socialised together all the time, and every team was the same. Bobby Moore even bought a little chauffeur's hat because he worked out the police never pulled over chauffeur-driven cars. If he was driving when he'd had a few, he would sit us in the back, put on his hat and off we'd go.

It was around then that I met Sandra. The Two Puddings pub in Stratford used to have a dance upstairs on Sunday nights. All the teenagers from the East End went there, and I would go with my mate Colin Mackleworth. There were two girls there that we asked to dance, Susan and Sandra. Colin got Susan; I got Sandra. Colin was better looking than me and I think Sandra thought she'd pulled the bad draw. She was hoping Colin would ask her to dance. I loved Sandra to bits from day one. I've been married forty-six years, and I always say she was my best signing. Jamie tells me I won the lottery the day I met her – and I did; I've never felt anything less than very, very lucky.

When people hear that Frank Lampard and I ended up marrying sisters, they always think the girls must have gone out hunting for footballers, but it wasn't like that at all. It was pure coincidence. Pat and Sandra had no interest in football – nobody in their family really liked the game – and neither of them had a clue who we were. We didn't even meet through each other. A few weeks after I started going out with Sandra, Frank came into Chadwell Heath one morning and said, 'I took a girl home last night, and you're seeing her sister.' He had met Pat by chance at the Ship in Stepney. What are the odds of that?

Sandra's dad, Bill Harris, was a foreman down Albert Dock. He was a huge bloke with arms bigger than my legs. You didn't want to mess with Bill. Sandra and Pat were hairdressers, and the whole family lived in Barking, in a house with a proper little garden, which I thought was very upmarket, coming from a block of flats on the Burdett Estate. I used to take Sandra back to her house after going out, and if I was there longer than ten minutes the old man used to bang on the floor from the bedroom upstairs. He was fantastic, Bill, an absolutely lovely man, but not the sort you wanted to cross. Frank was scared stiff of him as well – and Sandra and Pat's brother, Brian, was every bit as big. They were a wonderful family, though, and it wasn't long before we were making plans to be married.

I had to save up first – I told you times were different for footballers then – and to help us buy our first house I got a job in Mr Wilson's supermarket in Green Street. Turn right out of Upton Park, the station is on the left, and opposite was Mr Wilson's. He was a nice man, he came from Newcastle, and loved his football. We used to eat in Porkies Café, which was next door, and when I told him I needed extra money he offered me a job stacking shelves. I started on Monday and on the Friday of the first week walked down Green Street to pick up my wages from West Ham. Nobody got their pay sent directly into a bank account then. We all had to collect our little envelopes, and mine had twenty quid in it, plus a bit of silver and the wage slip. Ron Greenwood must have seen me arrive in my white coat because he came straight out to meet me. 'Hello, Harry,' he said. 'What are you up to? A bit of decorating?'

'No,' I told him, 'I'm working in a supermarket. I'm saving up to get married, but I want to buy a house and I can't afford it on what West Ham pay me.'

'You're working in a supermarket?' he replied. 'Not any more you're not. You're under contract to us.' He managed to get me another two quid a week, but I wasn't the only one doing two jobs. A lot of the lads took a shift on, certainly in the summer. Bobby Moore worked in a factory in Barking for a year at least.

The most I ever earned at West Ham was £50, and none of the young players had cars. It would be a few years before I bought my first one, a little green Austin 100 which cost £640. Players went to the match by bus, some of them even walked. John Bond lived no more than fifty yards from the ground: right, then first left, in a little terrace. The only person who had a big house and moved out was Bobby, to Manor Lane, Chigwell. Then Geoff Hurst and Martin Peters moved to Wingletye Lane in Hornchurch, but they didn't have mansions. Sandra and I were going to move to Barking, near Frank and Pat. I remember my dad thinking I was off my head, buying a house for £6,200. He didn't know anyone who owned a house. He and my mum still lived in their old council flat. He didn't understand what I was doing.

We got married in 1967 in a church in the centre of Barking. Frank was going to be my best man, but he broke his leg badly. Willie Carlin went over the top on him at Sheffield United, one of the worst tackles I've ever seen. Frank was only a kid, 18 at the time. His leg was in pieces. It took all his willpower – and more running up and down the terraces at Upton Park – for him to make a complete recovery.

We had the wedding reception at a club in Loxford Lane, Ilford, where Sandra's dad was a member, and went off on honeymoon – to Torquay. These modern players have got nothing on the glamorous life we lived then. What I remember most about the trip is the new car I had bought, so we could travel in style: a bright red Jaguar, formerly owned by John Bond.

After training, John used to hang out with his mate, who ran a garage opposite the Central Café called Birkett Motors. One day, Frank and I came out of the café and starting chatting to them.

It was Frank's idea that I buy the car. I'll admit it was a beauty: wooden steering wheel, lovely red paintwork, immaculate. We took it for a spin along East Ham High Street, and that was enough. John wanted £250. Deal done. I'd only had it a few months when I took it on honeymoon and on the way back the head gasket went. It took us nine hours to get home. Very romantic. Not only that but when I inspected the log book properly, the car was from 1960 and John had told me 1962. We ended up having a huge row.

Meanwhile, football was going through major changes. The step up to the first team had not been a problem for me initially, but between 1965, when I made my debut, and 1967, when I married Sandra, England won the World Cup, and wingers were no longer fashionable. My early form was good and, as a local boy, the fans were right behind me, but once three of my teammates had helped England lift the World Cup, in a team without wide players, the euphoria gave way to a more pragmatic approach. The wingless wonders altered how people looked at my position. It's true that I failed to fulfil my early potential but the revolution in the game certainly did not help. For years, full-backs had been the slowest players in the team. Now coaches had caught up and many were as fast as the wingers. They were told to get tight, not to give that yard of space to get the ball under control. A winger in a good team would still get enough chances to beat his man, but it wasn't like that at West Ham. I'd be out by the touchline, never allowed to come inside, and when we finally did get the ball to me – bang – the full-back came in hard. There wasn't the protection that exists for players these days. My form dipped, and so did my popularity. Upton Park is a terrible place to play if the fans are against you, and they came to be always on my case. The Chicken Run, the lower tier of the East Stand, was the worst. You could almost feel them breathing down your neck. The moment you got the ball they expected you to turn your man inside out like George Best. That's hard when your confidence is on the floor.

'Were the tackles as bad as people say back then?' I am often asked. I think they were worse. It was an open secret in football that at Leeds players were as good as coached to go over the top. Any fifty-fifty tackle and there was a good chance you would be done. Giles and Bremner are two of the finest players I have seen, but to say they could put it about is an understatement. They were horrible to play against. I think it was the dirtiest era there has ever been in football. Yes, there were some rough challenges in Sir Stanley Matthews's time, too, but the players were not as athletic. Have a look at the famous FA Cup final between Blackpool and Bolton Wanderers in 1953, and when Stan gets the ball, it takes about ten seconds before the full-back comes into the picture. He's had to run over from forty yards away. By the time I played for West Ham, players like Tommy Smith were on you as you got the ball – there was no space wide any more, and the only player I ever saw operate there consistently was George Best. Eventually, even he started coming inside to avoid a kicking, though. George at his peak was unstoppable, but for the rest of us mortals it was hard. I don't think football has ever changed as much in such a short space of time as it did in the mid-sixties.

I was seven years a West Ham player but, looking back, I was on my way out after 3 October 1970, when my relationship with Ron Greenwood hit a low. We had made a dismal start to the season and had only won one game – against Hull City in the League Cup – when Newcastle United came to Upton Park. Our bad form continued that day. I was about the only player who was performing for us, but when we went 1–0 down, Ron took me off for Trevor Brooking. I was furious and couldn't help showing it. I walked as slowly as I could from the far side of the pitch to the tunnel, with all the fans booing Ron's decision. It made a change from them hating me. We lost 2–0 and I was sitting in the medical room after the game when Ron burst in. 'Don't you ever do that to me again,' he snapped. 'When I take you off, you run, you don't walk.'

I wasn't having that. 'And don't you fucking do that to me again, either,' I shot back. 'You could have taken any one of us off – but it's always me, isn't it?'

Ron stormed out, but as he was leaving I picked up a bottle of beer from a crate that Jimmy Greaves and Bobby had been working on, and threw it against the closing door. 'That's nice,' said Jim. 'You could have thrown an empty one.'

I played about half of that season, and half of the next, but my time at West Ham was done. In 1972, I went to Bournemouth, where John Bond was now manager. I played 175 games for West Ham, but only scored eight goals. He wasn't a bad judge, Bill Nicholson.

CHAPTER FIVE

BESIDE THE SEASIDE

I joined Bournemouth on 1 August 1972, for what was then a club record fee of £31,000. John Bond, my old West Ham teammate and used car salesman, was the manager, and he was throwing a lot of money at a big rebuilding project. He'd bought Ted MacDougall, a Scotland international, who had scored nine goals in an FA Cup tie with Margate the previous season, and would go on to play for Manchester United. Ted's partner was Phil Boyer, and they had played together at four different clubs, scoring 195 goals. On the day I signed, John also bought Jimmy Gabriel. He had won the title and the FA Cup at Everton, but had lost his place in the team to Howard Kendall and had moved to Southampton. He was a Scottish international too, and rock hard in midfield. Bobby Howe, who played with me in the FA Youth Cup final, was another that had been brought to Bournemouth from West Ham.

I was only 25, but it didn't feel like a huge step down going to Bournemouth. John was a bold thinker and the club had ambition. We were building a new stand, and John switched the first-team strip from plain red to red and black stripes, like AC Milan. He even changed the name of the club. We were no longer Bournemouth and Boscombe Athletic as we had been since 1923. We were AFC Bournemouth. With the good players we were signing, even the standard didn't feel low. Whenever a good player became available who was within our reach, John would open the chequebook and sign him. The running joke was that if you had a good game against Bournemouth, they bought you the next day.

The best of the lot was a left-winger called Alan Groves. We had taken him from Shrewsbury Town and he had ability like I have rarely seen, not even in the top division. He was six foot, 14 stone, muscles on muscles, and nobody could get near him. I had played against him once before with West Ham, and I knew he was good: there were about eight of us chasing him all over the park like a Benny Hill sketch. We couldn't get near him. He was hard as nails: the more you kicked him, the more he liked it. 'Don't do that, son, you'll only hurt yourself,' he'd say to full-backs. It used to drive them mad. He was just one of the greatest characters I met in football. Smoked eighty fags a day, drove a Jag; if we were doing shuttle sprints in training he'd run ten yards, hop ten yards, then run the last ten pretending to be smoking a cigar. And still keep up! He was that athletic.

Alan was an orphan. He started off as a Dr Barnado's boy, became a long-distance lorry driver, and got into football by an alternative route. Having worked hard for a living, he knew it was only a game. He was one of those guys that was always laughing. John was a flamboyant sort, too, and when Alan bought an E-Type convertible Jag, he loved it. It had one of those fancy horns that play a tune, and you could hear him roaring about all over town. John turned it into a speech. 'I see one of you boys driving about in an E-Type Jag,' he said. 'Fantastic. I want the day to come when you've all got E-Type Jags; all got Mercedes. I don't want to see Minis and Morris Minors out there, just beautiful cars. Because that means we've all been successful together.' He turned to look at Alan. 'Grovesey – different class, son,' he said. The following week, we got beat and Groves had a quiet one. John came in like a whirlwind. He blasted the lot of us, then turned to Alan. 'And you,' he said. 'If you think you are going to drive around town, showing off in that fucking E-Type, you've got another thing coming. Get rid of that car. I don't want to see that fucking car at this club ever again.'

For a time, Alan was killing every defender in the division. I told Bobby Moore about him one night. 'He's the best I've seen, Bob,' I said. Bobby had just played for England against Yugoslavia. 'Oh yeah,' he replied. 'Is he as good as Dragan Džajić?' 'He's better,' I told him, because by then I'd probably had a few and wasn't going to back down. Bob brought a few of the West Ham lads down to watch one of our games just to check out Alan. He was brilliant that night. Scored two goals, beat four players for the first, five players for the second, won the game on his own. 'You may be right,' Bobby said afterwards. 'What a player.'

One day we went to an away match at Chesterfield and, as we got off the coach, a girl was waiting for us. We heard this huge row taking place, at the end of which the girl was marching up the road with Alan running after her, holding a baby. It was his, apparently, from when he played at Shrewsbury. The time came to warm up, we were all in the dressing room, and Alan was still standing there with the little boy. In the end, he gave it to these two fans, a couple of old girls who used to follow us everywhere, and they looked after it during the game. You never knew what was going to happen next with him. Trevor Hartley, the manager that succeeded John Bond, sold him to Oldham Athletic in the end. Alan didn't want to go, but Trevor had been promoted from our youth-team set-up and didn't know how to handle him. Alan was just too lively for him. The next time Bournemouth played Oldham, Alan got the ball on the far side of the pitch and began dribbling it along the halfway line. We were in pursuit, but nobody had a clue where he was going. He finally veered off slightly right until he got directly in front of the Bournemouth dug-out and then he hit the ball as hard as he could straight at Trevor Hartley. The ball was bouncing about inside the concrete shell like a pinball. At the end of the game, Hartley ran off and locked himself in our dressing room to stop Alan trying to get him a second time. The player had the last laugh, though. Bournemouth were in a promotion position when Alan was sold, but missed out, and who went up in our place? Oldham, mostly thanks to the impact that Alan made. You may wonder why you have never heard of this incredible, larger than life man, and I'm sad to say the story doesn't have a happy ending. Alan died of a heart attack in his home, at the age of 29. He was about to start preparing for the new season, 1978–79, with Blackpool.

I certainly can't complain about my time at Bournemouth, though. All of John's new signings moved into the same little housing estate in Christchurch, me with Sandra and our oldest son, Mark. Jimmy Gabriel and Bobby Howe lived nearby and we'd share a car into training every morning, talking football all the way. Little did I know that those journeys were going to lead to more than thirty years in football management. And despite narrowly missing out on promotion on two occasions, we all knew

Bournemouth were going places thanks to John's ideas and the money invested by Harold Walker, the chairman. Unfortunately, as often happens to a promising project in the lower leagues, it was not to last. In November 1973, John got an offer to manage Norwich City, who were in the First Division, and Bournemouth accepted £10,000 compensation for him and first-team coach Ken Brown. He promptly bought MacDougall and Boyer, too, and he tried to sign me, although by then a long-standing knee problem had deteriorated to such an extent that I could barely run. Bournemouth went on a gradual slide once John left with our best players and, by 1976, after a lengthy period in plaster, I gave up. I made one last attempt to revive my career at Brentford, with a month-long trial. My only game away at Aldershot lasted 38 minutes before the knee problem intervened and the manager that set up the trial, John Docherty, got sacked at half-time. I took that as a sign. There was no way I could continue as a professional footballer in England. America, however, where my friend Jimmy Gabriel was embarking on a new career, was a different matter.

Jimmy's time at Bournemouth had not ended well. He was eased out after a very strange row with John Bond. I couldn't see why they didn't just patch it up. We were playing a league game away from home and one of our players had been taken out by this big lump shortly just before half-time. 'Don't worry,' said Jimmy, 'I'll snap him in half.' He meant it, too – Jimmy was a seriously tough guy when he needed to be. John Bond overheard and rounded on him. 'What do you mean by that?' he asked. John had been around. He knew exactly what Jimmy meant. 'I'll do him,' Jimmy said. 'I'll go right over the top.' 'Not in my team you won't,' John shouted, and they ended up having a huge argument. And that was the end of Jimmy at Bournemouth. He was shipped out on loan to Swindon Town and ended up at Brentford. By the time I retired in 1976 he was player-coach of Seattle Sounders under John Best, an ex-Tranmere Rovers defender who had been playing and managing in America since 1962. Best had moved upstairs to be general manager and Jimmy had succeeded him as coach. We had stayed in touch since our time together as players and when I told him I was retiring he immediately suggested coming out to Seattle to play for him. It was a big decision, but what options did I have back home? In March 1976 I flew out with Sandra and our two little boys, Mark and Jamie, who had been born during my time at Bournemouth, to begin our new life in America.

A lot of us ended up out there in the end: Bobby Moore, Geoff Hurst, Alan Hudson, Bobby Howe. The social side was great, and the football wasn't bad either. It was the time when Pelé and Franz Beckenbauer were playing for New York Cosmos, and there was real interest in this new sport called soccer. We averaged 28,000 for home matches in Seattle, and in my first game against Cosmos the crowd was 66,000. As for the lifestyle, that was fantastic. We all lived on the same complex and, while we went off to train, our wives would go to Green Lake and get a barbecue ready. We'd come back, eat, have a swim and play with the kids until nightfall. It was like being on holiday. There was none of the hooliganism that was blighting the game back in England, and the fans loved the foreign players, who were the stars of the league. There was a real feel-good atmosphere around football in America.

And Jimmy must have liked what he heard during those short trips into training in the car from Christchurch, because he made me his coach. I had played most of the first season, when we reached the final of the Soccer Bowl and lost to New York Cosmos, but although I still turned out as regularly as my knees would allow, I was more involved with Jimmy and the staff. The reserves at first, but then with the first team. I liked it immediately.

To be fair, Ron Greenwood had whetted my appetite for coaching when I was at West Ham. We used to be paid £2.50 an hour to train the kids at the local schools. I started with Forest Gate School and then one in Howard Road, East Ham, and ended up at Frank Lampard's old school off Green Street. We'd do Monday to Thursday, £10 per week. You don't see that sort of thing any more, but I thought it was very important because it kept the players and the club connected to the local community. Ron didn't want me working in a supermarket, but he didn't mind any of us coaching school children. I think all the players in the first team did it at one time or another.

So things were going well in America. We had twelve-month contracts but were allowed to spend the close season back home. It was a great little job. And then Jimmy rang up and said he'd been offered a job in Phoenix, Arizona, and that's where it all fell apart. Phoenix Fire were not in the North American Soccer League, which was the top division, but in the second tier, known as the American Soccer League. The club owner, Len Lesser, had told Jimmy that this inferior status was strictly temporary and with the money he was investing they would be promoted within a season. Jimmy had signed up and wanted me to come with him. When Lesser called he talked telephone numbers. The best money I had ever received in my life. A housing budget, a convertible for Sandra – and she couldn't even drive. For a bloke who had ended up playing for Bournemouth it seemed too good to be true – which it was.

Lesser wanted me to bring some players back with me from England, and I did. Not the greatest talent, but plenty good enough for the American Soccer League. Families in tow, they returned with me to Phoenix to begin our new adventure. The first warning sign came when Jimmy and I had lunch with Lesser, and I saw him altering the bill. I tried to tell Jimmy, but he wasn't having any of it. With ten minutes to go before our first game with Chicago Fire, we had no kit. When it finally arrived there was no goalkeeper's shirt. 'We'll be the smartest team in America,' said Lesser. 'We'll all wear the same, none of this different shirt shit.' I tried to explain that the goalkeeper had to dress differently because he was allowed to pick the ball up, but I couldn't make him see sense. In the end, Kieron Baker, a goalkeeper I had got from Ipswich Town, borrowed an alternate shirt.

Kieron's wife had stayed back in England because she was pregnant so, when he returned home, I instructed him to bring out all new equipment – boots, shin pads, gloves, everything we would need to become a serious football club – with him on his return. But, by the time he came back, the full reality of Lesser's con had started to dawn. It was my birthday, 2 March, and I was going to take the family out for dinner. I went to a bank to get some money out, only to be told the account had been closed. The Phoenix Fire tab was three quarters of a million dollars overdrawn, and had subsequently been shut and all money reclaimed – including that from my account, which held £5,000 of my own savings. I got that back after an argument with the bank manager, but it was cold comfort. There were no wages, backdated or current, and when I rang Jimmy, his wife Pat told me that her cheque had bounced at the supermarket, too.

Jimmy and I confronted Lesser at his office – he had a huge photograph of himself and former President Jimmy Carter on the wall – and he assured us it was all a misunderstanding caused by the transfer of money between Phoenix Fire accounts. Then he offered me twenty dollars to fund my birthday dinner. He must have thought we would be driving through McDonald's on our way home. 'It will be sorted out by Monday,' was his promise. Of course, it wasn't.

Phoenix Fire was just Lesser's scam. On the back of appointing the management team – 'our super coaches', he would call us – that had taken Seattle Sounders to the Championship final, he had persuaded five investors to stump up two and half million dollars. That had now disappeared, and Lesser just brazened it out. He knew he was in trouble, but had hidden the money away. Meanwhile, Kieron Baker was returning to Phoenix all smiles, with forty pairs of boots and a heavily pregnant wife, to play for a team that no longer existed.

Lesser ended up getting two years, but nobody recovered any money. All our cars were repossessed, except mine, which I used to ferry all the players back to the airport with their wives and families, our American dream at an end. The repossession company were hunting everywhere for me, and I kept moving from motel to motel to stay out of their reach until the job was done. We stayed a little longer in Phoenix, trying to get a second team off the ground, but it was a dead end. About five months later I came home.

Considering that my first jobs in management ended in that nightmare, to be followed by a period of going nowhere fast with Bobby at Oxford City, you might think I would be sick of it – but when David Webb called to offer me the job as his coach at

Bournemouth, I jumped at the chance. The money wasn't great, but it was close to home and the club was ambitious. Well, Dave was anyway.

He wasn't the greatest coach, but Webby was a good motivator and he could spot a player. I haven't see too many better than him at mining talent from the lower leagues. He went to watch Andover one night – they had a player we fancied – and came back with Nigel Spackman, who went on to play four years at Chelsea and won the league at Liverpool. Dave paid £2,000 for Nigel and Andover couldn't believe their luck – he wasn't even getting in their team at the time. The night Dave went, Spackman didn't so much as start. He came on as a substitute and Dave liked what he saw immediately: a 6 foot 1 inch midfield player, good technique, and could run all day. I don't know too many managers who have dug one out like that.

Dave's problem was that he was always on the lookout for something bigger and better. He had petrol stations and property interests outside football, and if there was something going, he wanted in on it. He didn't want to manage Bournemouth, he wanted to run Bournemouth; and not even Bournemouth, but Chelsea. He would persuade a hotel receptionist to announce a telephone call for him, so all the board could hear. 'Mr Webb, Mr Ken Bates is on the line for you.' And every time he pulled a stroke like that, his wages would go up. He was a great one for telling doormen, 'Do you know who I am?' They didn't always. Then Dave would tell them to fetch the manager because he was going to buy the place and give them all the sack. Meanwhile, I would be trying to hide in a corner with embarrassment. Sometimes he just pushed it too far. Dave's big mistake was thinking Harold Walker, the Bournemouth chairman, was a mug. A couple of times he called Dave's bluff when he was threatening to quit, saying he was too big for Bournemouth, and one day he simply talked himself out of a job. The chairman had been courting a couple of investors, but Dave had it in his mind to pull off a coup. He had Jim Davidson, the comedian, onside, plus Barry Briggs, the former World Champion speedway rider. When the two investors arrived at Bournemouth, Dave was there to meet them, heading them off before they went inside. 'Don't go in with Harold Walker,' he told them. 'I'm taking over. Come in with me, I've got big plans.' Unfortunately one of the prospective directors was the chairman's best friend from his time at university: two days later, Dave was sacked.

Typically, though, he believed he could sweet talk his way out of it. Walker had given him until the end of the week to clear his desk, but on the Friday, Dave attempted his final stunt as Bournemouth manager. He phoned the chairman. 'I've got two fantastic players I can get on free transfers,' he said. 'We could sell them later for a fortune. Obviously, though, there's no point if you meant what you said about me leaving.' He waited for the chairman to climb down. 'Don't sign them, then, Dave,' said Mr Walker, 'because I meant every word. Goodbye.'

Frankly, my first thought when I heard Dave was leaving was for myself, my family and our future. Dave was always going to get fixed up somewhere – and he did end up managing Chelsea, with Ken Bates as chairman – but I had barely got a chance in English football, and now it looked like I was about to get sacked as well. I was earning £90 a week and we were only making ends meet because Sandra had started hairdressing again. She had one of those big hairdryers and was doing a £1.50 shampoo-and-set for a few old girls around our way. It was a struggle. I didn't even have a contract. I was cursing Dave. I had told him to sort it out with the chairman. Now what was I going to do? 'You'll be all right,' he said. 'They'll give you a couple of weeks' wages.' Great, two hundred quid if I was lucky. And after that?

Dave had left and I was sitting at the ground wondering what my next move could be, when there was a knock at the door. 'Would you take the team tomorrow?' asked Mr Walker. 'We've got no one else.' Suddenly, from being close to unemployed, I was caretaker manager of Bournemouth, and we were away to Lincoln City, who were top of Division Three at the time.

Lincoln were managed by Colin Murphy and, although they faded that season and failed to win promotion, they were still a very strong team in our league. They had John Fashanu and Neil Shipperley upfront and Steve Thompson, who was an imposing centre-half. They played West Ham in the League Cup the following month and took them to a replay. They were three points clear going into our game and would have been hot favourites for a home win.

As for me, I had John Kirk as my only member of staff. John was a former goalkeeper and his official title was physiotherapist, but he was an old-fashioned trainer, really. If someone broke a leg, John would run a cold sponge over them first just to make sure. He didn't really have a clue. It was a bitterly cold day, 18 December 1982, and there were games off all over the country due to frozen pitches. Lincoln had a pitch inspection at their ground, Sincil Bank, too, and we expected our match to be among those postponed. I hadn't counted on Colin's desperation to play Bournemouth, in turmoil with a rookie manager. When I arrived he had lit small coal fires all over the pitch, about eight of them. God knows what they

Above: Me as a shy youngster at West Ham. We'd won the FA Youth Cup in 1962–63 when I was just 15.

Below: Happy Hammers – the West Ham youth team. The keeper Colin Mackleworth had come from the same Burdett Boys side as me.

Above: Here I am at the beginning of the 1968–69 season, well established by that time in Ron Greenwood's first team and looking a bit more cocky and sure of myself.

Above: I met Sandra at a dance in the Two Puddings pub in Stratford. I was lucky enough to be the one that got to dance with her.

Below: When Frank Lampard broke his leg in a game, it ruled him out of being my best man. But he did end up marrying Sandra's sister.

Above: Waved off by a boy with a Hammers bobble hat and a
rattle – you don't see that often at a wedding these days.

Left: My mum, Violet, and dad, Harry Senior, at our wedding. My dad took me from an early age to see his beloved Arsenal and, though never professional, was quite a player in his own right.

Above: And still mates all those years later.

Below: We've been married 46 years and I always say she was my best signing.

Above: A classic West Ham side, including myself, Bobby Moore, Billy Bonds and Frank Lampard Senior. 1971–72 would be my last year with the Hammers.

Below: In action against Hereford in 1972. The great Bill Nicholson marked me out from the off as a winger who didn't score enough goals. I was certainly no Gareth Bale, registering not a single goal in my final season at Upton Park.

Above: Me and Bobby and some of the West Ham lads out for a few beers at Raffles in Canning Town.

Above: Me and Bobby with Mark and Jamie out on the pitch during our American adventure with the Seattle Sounders.

Above: Winning the Bell's Manager of the Season 1986–87, having taken Bournemouth to the dizzy heights of Division Two for the first time in their history.

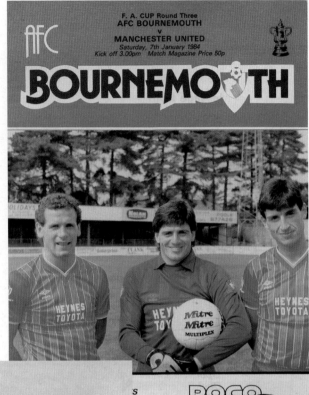

F. A. CUP Round Three
AFC BOURNEMOUTH
v
MANCHESTER UNITED
Saturday, 7th January 1984
Kick off 3.00pm   Match Magazine Price 50p

BOURNEMOUTH

Club
COMMENT

POCO HOMES
PLEASING PEOPLE

It gives me great pleasure today in welcoming Manchester United to Dean Court in the Third Round of the F.A. Cup. Since our last meeting in the Milk Cup many changes have taken place here at Dean Court culminating in myself taking over the hot seat as Manager, but I will not forget that first leg tie at Old Trafford when I made my sudden come back to competitive football, and the moment I diverted that cross from Ashley Grimes into our own net.

In recent games we have created more chances than at any other time in the season, putting them away has been a problem, but as long as we are playing the style of football that creates these chances then the time will come when we will convert them into a number of goals, and it will give us all a great thrill if that time comes today.

I must remark about Bob Savage our latest signing a lad full of enthusiasm and a will to win. His goal within forty seconds of the kick off against Exeter was the first of the many he is capable of scoring from a mid field position. He is a lad with the type of character that I have been seeking since I have been Manager and I know he will prove an asset to AFC Bournemouth for the future.

Give us your extra support today and let us look forward to an exciting game.

HARRY REDKNAPP

Above and left: In my first full season as manager with the Cherries in 1984 we pulled off the mother of all upsets by knocking Manchester United out of the FA Cup. In my programme notes I wax lyrical about my stunning own goal the last time we'd played them in the Milk Cup.

Above: We might look like mechanics, but that was our training gear. Me, Geoff Hurst, Clyde Best, Trevor Brooking, Pop Robson, Ronnie Boyce and John Ayris – probably thinking about the steak and kidney pie we would be having for lunch in Porkies Café.

Left: My first season at Bournemouth under John Bond, 1972–73. The hair was getting longer, the goals fewer and the knees dodgier.

Relaxing at home 70s style: me and Sandra, son Mark and dog Matty.

Above: Going up, going up, going up. The only way to celebrate was to get in the bath with the team.

Below: My friend Brian Tiler and me in our pomp at Bournemouth. He would never make it out of the wreckage of our minibus on that fateful night in Latina during Italia 90. I was luckier. I still sorely miss him.

Above: Stormy weather – me and Bill in 1992. I didn't have to think twice when I got the call from West Ham, but our relationship was destined to not always run that smoothly.

Below: Signing big John Hartson for West Ham in 1997. With desire and commitment like his, you could forgive him almost anything. His goals saved us from relegation that year.

Above: Losing 0–1 to Charlton in 1999. Standing anxiously on the touchline is something I've made a career out of. It is always easier to suffer the disappointments though when you have men like Frank Lampard Senior beside you.

Below: 'Yes Paolo, I know Paolo, don't worry Paolo'. Di Canio might have always bent my ear during training sessions, but it was worth it come Saturday. Among a small legion of foreign disasters, he stands tall as West Ham's greatest ever import.

Opposite: Here I am at West Ham in classic manager's office pose – a phone, a fax, a video tape, a copy of Rothmans, a nice cuppa and I'm ready for business.

Below: I'd first met Milan when he ran the San Jose Earthquakes back in the 70s. From the minute we met to talk about Portsmouth we hit it off. He's a true character.

Above: 'Harry and Jim' the fans would sing at Fratton Park and with his 30 years of experience we really were a winning double act. But Milan didn't see it that way and never truly took to Jim. The bust-ups over him would eventually result in me leaving the club.

Above: Winning promotion to the Premiership with Pompey, with a 1–0 win over Burnley, was a special moment for me and the fans.

Below: Finally getting our hands on the Championship trophy after a win against Rotherham on the final day of the season.

were supposed to do, but the referee fell for it and announced that we would play. How these fires were meant to thaw anything out, I don't know.

It was at this point that John Kirk announced that all our footwear had long studs, not rubbers. 'I've been telling them about this for weeks, Harry,' he said. 'They don't listen to me.' I went out for the warm-up and Lincoln were there, wearing boots with little pimples on the soles, running, checking, turning, knocking it about like Brazil. Our centre-half took two steps on to the pitch and went arse over tit. The next two followed him. We walked out like Bambi on ice. It would have been funny had I not known what was going to happen next. Stone me, were we in trouble that day. At 8–0 down we got a corner. John Kirk, who had barely said a world all game, suddenly sprung into life. He was on his feet and charging over to the touchline, screaming to the players, 'Get up, get up!' 'Get up?' I echoed. 'What are we going to do, win nine fucking eight? Get back, get back!' With about 25 minutes to go they scored the ninth and it could have been anything by the end. Luckily, they did not push for double figures and we hung on until the whistle. I thought my world was at an end. I was really looking forward to my first shot as a manager. I had been doing all the coaching under Dave and it was going well. The players had responded to me, but there was nothing I could do that day. We drew the following game, at home to Reading, 1–1, but we didn't even have the boots as an excuse in our next match, away at Leyton Orient. We lost that one 5–0. I just felt embarrassed by then. What a start – no wins in three and 14–0 down on aggregate in two away games. I hung in there, though I knew the club was looking for another manager.

But, slowly, it started to turn around. We beat Brentford 4–3, we won 3–0 against Millwall, we got a draw at Sheffield United, and then beat Oxford United who were challenging for promotion. We played Gillingham away on 5 March and won 5–2. Before we left their ground, Alec Stock, the old Fulham manager who was by then a director at Bournemouth, got on the team bus. 'Well done, Harry, well done,' he exclaimed in his posh accent. 'I've been over at the training ground, I've watched you working, I like what you are doing. There is a board meeting on Monday and we'll be discussing your situation. You've done really well and they are going to make you the manager, full-time. Over the weekend, write down what you are looking for: a bit of petrol money, some of your telephone bill paid, we'll find you a little club car, a runabout, I'm sure.' I went into work that Monday feeling very happy with life. I sat in my office, waiting for the knock on the door from the chairman. Sure enough, it came. 'Harry, you've done really well,' he said, 'but I'm sorry, I've just sold the club and they want to bring in their own manager. I couldn't guarantee your position, I'm afraid.'

I sat there, stunned. Two minutes later, another knock and in walked Brian Tiler, the former captain of Aston Villa. I'd met him a few times in America, where he played for the Portland Timbers, and now he was at Bournemouth as a representative of Anton Johnson, the new owner. 'Anton wants to appoint his own manager,' he explained, 'but we want to keep you.' I wasn't sure. 'We're serious,' said Brian. 'We want you here. We see you as a big part of this club.' I didn't really have much option other than to stay and see how it panned out.

Don Megson was Anton's appointment and, frankly, he was a disaster. The results were not good and they quickly fell out. Now

I liked Don as a bloke, but the writing was on the wall at the end of the 1982–83 season when we went on a brief break to Portugal. We were talking about a transfer target, a boy at Rochdale, who I described as a winger. 'He's not a winger,' said Don, 'he's a striker.' This went back and forth, until Anton intervened. 'Don, he's definitely a winger,' he said. 'How do you know, Anton?' asked Don. 'Because Harry says he's a winger and he knows ten times more about fucking football than you,' Anton replied. When results did not go well at the start of the 1983–84 season, it was only a matter of time before Don left.

I was in a stronger position by then. Jimmy Melia kept ringing me up to ask me to go to Brighton and Hove Albion, and Anton knew he had made a mistake not giving me the job in the first place. At first, when he asked me to be the manager, Don volunteered to work as my assistant. I wasn't having that. You couldn't have players wondering which of the two of us was in charge. 'That isn't going to work, Don,' I told him. 'You can't go from being a manager to being assistant.' I was determined to be my own boss, with no interference.

What a great year that turned out to be for Bournemouth. We won the Associate Members Cup, the inaugural competition for lower-tier clubs, now called the Johnstone's Paint Trophy. It may not sound much, but for Bournemouth it was a huge deal. We played Hull City in the final and my only regret is that the Bournemouth lads did not get to play at Wembley. The Horse of the Year Show had destroyed the turf, so, after beating Millwall in the semi-final, we went into a draw for home advantage in the final, and Hull won. They were a strong team and had finished level on points and goal difference with third-placed Sheffield

United that season, but had missed out on promotion to Division Two on goals scored. Colin Appleton was the manager and he had Billy Whitehurst as a striker and Steve McClaren buzzing about in midfield. We went 1–0 down but won 2–1, and had a big party on the coach all the way down. Anton had sold the club by then, and it was back in the hands of Bournemouth people. The next season we knocked Manchester United out of the FA Cup.

I'd like to say there was some wonderful secret plan that day, some masterstroke of tactical imagination – but it was sheer hard work, nothing more. We weren't lucky, don't get me wrong. The best team won. There were no issues with the pitch or bringing United down to our level. We raised our game, inspired by the occasion, and played better than we had done all season, and maybe United took us a little lightly. We certainly weren't in any trouble. Once we got in front, there was never a moment when I thought we would lose it.

It wasn't an upset you could really see coming. We had played Walsall in the first round, and won comfortably, 4–0, but Windsor and Eton, a non-league side, had really given us a scare in round two. We drew the first match 0–0 at their place, hanging on for our lives in ankle-deep mud, and only went through in a replay. By then we knew Manchester United were waiting for us if we won, and it was definitely an incentive. In the end, we beat Windsor in the replay by the same margin, 2–0, that we beat Manchester United – and I still say the non-league lot gave us more of a game. We had a team that hadn't cost a penny, really, and they came down with all of their big stars: Norman Whiteside and Frank Stapleton, managed by Ron Atkinson. They were the FA Cup holders, too.

I could tell my players were nervous the day before, so that night I took them all out to an Italian restaurant in town. The chap that ran it promised our goalkeeper, Ian Leigh, free pizza for life if he kept a clean sheet.

We were a middle-of-the-road team, nothing more, but we didn't play like it that day. The crowd got behind us and we never stopped working and closing them down. We ran and ran, fought for every ball, never let them play – it was a typical underdog victory in that way. More perspiration than inspiration. Milton Graham and Ian Thompson scored and, out of the blue, we won. Unfortunately, 'Nipper' Leigh never got his lifetime of pizza. A few years later that Italian restaurant changed hands and the new owner refused to honour the existing arrangement. The name of that miserable, skinflint proprietor? Harry Redknapp.

Three seasons later we won promotion to Division Two – the highest up the league that Bournemouth had been. Putting that side together probably made my reputation as a manager who knows his way around the transfer market. They were great times. Some of my best signings were at Bournemouth – even if I had to pull the odd stroke on the way.

Colin Clarke was my first big transfer there. He was available from Tranmere Rovers for £20,000. The only problem was that Bournemouth did not have £20,000, according to our chairman. So I hit on a plan. I spoke to three friends, who were all vice-presidents of the club, and persuaded them to put in £5,000 each. I would put in the remaining £5,000. 'When we sell him,' I told the chairman, 'we split the profits. In the meantime, the club gets the benefit.' He eyed me suspiciously. 'You sound very keen to buy this player; he must be good,' he said. And, hey presto, the

£20,000 was found. I was right about Clarke, though. He played 38 times for Northern Ireland and later had two cracking seasons with Southampton in the First Division. And he was the straightest boy I've ever met – as I discovered on the day he signed.

Colin came down from Merseyside to do the deal and we put his wife up in a little guest house around the corner to the ground, while we talked business. I was sitting drinking tea waiting for his contract to be formally prepared when the phone rang. It was Colin's wife to say that Chelsea had been on and their manager, John Neal, wanted to buy him.

I could only hear Colin's end of the conversation but I knew it was bad news for Bournemouth. When he told me what had happened, I thought the deal was over, particularly when he added that he was a Chelsea supporter and the club were sending down a car down to collect him. I could have strangled our secretary. He had been messing around with the contract all afternoon and because of that we were going to lose the player. But what could I do but accept it? 'Colin, I understand,' I told him. 'Chelsea are in Division One, we're in Division Three, I know there is nothing I can do or say. You've got the chance to go and play in the best league, I don't blame you for taking it.'

He kept repeating that he was a Chelsea fan, which made it difficult when, out of nowhere, he changed his tune. 'No,' said Colin, suddenly and very definitely. 'I shook hands with you two hours ago on this deal, and if we've shaken hands, that's enough. I gave you my word and to go back on that wouldn't be fair.'

I was so surprised I nearly let him slip away again. 'Are you sure, Colin?' I asked.

'Yes,' he said. 'My handshake is my word. As long as if in a year or two if I do well and a big club comes in for me, you'll help me move.'

'Colin,' I promised, 'that won't be a problem. I cannot believe what you've done.'

We had Colin for one season. He played every game, scored 26 goals, we won promotion and sold him to Southampton for £500,000. What a boy. That just wouldn't happen these days. There would be an agent and the whole deal would go through an owner or the chief executive without that personal touch. The idea of a player like Colin sitting in the manager's office on his own would seem strange to most modern chief executives or chairmen. I cannot remember the last transfer deal that did not involve an agent, and these days they don't want to know the managers anyway. We don't do the deals any more. We come and go and a lot of the time have no say in buying policy. The CEOs and the chairmen are the friends of the agents these days; they are the ones getting wined and dined.

Jimmy Case, the Liverpool and England midfield player, was another old-school transfer, although this one took place many years later at the start of my last season with Bournemouth, 1991– 92. I was sitting at home watching the local news on television when it said Jimmy had been released by Southampton, despite playing almost every match of the 1990–91 season in Division One and being selected for a representative Football League XI. Ian Branfoot, the new Southampton manager, did not want to renew his contract. I was straight on to it. I knew Jimmy only lived twenty minutes up the road; I phoned him up immediately. 'Jimmy, I've just seen the news, can I have a chat with you? How about a cup of tea? Where can we meet? Is now a good time?'

We got together at a service station on the M27. No agent, just Jimmy. He said he was interested.

'Jim, you've only been released half an hour ago,' I told him. 'You probably want to have a hunt around as well, yes?'

'No, that's fine,' he said, 'I'd like to come and play for you.'

We hadn't even talked money. 'What are you looking for,' I asked, nervously.

'Make me your best offer,' said Jimmy.

Now, I couldn't sugar-coat it any longer. 'I'll be honest, Jim, we're struggling,' I said. 'It's Bournemouth. We've never had a lot of dough. I can stretch to £300 per week.'

'Fine,' he said. And we shook hands. 'If someone comes in and offers me a grand now, Harry, the answer is no. I've given you my word, so don't worry.'

I could still hear alarm bells. 'Tell you what, Jim,' I said. 'Let's go back to the ground and get that contract done.'

'Don't sweat,' he assured me. 'We can do it in the morning.' He could obviously see the look on my face because he kept repeating, 'Harry, I'm signing for Bournemouth.'

And he was a man of his word. The next day, his phone was ringing off the hook, but he came in and put his name on a piece of paper with us.

If only they were all like Jim. One of the reasons I am still so insistent on the need to move fast for a transfer target is that, in the early days, as my reputation for spotting a bargain grew, so did the chances that other clubs would profit from my hard work. Each week there were the nightly slogs up and down the motorway that made losing a player particularly frustrating. One of the minuses of managing, and living, on the south coast is that unless a fixture involves one of a handful of local clubs, scouting usually demands a good two or three hours in the car – and then back. It is a little galling to later see the object of those visits spirited away by another manager. Ian Woan was a perfect example.

I went to watch him twice in the bitter cold at Runcorn with Stuart Morgan, my chief scout at Bournemouth. A long old journey, but what a player. Great left foot, great ability, played on the wing. We had the deal done at £40,000. Met his dad – nice guy, used to be a professional at Aldershot but had since qualified as a quantity surveyor. It was all arranged for him to come to Bournemouth and sign. The night before, his dad called. 'I can't get down tomorrow,' he said, 'we'll come down later in the week.' I was a tactful as I could be in the circumstances. 'Well, we don't really want you, Mr Woan,' I said. 'It's Ian we need. You don't have to be there at all.' But he sounded a decent guy. He said it had always been his ambition for his son to be a professional footballer and he wanted to be there when it happened. I had no reason to disbelieve him – or to think this small delay would cost us such a talent.

'We'll be there Friday morning,' he promised. 'I've got the day off, we'll be there, for sure.' I don't think he was pulling a fast one, he wasn't angling for more money or a longer contract. In fact, I don't think even he could have known what would happen next. It was Alan Hill, Brian Clough's assistant at Nottingham Forest, who told me the rest. The news of the prospective transfer made it to the local papers and, from there, to the news service Teletext. Clough was sitting in his office reading through the transfer gossip. He saw the story about Bournemouth and Woan. 'That Redknapp does well with non-league players,' he announced. 'Who is this fella Woan?' Forest didn't know him, didn't have any reports, but Ronnie Fenton, another of Clough's backroom staff, was a pal of the manager of Runcorn. He made the call. 'Is Woan any good?' he asked. 'He's too good for bloody Bournemouth,' came the reply. And that was the end of our deal. Forest doubled our offer, paid £80,000, and his dad phoned me at 11.30 p.m. on Thursday night. 'You won't believe this, Harry, but Nottingham Forest have come in.' We lost a good lad that day, with a great attitude, too. He played ten years at Forest.

One of my most important signings was John Williams, a big centre-half who I got for £30,000 from John Rudge at Port Vale. He helped us win the Third Division title in 1986–87, one of three promotions he won with as many different clubs. John was different class. We only lost two games after Christmas that season, and for one of them he was suspended. He was a bit of a lad, John, but I loved him. What a competitor – if I made a list of my best signings, he would be on it. When he retired he came back to Bournemouth as coach and was caretaker manager for a short while. He still works in the local media.

Sometimes new players came from the strangest sources. As well as Bournemouth, I was coaching an under-10 team that Jamie played for, Mudeford Boys Club. Jamie was only about seven, but he was good enough to go up against the older boys. Our secret weapon was that our goalkeeper was a complete ringer. He was actually 14 but was quite small for his age and could pass for ten. He was a cracking keeper, too, when needed, which wasn't often because the rest of our team was quite useful. Then one day I looked over and he'd got bored and lit up a fag while leaning on the goalpost. So that was the end of our cunning plan. It was a bit hard to pass him off as ten after shouting at him to put the fag out. Anyway, one Sunday another manager from our boys' league rang up and said one of the older teams at his club had a lad who was outstanding. He thought I might like to give him a trial for Bournemouth. 'He was at Portsmouth, but they let him go,' the chap said. 'He's too good for Sunday morning; can he come training with you?'

I was reluctant at first. 'If I let him in, I'll have everyone asking,' I said.

'Well, he's old enough to work, but he isn't working,' the chap continued. He made it sound a matter of some urgency that this lad got a trial.

I decided to take a chance. 'What's his name?' I asked.

'Steve Claridge,' I was told.

'Well, if he's doing nothing, tell him to come tomorrow morning,' I said.

Within half an hour, I knew he was good enough to play professionally.

We ended the training session with a little competition, one on one in the penalty area. Steve won it. His last goal was bent into the top corner, an absolute beauty. 'We've got to have him,' I said. 'What were Portsmouth thinking?'

He went on to have a super career, playing over a thousand games for clubs across the whole spectrum of league football, and Steve is now a respected media pundit – but back then he had a few strange habits. The penny soon dropped about why Portsmouth may have let him go. Boots, for instance, were an obsession with him. He thought certain pairs were lucky and would just pick them up and wear them, whatever the size, whoever the owner. It was superstition, not stealing, but it made for some bizarre moments.

The first match he played for us was at York City. Someone had told him that glucose gave you energy, so he had six packets of glucose tablets and two Mars bars on the coach on the way there and ended up being sick. Next thing, during the warm-up, I noticed he was walking like an arthritic old man, as if he was in pain. It turned out he was wearing new boots, size six and a half, and Steve is size eight. I got hold of John Kirk. 'Sort him out, John,' I said. 'He's driving me mad.' John came back and said that Steve didn't want size-eight boots. The person in the shop had said these ones would give out. Fine if we were playing ankle deep in mud and water, they might let a little bit – but York's pitch was rock hard. 'Let him get on with it,' said John. 'He says he'll be fine.' The game was two minutes old when Steve came over to the touchline. 'Have you got any bigger boots?' he said. 'These ones are killing me.'

It was all nerves with Steve. When he felt under pressure he would shave his head. I'd come into a team meeting and it would be like that Tommy Cooper routine where he plays two characters by turning sideways. On one side Steve's hair would be normal, on the other it would be half-bald. He would claim his dad had given him a bad haircut. I hit on the idea of making Billy Rafferty his roommate on away trips, to try to calm him down. I'm still good friends with Billy; he's a lovely, sensible lad and was a very decent centre-forward. One night in a room with Claridge, though, and he came down as white as a sheet. 'Boss, it was like fucking *Psycho*,' he said. 'He kept going into the bathroom and every time he came out, he'd shaved more off his head. I haven't slept a wink all night.'

But Steve was a good player for us – so much so that I bought him twice. I sold him to Weymouth Town and when they messed his contract up, I bought him back on a free. Then I sold him to Crystal Palace. He was a strange one, an oddball – but he ended up with a great career. And all from a tip from the manager of a Sunday boys' team.

Brian Clough was right, though – I could spot a diamond in the non-league game back then. Maidstone United had a cracker called Mark Newson, who had been selected for the non-league representative team. I had been tracking him for a while and when Stuart Morgan rang and announced Mark was going to Tottenham Hotspur on trial I was choked. He was the best player in non-league by a mile. Stuart said Spurs had a match at their training ground the next Tuesday, Newson would be playing and he would find a way to watch. He phoned me immediately after. 'Best player on the field by a mile,' he confirmed. Tottenham had put four past Norwich City and he had played at centre-half and right-back.

'We've got to get him,' I said.

'We've no chance,' Stuart replied.

But that night I got the luckiest break. An old mate who had contacts down there called me. 'Harry, I know you're after Mark Newson,' he said. 'I wanted to tell you, Newson's not under contract. He's not registered. He's a free transfer, Harry. Tottenham want him and I think they are ready to pay £200,000 for him, but he's unsigned.' I couldn't believe what I was hearing. 'I've got Mark's number if you want it.'

He didn't need to ask twice. Mark lived in the Isle of Dogs and he took a little persuading at first. 'I'm at Tottenham at the moment, Harry,' he said. 'I'm having a week there and things have gone well for me – I think they might sign me.'

'Just come and meet me, Mark,' I pleaded. 'Get on the train, I'll pay your fare and pick you up from the station.'

'Well, we do have a day off tomorrow ...'

I could tell he was wavering, so I went in for the kill. 'Mark, you're different class, but you're not going to get a game at Tottenham, you know that. If you come to Bournemouth you'll play every game. You'll be a star for us. We're putting a good team together.'

We agreed to meet and our conversation continued at an Italian restaurant. Every time Mark mentioned Tottenham, I had my answer ready: 'They might take you, they might not take you, and even if they do, if you don't make it you'll be out on your arse and then what happens? You might not be able to get in anywhere else. You might end up on less than you earn at Maidstone.'

In the end, we offered £200 per week. 'I want some time to think it over,' said Mark.

'No way,' I insisted. 'You are not leaving here until this gets done.' Brian Tiler came up with an extra £20 and Mark seemed happy. Now the deal was finalised.

The next call was to league registrations to confirm what my source had said was true. Yes, it was confirmed, there was no contract between Mark Newson and Maidstone United. It only remained for me to tell genial Barry Fry, the Maidstone manager, the good news. Barry was his usual self. 'How you going, Harry?' he asked. 'How have you been, son?'

'I'm feeling great, Barry,' I told him. 'I've just signed Mark Newson.'

Barry didn't want to believe what he had just heard. 'You want to sign Mark Newson?' he replied. 'I'm afraid not, mate. It looks like he's going to Tottenham. We're getting two-hundred grand plus another hundred in add-ons. I don't think Bournemouth can match that.'

'You misunderstand, Barry,' I said. 'I've signed him.'

There was a brief pause. 'Have you been drinking, Harry? he asked.

'No, you didn't have him under contract, Barry, so he's a Bournemouth player now,' I explained.

Quickly, the gracious mood changed. Now Barry was shouting, 'Don't fuck with me, Harry. I'll tell you what, I'm gonna send two geezers – there'll be two blokes coming down to see you and shoot your fucking knee caps off, you—'

'Unlucky, Barry,' I said, as I put the phone down. 'That's the chance you take.'

Ten minutes later, the telephone rang again. Now it was Maidstone's chairman, trying a more conciliatory approach. 'I must apologise for the way Barry spoke to you there, threatening to have you shot and heaven knows what,' he began. 'We don't work like that here. So let's all be gentlemen about it. We've made a mistake, you've clearly been clever and capitalised on our mistake, so let's come to an arrangement. Now we're obviously not going to get what we would have been paid by Tottenham, but I'm sure we can find a fair way forward.'

'I'm sorry,' I said, 'there's nothing to pay because he's a free agent. We don't need an arrangement with you.'

Then it was back to kneecaps. 'You fucking bastard,' he said. 'I'll come down there and do you, and your mate, Tiler.' The phone went down. The following day, Brian and I were in the office when we saw a car pull up outside. Out got Barry, his chairman, and another chap we didn't recognise. We decided not to hang around and find out what they wanted. We dived out the back way, across the pitch, over the turnstiles and someone got a car to come around and drive us away. They didn't bother coming back, luckily, and Mark was great for us. He captained the team when we won the league and I sold him to Fulham three years later for £100,000.

One of my favourite signings, and not just from my Bournemouth days, was a striker called Carl Richards. I took him from Enfield and he was a real one-off. He was a big lad, and looked more like Carl Lewis. I remember driving to Nuneaton Borough's old ground, Manor Park, on a bank holiday Monday in 1986 to watch him play in a representative game between the non-league teams of England and Wales. After the game, there was a trophy and speeches and sandwiches, and I went and hid round the back of this little hut because I didn't want any of the other managers to see me. Carl came out on his own. 'Psst,' I said, from behind a fence. 'Carl, I want to talk to you.'

'Who are you?' he asked. 'What do you want?'

But he came over. Massive shoulders, trim waist, really fit. 'I'm Harry Redknapp, manager of Bournemouth,' I said.

'Bournemouth?' he replied. 'Never heard of you. What league are you in?'

I told him we were in the Third Division.

'Well, I'm not dropping down to the Isthmian,' he said. 'Not the third division of the bloody Isthmian,' I told him. 'The Football League. We're in Division Three.'

'What, professional?' he asked. Now he was interested. 'I always wanted to be a professional,' said Carl.

'Well, that's handy,' I told him, 'because we're professional, and we want you.'

'Train every day?' he asked. He really didn't have a clue. I bought Carl for £10,000, went to pick him up from Enfield, and while he went in to say goodbye to his manager, he left me with his mate. 'What are you signing him for?' said this kid. 'I'm ten times better than him. I've got twenty-six goals this season, he's only got twelve. I'm different class than him. Why don't you sign me?' Now I was worried. Stuart Morgan, my assistant, had recommended Carl. I had never seen him play for Enfield, only that one game up at Nuneaton. He was great that day and I loved him, but I couldn't help wondering if I had bought the wrong player. 'I can't buy you, I'm buying him,' I told Carl's mate, 'but I'll keep an eye out for you, don't worry.'

So we took Carl and he was absolutely useless. He could run, but that was about it. The pre-season was a nightmare. Yeovil Town, we got beat. Weymouth Town, got beat. Bath City, got beat. We played about six games, couldn't win one. Carl was terrible. After about four games of this, he came to see me. 'I've got a mate,' he said. 'He was asking if he could have a trial. He's a striker, like me.'

'And is he as good as you, Carl?' I asked, suspiciously.

'No, he's not as good as me,' he said, 'but he's decent.'

'Well, tell him not to fucking bother then,' I snapped, and that was the end of it. The following Saturday, we went to play Crystal Palace. 'My mate, the one who wanted a trial, he's playing for Palace today,' said Carl. 'Oh good,' I thought. 'No problem there then.' Anyway, three goals later I realised Carl wasn't much of a scout, either. His mates's name? Ian Wright.

Yet Carl ended up doing fantastic for Bournemouth and I loved him to bits. He didn't have a clue about the real world. On his first payday he knocked on my door, accusing me of having him over. 'You told me I was getting £220 a week and I'm only getting £150,' he said.

'That's your deductions, Carl,' I explained. 'Income tax, national insurance.'

'What's that?' he asked. 'You never told me about that.'

'You've got to pay tax and insurance, Carl,' I continued, as soothingly as I could. 'Everybody does.'

He wasn't having it. 'When I did some painting for Leroy,' he insisted, 'he said he would give me a hundred quid, and he gave me a hundred quid.'

'What about your other jobs?' I asked. 'You would have paid tax and insurance then.'

'I ain't had no other jobs,' said Carl. 'Just painting with Leroy.'

And it didn't stop there. Carl had a wife and a little baby, but no house. I said he should buy one. 'How do you do that?' he asked. He wasn't kidding. I told him to go to the high street and look out for one of those shops with pictures of houses in the window. I said he should try to find a home for about £35,000. The next day he came in, and said he had bought one. I was a little stunned. 'What sort of house is it, Carl?' I asked.

'Oh, three bathrooms, one bedroom,' he said.

'You mean, three bedrooms, one bathroom?' I queried. 'Something like that,' he said. He told me he had paid £38,000.

'And how much were they asking for it,' I wanted to know.

'I told you,' said Carl, '£38,000.'

He hadn't made an offer, he hadn't even seen the house. 'I've never met anyone like your Mr Richards,' the estate agent told me. 'He bought the first house we showed him, in the office, for the asking price.' I managed to negotiate it down to £36,000 for him. The agent turned out to be a big Bournemouth fan. He was right about Carl, though. I have never met anyone like him either. After that poor start he became a great player for us, strong and quick, and the year we went up he murdered defenders every week. Birmingham City bought him after two seasons for £85,000. He had a season with them, another with Peterborough United and two years with Blackpool. He ended up going back to Enfield after that. I often wonder what he is up to now. A bit of painting with Leroy, probably.

When I look back, Bournemouth was probably the most fun I ever had as a manager. There wasn't the money, or the success, obviously, and it certainly didn't compare to working with great players like Paolo Di Canio or Gareth Bale, but there was a sense of adventure back then, taking a chance on someone like Carl or scouring the leagues for an undiscovered gem. And when a really good player did drop down the league to work at that level, you appreciated it. I can remember Luther Blissett joined us from Watford in 1988. He was one of those players that changes the attitude of a football club. He was a great trainer – he'd been to Italy, he had played for England – he had a different work ethic to the rest. He taught the players about eating right, and coming in with the proper attitude. We beat Hull City 5–1 on his debut and he scored four goals. The chairman gave a big speech in the boardroom afterwards. 'The great thing is,' he said. 'We haven't even seen the best of Luther yet.' 'He's just got four goals in one game, Mr Chairman,' I said. 'I think we have.'

Yet those leagues have a way of keeping your feet on the ground. Even in 1984, when we knocked Manchester United out of the FA Cup, we weren't allowed to bask in the glory for long. We were 21st in Division Three that morning, and Manchester United were second in Division One; it was probably the biggest result in the history of the club. A full house, the greatest FA Cup upset in years. The next morning they wanted me on breakfast television and all the players were doing interviews with the newspapers. It was a huge story. 'Can we come down to your training ground?' one TV crew asked. I told them we didn't have a training ground. We trained in King's Park, which was public land. People used to walk dogs there, and the first job for the apprentices each morning was to clear the mess so we could play. In winter, it would get quite boggy, so if we could we would use a red cinder all-weather surface, the sort of thing I used to play on in the East End as a kid. It had some small floodlights and the council used to hire it out to teams at night.

On the Monday after we beat Manchester United, the gates to the ochre pitch had been left open, so in we went. The players were buzzing, as you'd expect, and we had a really good session. When we came to leave, though, there was a giant padlock on the gate. The park keeper had come round on his bike and locked us in without saying a word. He was another Cheyenne, a nightmare to us at the best of times, but this was really special. We had to scale a twenty-foot fence to get out. I had one leg over and couldn't get the other one across, and the frame was swaying in the wind. All the lads were laughing. And that's what it was like: Bournemouth always had a way of bringing you down to earth. We had a dozen footballs at the start of the year and when one got lost, we would have the kids searching for it for hours. Now players boot balls over the fence and don't give a monkey's. They forget where we all came from. I remember Sol Campbell at Portsmouth telling me the training-ground pitch was crap, which it was. It was in a disgusting state, really. But you can't let players use that as an excuse. I remember watching Sol play for an east London boys' team called Senrab – they came from Barnes Street in Stepney originally, and Senrab is Barnes reversed – and they would play on Wanstead Flats or Hackney Marshes. I reminded him of those days and he got my point. That's where we grew up. 'You've played on worse than this and loved every minute, Sol,' I told him. Nowadays, it's a different world. Modern players, certainly those who have come through elite clubs in the top division, don't realise how lucky they are. All they have ever played on is billiard-table surfaces.

Life at Bournemouth made you appreciate the good times more. One of my chairmen, Jim Nolan – I had about nine in my time there but he was one of the best – came over the park one day and announced he wanted to take me somewhere after training. We pulled up at a Mercedes garage and he presented me with a little 190E for getting promoted. I was still driving a Morris Marina at the time. The 190E was a £17,000 car, and it felt like I had won the pools. It was different for ex-players in those days. We hadn't made fortunes out of the game. I'll never forget Jim for what he did. He didn't have to do that. I felt so proud of my little black Merc.

Almost all of my chairmen did their best for me and the club. Another time we were going to play York City away on a Wednesday and Darlington the following Saturday, so I asked the chairman if there was any chance of staying in the north for three nights. He said we didn't have the money, but I knew that by the time we'd paid for the coach there and back twice it would come to roughly the same. So I rang around until I found two guest houses next to each other that could take us, two in a room, three in a room, and if we did the journey in two hired minibuses we could make it pay. You had to see these mini-buses. They were the worst. Old and green, they looked like they'd carried troops in the war. We took the smallest squad we could cope with to keep the costs down, and Keith Williams, my assistant, drove the second vehicle. When we arrived at Darlington they wouldn't let us in. I said I was the manager of Bournemouth and this was our team, and the bloke on the gate fell about laughing. It was only when one of his mates recognised me that we got through the door at all. But we won both matches. The two nights in the guest house really helped with team spirit, too.

It worked so well that, later, when we were going for promotion, I tried the same tactic on the north-west coast. We won at Port Vale on the Wednesday and stayed in Blackpool waiting for our Saturday match, which was at Carlisle United. The hotel accommodation was a little more upmarket this time, and the temptations of Blackpool very different to Darlington. The night before the game, I called a team meeting. I kept it simple. Massive game tomorrow, nobody goes out tonight, early to bed, prepare right, we're going great, don't spoil it, don't take liberties – they all listened, all agreed. Lovely. Sam Ellis, who was the manager of Blackpool at the time and a good friend, came over to see me in our hotel. We had a cup of tea and a chat and by 10 p.m. all the players were tucked up in bed. I had another half hour with Sam, said see you later, and got in the lift to go up to my room. Before I had the chance to press a button the doors closed and the lift started going down to the basement. I got out – where was I? With that, the lift doors closed behind me and up it went. Now I was stranded, in what I realised was the underground car park. Terrific. I was pressing the button to call the lift when the doors opened again, and who was there but John Williams, my captain, done up like John Travolta. Behind him, five other players, all ready to hit the town. Flowered shirts, plenty of aftershave, the lads were well for up for it. Unfortunately, the doors had opened to reveal their manager, who was not best pleased. John walked straight into me. 'Oh my God,' he said.

I looked him up and down. 'What do you think this is, fucking *Saturday Night Fever*?' I asked him. 'See you – you're going fucking home in the morning.'

'It's a fair cop, boss,' he said. 'What can I say?'

I was livid. 'Fuck off, that's what I'm saying,' I told him. 'I don't care what you want to say.'

But I couldn't stay angry at John for long. I knew he wasn't the only one with plans that night. I went storming up to their floor and I could see the little crew from the lift scarpering back to their rooms, and a few others too. I let John stew the night and then pulled him the following morning, gave him a bollocking and let him remain with us. We got the result we needed at Carlisle and we were better off with him in the team.

I loved Bournemouth. I still do. When the club was in financial difficulty I worked without pay for four months, and I even loaned them money, interest free, to make up the shortfall in a rescue package under Trevor Watkins, one of my many chairmen. I turned down good jobs in order to stay at Bournemouth, too: Aston Villa, Stoke City and even West Ham United, the first time.

It was in February 1990. They had sacked Lou Macari after just a year at the club, which was very unusual for West Ham, and were dithering on appointing Billy Bonds as his successor. I got a call from the chairman, Len Cearns. 'We have had a lot of applications for the job, but we didn't have the one we wanted, which is yours,' he told me. I couldn't understand why, if I was their man, they didn't just try to speak to me without waiting for a letter. I told Brian Tiler and Jim Nolan about the conversation, but they refused West Ham permission to speak to me, and I didn't make a fuss. They had treated me very well at Bournemouth and I had signed a new three-year contract little more than twelve months earlier. I didn't want to rock the boat.

And as for the contract, what a night that was. We were playing away at Hull City, but Brian Tiler insisted on going out to celebrate, even though it was Friday, the day when professionals are supposed to be tucked up in bed early in readiness for the match. Some Bacardi and Cokes, three bottles of red wine and two bottles of champagne later I was stumbling down the hotel corridor, back to my room. It is a good job our season was as good as over, because the next day I wasn't much use to anybody. We were 4–0 down at half-time, but all I could think about was the pain in my head. If the players were expecting some instruction, guidance, or maybe even an informative rucking, they would have been sorely disappointed. I stuck my aching bonce around the door. 'Come on, lads,' I said. 'We've got to do better than that.' I could have been talking about myself. Then I staggered off in search of some aspirin.

Bournemouth was always punching above its weight in the second tier, though, and at the end of the 1989–90 season, we were relegated. We had done fantastically well to get as high as we did, but it couldn't last. We were a decent team, but our resources were always stretched. I remember one game at Portsmouth, on the last day in March, when we lost our entire starting back four, plus the goalkeeper. It was just injury after injury and we didn't have the squad. From being in the top half of the table on 29 December, we only won two league games between February and the end of the season and ended up needing to beat Leeds United at home on the final day to stay up. Leeds needed to win to get promoted to the First Division and their fans just took over the town – and wrecked it.

It was a May bank holiday, blazing hot, a seaside location – a real recipe for disaster. The Leeds supporters left Bournemouth in a horrendous state. Streets and property were smashed to pieces. The police estimated there were as many as 15,000 of them. They were taking the tickets off Bournemouth fans, and every vehicle in the club car park was damaged in some way. It was horrendous behaviour: windows caved in, cars ruined. Our chairman had a Rolls-Royce, and by the time they had finished with it there wasn't a window intact and all the doors were missing. The police tried to intervene and were chased off. There was a charge – and the next thing we knew the police had turned tail and were running the other way. The fans had been on the booze all weekend and just ran riot. It was as well we lost 1–0 because I don't know if we'd have had a ground left had we beaten them. It was one of my worst days in football.

Looking back, I think the support of Brian Tiler was the main reason I stayed at Bournemouth so long. I could never take a liberty with Brian. I would never have threatened to walk out, or tried to back him into a corner over interest from a bigger club.

Peter Coates offered me the job at Stoke, and Villa said they wanted me too, but I loved the relationship I had with Brian and the staff at Bournemouth. He was one of those guys that always knew when to say the right thing. He knew my moods, he knew when I had the hump, and he knew his football, too. It was the perfect combination. If I was about to blow with the chairman, he would swoop in and we'd go racing, to Ascot or Sandown Park. If there was something wrong or someone was upsetting me, Brian would sort it out. He was just a man that I felt was always in my corner, fighting.

CHAPTER SIX

UP THE HAMMERS

I'm lucky to be here. I try not to think about it. On the night of 30 June 1990, a minibus in which I was travelling was involved in a head-on collision on a road near Latina, in the region of Lazio, near Rome. I was sleeping in a passenger seat and had no idea of the horror that had occurred. My friend, Brian Tiler, was killed. So were the three teenage Italian soldiers in the other car. I woke up in hospital with terrible injuries. Apparently, a sheet had been placed over my face at the scene of the accident with the presumption that I must be dead. Another friend, Michael Sinclair, the former chairman of York City, had pulled me clear of the wreckage – I was soaked in petrol, and he feared an explosion. When people ask me about it now, I am afraid I plead ignorance. I have no memory of it and am happy for it to stay that way. All I know is that I lost a wonderful pal in Brian, and a moment of recklessness cost three young men their lives.

The accident happened on the SS148, one of those three-lane carriageways that are commonplace in Europe: a lane for traffic north, another for traffic south, and one in the middle for whoever is brave enough. It was a bad road, notorious for accidents, and the three youngsters were on our side of it, attempting to overtake a vehicle at 90 m.p.h. when the collision occurred. Losing Brian really affected me. I have had good relationships with a number of my bosses at football clubs, but there was never anyone quite like him.

Brian was a fantastic character – what I would call a proper boy. He was Bournemouth's chief executive, but his background was more football than business. In any disputes with the board, his instinct was to side with the football people, and he'd steam in for me at the first sign of trouble. He knew when to lay it on the line, and when to get out for a game of golf to clear our heads. And he knew the game. He would never interfere, never tell you what players to pick, but it was great to seek his opinion when there was a big decision to make. I liked his company and I miss our glasses of wine on a Friday night before the match. I couldn't have had a better boss than Brian.

I can't remember whose idea it was to book a trip to the World Cup in Italy in 1990, but I wouldn't call it work. It was the holiday of a lifetime, really. There was no way Bournemouth could afford any of the players on show, so we just treated it as a summer break. The travelling party was Brian and me, Michael Sinclair and Eric Whitehouse, a big Aston Villa fan and Brian's friend from way back. Some of the chaps took their sons with them, too, and we booked a beautiful hotel on the coast, spent the days around the pool and the evenings watching games. On the night of the crash we had seen Italy beat the Republic of Ireland, thanks to a goal from the local hero of the tournament, Salvatore 'Toto' Schillaci.

After the match we stopped for a pizza at a little square around the corner from the Stadio Olimpico, and some Irish fans joined us. They recognised me as the manager of Bournemouth, and we struck up a conversation about Gerry Peyton, who was my goalkeeper and Ireland's second choice behind Pat Bonner. Brian was anxious to go because we had to be up early the next morning to get to Naples, where England were playing Cameroon. I must have held us up about ten minutes, chatting to these lads. I often think about those ten minutes. If we had gone when Brian wanted, he would still be here today, and perhaps those kids would still be alive, too. I'm not saying I'm tortured. I wasn't to know the consequences, I understand that. Yet when I play back what I remember of that night, there are so many little twists, things that were, quite literally, the difference between life and death. Brian nicked my seat. That was my punishment for keeping everybody hanging about. I usually took the aisle position, Brian sat by the window because I didn't like the breeze. But when I got on board that night, he had switched spots. How fateful was that little wind-up? Sitting in that window seat was the last I remember of our holiday. I went to sleep and the accident happened. I woke up in hospital, not knowing a thing. I don't remember seeing the car coming, I don't remember the impact, not one single event after I nodded off. I just remember the hospital in Latina, coming around in bed two days later. I think it was about another two days on when I felt well enough to begin piecing it all together. That is when I found out Brian had died. I was still having lots of scans and doctors visiting, but was finally able to ask what had happened. It was then I was told the whole bloody nightmare.

From the recollections of the other passengers, I have recovered fragments of the events on the night. I had been thrown clear of the wreckage, and then dragged farther away by Michael, but the paramedics on the scene thought I was already dead. The doctors shared that opinion when I arrived at the hospital, too. Somebody certainly thought I wouldn't be needing any money where I was going, as my valuables, including my watch, were never recovered. I had fractured my skull and many other bones, and suffered a horrific gash to my leg that still bears a scar. I don't think my life was ever in danger, although when I look at pictures of the accident scene I can hardly believe that any of us survived. Both vehicles were a write-off, there were four fatalities and our driver spent nine months in hospital. Incredibly, the rest of the passengers had only minor injuries. It was a miracle, really.

I felt so desperately sad when I heard Brian was gone. So sad for Hazel, his wife, and his daughter, Michelle. We had been through a lot together at Bournemouth, shared some great times, had so many laughs. He wasn't my boss, he was a friend. Later that year, we organised a fundraising night to help his family, and I saw a side of one man that I never knew existed.

I didn't get off on the right foot with Ken Bates, one of football's most controversial chairmen. When Bournemouth played Chelsea in Division Two, he came down to the dug-out to have a word with his manager, Bobby Campbell. We were winning at that point in the match, and he didn't seem too happy. After the game I was asked if I would allow my chairman to speak to me on the touchline while the game was in progress, and I gave a straight answer: 'No, he wouldn't do that anyway,' I said. 'He's too busy.' The next week I got a letter from Ken Bates, and you can imagine the contents. He absolutely slaughtered me. Put me in my place good and proper. Then, after Brian died, a director of Bournemouth called Brian Willis organised the fundraising dinner at the Royal Bath Hotel. Ken Bates came down and bought everything in the auction. Quietly, though. He didn't show off, he just pulled the organisers aside and said he would top every bid that night, whatever it was. When we sent the invoice off, he returned a cheque for double the amount. So I have never thought ill of him, no matter how much criticism he received at Chelsea and then Leeds United. That was a fantastic gesture and I'll never forget him for it.

After the crash, recovery was difficult. The club paid for a company called Euro Assist to fly me home, because the plane had to travel low due to my skull fractures; I couldn't afford to be subjected to significant air pressure. I have never regained my sense of smell, not a complete disadvantage in some dressing rooms, and I lost my sense of taste for about six months after the accident, although it has slowly returned over time.

Once home, I thought my life would change. I still felt a real sense of loss over Brian, and I determined never to get uptight again about football – but that new outlook didn't last long. That's the way I am, and it proved impossible to change. So, soon, I was back into it full-on again. As soon as I was up and able, I went to watch Bournemouth play at Reading, The doctors had said that under no circumstances was I to get involved with football until I had made a full recovery and been signed off, but a mate of mine took me in disguise. He drove, and I had a bobble hat on, a hooded top over that, a big scarf wrapped around me, and we sat up the back of the stand in the crowd. While I was ill, Stuart Morgan, my assistant, had signed a goalkeeper called Peter Guthrie from Barnet. He used to be at Tottenham Hotspur, who had bought him for a lot of money, but he didn't do well there. Stuart knew him from one of his earlier clubs, Weymouth, and rated him, but this afternoon he was useless. He didn't come for crosses and we got beat 2–1. He must have got a bit of a shock when this mad bloke in a bobble hat suddenly burst into the dressing room at the end of the match and gave him a bollocking. Harry's back! The doctor would have gone mad had he known.

Sadly, though, once Brian was gone it was never quite the same at Bournemouth for me. I'd had a great nine years there, I was back into it, and as committed as ever, but I missed him and the club was changing. It was difficult without Brian, and I felt quite low. We finished eighth in 1992, but by then I felt it was time to go. I had fallen out hugely with the latest chairman, Ken Gardiner, and there was no way forward from there. Our last home game of the season was against Reading. We won 3–2, and in the vice-presidents' lounge Gardiner was about to make a presentation to a barman who was leaving having been with us for nineteen years. He was calling for order when Kevin Bond, our centre-half, came in and ordered a lager. Gardiner loudly put him down, in front of a lot of people and, after the presentation, I approached him about it. We had words at the end of which he made a very hurtful and disparaging comment about Brian Tiler. That was the last straw. I grabbed Ken by the throat and we had to be separated. The final game of the season, away at Hartlepool United, was plainly going to be my last for the club.

I'd had a great time at Bournemouth and absolutely loved it for the most part, but I wasn't happy there any more. I knew the club had a manager lined up, too, in Tony Pulis, whom I had taken from Newport County as a player. Tony had retired from playing and was now part of my backroom staff, and I'm sure most of the league breathed a sigh of relief when that happened. He was a monster, Tony – the toughest tackler I have ever seen. I remember the day we bought him, it took me about three hours to get to Newport, it rained all the way and, as I made my journey up the motorway, one by one every game was called off. Plymouth Argyle – gone; Cardiff City – gone. I arrived in Newport and sat down in this little wooden hut where all the scouts went for a cup of tea before the game. It must have been 7.20 p.m., ten minutes before kick-off, but the first person I saw in there was Tony Pulis. Terrible journey, waterlogged roads all the way, and the bloke I've come to watch has been dropped. The look on Tony's face suggested he knew why I had travelled. He'd played against us earlier that year and had a blinder. He wasn't a stylish footballer, but he made it bloody hard for those that were. You hear legendary stories about Ron Harris and Tommy Smith these days, but Tony would be up there with any of them when it came to the hard stuff.

Some of his stunts were unbelievable. We had our own tough nut, Keith Williams, a lad I'd bought from Northampton Town. Hard as anybody, a wicked tackler, he always did a great job for us. I didn't know Tony Pulis from Adam, but ten minutes in he had sorted out Keith like nothing I had ever seen. He'd come in quick, sharp as a razor. He couldn't actually play. He couldn't pass it more than five yards, really, but when he set off for a tackle you wanted to dial 999 just to be on the safe side. And players would get away with it in those days. Times have changed but, back then, I'd rather have a lad like Tony in midfield for me than against me, and he knew he was the player I had come to watch. It gave us time to have a little chat, though, and he said he'd love to play for Bournemouth. He wasn't getting on at Newport and was available as a free transfer at the end of the season. Tony did a great job beside Sean O'Driscoll in our midfield and he eventually became my assistant. He was tough as a manager, too. After I left, he got in trouble for chinning one of the players.

Yet Tony's experience and ambition helped me, because it meant Bournemouth did not fight too hard when West Ham United came calling that summer. By then, we had another chairman, Norman Hayward, and he was Tony's mate. I knew they would do well together. I also knew then the sort of manager Tony would be. He was a very good trainer, always into his fitness, and I thought that was how he would prepare his teams. They'd be conditioned, ready to run all day and they would work for him, or else … His Stoke City teams were like that, too – they may not be easy on the eye, but they always give you a game. I'm sure Norman wasn't bothered when West Ham offered me the job as assistant to Billy Bonds, because he had Tony to step in right away.

As for me, I didn't have to think twice when I got the call from West Ham. I knew something was up when I heard Billy's voice on the telephone, because Bill wasn't the type for social chit-chat. West Ham had been relegated that season, and he wanted an assistant. That suited me perfectly. Those last two years without Brian at Bournemouth had taken a toll on me and I was more than happy just to get out on the training field and coach players. I'd had enough of being the bad guy. When you are the manager, you put up that team-sheet and, straight away, half the club hates you. Their wives hate you, too. At Bournemouth, Shaun Teale's missus nearly ran me over after a row about one hundred quid. She marched down to the training ground over some minor contractual issue, gave me a mouthful, I told her to piss off, and the next thing I knew she was reversing out of the car park so fast, she nearly took me with her. That was one side of the job I wasn't going to miss. When you are the coach, as long as the results are going right, you can be everyone's friend. I was looking forward to being able to relax during the week again. It didn't quite turn out as I had planned.

West Ham were a shambles. It came as quite a shock. Bill didn't need someone looking for a quiet life, someone who would just sit back. They had gone down for a reason, and that was apparent to me the moment I walked through the door. Bill was upset that I said it publicly, but the club was too easy-going. Julian Dicks was our captain, but didn't return from his summer holiday until two days after pre-season training had started. His attitude was frighteningly poor at times. As for Ian Bishop, he had been with me at Bournemouth and I was appalled to see the state of him. He was 32 pounds heavier than he had been previously – and I had the evidence to prove it.

These days, sports science techniques address issues like Body Mass Index, which assesses how much players should weigh, taking variables such as height into account. I just had my old black book with the player weights written down. Old school, but effective. When Bishop denied that he had a weight problem, I could prove that he was wrong. I went to the boot of my car, found my book and there it was, documented and undeniable. I was looking forward to working with him again, too. I had bought Bishop from Carlisle United for £20,000, and sold him for £465,000 plus Paul Moulden a year later. He was a superb player, but his weight was symptomatic of a club that had let itself go. They were no longer top-notch players, because they had not behaved in a top-notch way. West Ham had finished bottom of Division One the previous year, with a total of 38 points in a twenty-two-team league. It would be like getting 34 points in the Premier League today, a stupidly low total. Bishop wasn't the same player I knew, and West Ham weren't the same club.

There was a lot of anger about. This was a relegated team, and the fans were not having the players at all. They hated Bishop, they hated Trevor Morley, the main striker. They were on their backs from the start. I went to a pre-season game against Hornchurch, and it was a brutal introduction. A lovely summer evening, the pitch in perfect condition, everyone tanned and happy – and yet the mood in the crowd was absolutely rotten. Hornchurch were a little Isthmian League club with a ground in Upminster that didn't hold more than 3,000. In this gentle setting, I could not believe the abuse our players were receiving. 'You tosser, Morley; you wanker, Bishop.' And that is just the printable stuff. Welcome to the new season, Harry. The punters are usually pleased to see you, simply delighted that football is back. This was spiteful, and the players were scared. There was no confidence about them at all.

It wasn't just the team that were copping it. There used to be a family with season tickets above the tunnel at Upton Park, and they would give Billy Bonds abuse like I've never heard. They had a little blond-haired boy with them but it made no difference. Billy was the manager that had got them relegated so, regardless of his fine standing and fantastic service to the club, he was a fucking wanker and deserved all he got. Every week, no matter the result. And the kid joined in. I was so disgusted, because I knew Bill could hear it – let's face it, everyone could hear it. The whole family: Dad, Grandad, even the old grandmother at one match. But the boy was the worst. Bill just shrugged his shoulders. 'It's always the same, Harry,' he said. 'Every game.' Unfortunately, I let it get to me. One week as the lad gave Bill some really horrible abuse, I turned and addressed the lot of them. 'You should wash his mouth out,' I said, pointing. 'Who you talking to?' the dad replied, aggressively. So they left Bill alone and started on me each week instead. By the end, I'd had enough. I complained and the secretary moved them to another part of the ground. Then, a few years ago, the strangest thing happened. I went back to West Ham as manager of Tottenham Hotspur, and when I came out of Upton Park a few people were waiting for autographs. I went over to sign and out of nowhere this big lump appeared – blond hair, about 6 feet 4 inches – and started giving me all kinds of abuse. It was vicious and very personal, and I was quite glad the fence was there. But I looked at him, and I'm sure it was that kid. He would be about the right age for it.

At times like that I think back to the days of going to the Blind Beggar with Bobby Moore and how much the game has changed. Yes, we came across the odd nutter who wanted to show off to his mates by having a pop at a footballer, but mostly there was a great atmosphere between the players and the fans. The locals loved West Ham, and we were the local boys that played for West Ham. We'd go to the Black Lion in Plaistow after the game, and there would still be a lot of fans in there who had been to the match. There was never a problem, even if we'd got beat. You couldn't do that now. Lose a match and people take it personally. And Billy's West Ham team had been relegated. So the early part of that season was hard for us.

We won the first game, away at Barnsley, but played Charlton Athletic at home six days later and lost 1–0. We had a meeting after that match because we could not carry on this way. Some of the players wouldn't even go on the pitch to warm up because the crowd were still so angry, and it was no surprise that we lost two out of our first three games. We were edgy but, slowly, we got it sorted. We won five and drew one in September and players like Bishop got back to their old selves – and their old weight. Meanwhile, I had unearthed another problem – and helping solve it came to define the future at Upton Park.

One morning I went along to our Chadwell Heath training ground and saw our under-13 team getting slaughtered 5–0 by Charlton. I found out we'd lost our last match by a similar scoreline, too. How are Charlton getting better kids than us? I asked. I was pointed in the direction of Jimmy Hampson, the man in charge of Charlton's youth set-up. 'If he's getting the best talent, then we ought to get hold of him,' I told our youth coaches. That afternoon I went over to Jimmy and began talking to him about coming to West Ham. 'Do you fancy it?' I asked. 'Do I fancy it?' he echoed, and pulled up his sleeve. He had the West Ham crossed hammers tattooed on his arm. 'West Ham's my team, Harry,' he said. 'I come from Canning Town.' So we took Jimmy. And because we took Jimmy, we also in time took Rio Ferdinand, Joe Cole, Michael Carrick, Glen Johnson and Jermain Defoe.

We made Jimmy youth development officer and that changed our whole operation. I'm very proud of his appointment, because it altered the path of the club. We ended up with six players in or around the England squad, and most of them came to us due to Jimmy's guidance. I've heard that Billy thought I interfered too much as his assistant, poking my nose in even with the youth operation, but what was I supposed to do, sit back and shrug my shoulders as the next generation of talent drained away? My attitude was that as a member of West Ham's staff I was going to do the job to the best of my ability. I didn't see that as interference then, and I don't now. If there is anyone who can find me the equivalent of Rio, Joe, Jermain and Frank Lampard for Queens Park Rangers, I would be happy. Good players make a manager's life easy. Yes, I was grafting, but only because I wanted to see West Ham do well.

And we did do well. In fact, we won promotion at the first attempt – but it wasn't easy. We looked odds-on to go up alongside Kevin Keegan's Newcastle United, but then we stuttered and Portsmouth, who were managed by Jim Smith, went on an amazing run. With two matches to go, they were three points ahead of us with a goal difference of plus 77 to our plus 76. We were playing on Sunday, away at Swindon Town, but Portsmouth were at Sunderland the day before. I went to watch a game elsewhere and as the news came through from Roker Park my smile must have got wider and wider. Portsmouth had lost 4–1. Now it was back in our hands. We won 3–1 at Swindon and it went down to the last.

Portsmouth were playing Grimsby Town, who had nothing riding on it, so I telephoned Alan Buckley, their manager, and promised him a nice case of wine if he could win on the final day. Grimsby lost 2–1. Our final match was against Cambridge United, who were managed by John Beck, fighting to stay up, and a right handful. John was one of my former players at Bournemouth. I took him from Fulham, and he was such a lovely player, a really good footballer, but with an incredible level of fitness. In that division, it really stood out. We'd go running up St Catherine's Hill near Christchurch and he was always the fastest. He decided when he became a manager that this was the way to go. Get the team fit as fiddles and compete physically. He made visiting Cambridge an ordeal for the opposition. No lights in the dressing room, so you had to go hunting for bulbs, and only cold water in the showers. He caught one of his players talking to Gerry Peyton, my goalkeeper, before a match once and I thought he was going to kill him. He manhandled this guy away, shouting and hollering about never talking to the opposition. I suppose he thought he had to do something to intimidate the visitors because, being frank, who would be scared of going to Cambridge? So he made it a different world up there.

One time when we played with Bournemouth, they had a young lad in midfield with a really nice touch. After about fifteen minutes, he played the ball backwards to his defence, and John came marching out of the dugout to shout at him, 'Forward! Always forward!' he yelled. About two minutes later, the kid passed one square. Out came John again. 'One more,' he told him, 'and you're off.' Next ball, it was really tight, we had a lot of players crowding in and he had absolutely no options, so he did the sensible thing and laid it off behind – and that was it. Up came his number, gone in 20 minutes. John wasn't interested in playing any other way. Everything had to go big. Help it forward. No matter where the ball was, it went forward. Turn it in behind you, get up and win the second ball. He had four signs in the corners of the pitch that read QUALITY, and the players were instructed to aim for them. He let the grass grow longer down there, too, so the ball wouldn't just run out of play. Then they put Dion Dublin upfront and bombarded you. I remember talking to John Vaughan, who used to be a goalkeeper at West Ham, and had joined Cambridge from Fulham. He said that when he went there to sign, Beck took him out on the pitch and made him kick balls to make sure he could reach those forward areas. He had to dribble it out ten yards and then launch it into the corners. John's plan was that the defending full-back would head it out for a throw, and Cambridge would work off a long throw. It could be very effective.

This day, however, Cambridge would not have it all their way. The match was at our place. So hot showers, bright dressing rooms and balls for the pre-match warm-up that had not been deliberately overfilled with air, so as it felt like you were kicking a cannonball. It was still tense, but we were winning 1–0 when, with about five minutes to go, their winger, Chris Leadbitter, hit a thirty-yarder that just flew into the top corner. That was it. We were done. But just as Cambridge were running back celebrating, thinking they might avoid relegation, we noticed the linesman on the far side had his flag raised. My old mate Steve Claridge had been standing out by the wing, but in an offside position. What a piece of luck. These days it would have been given, because there was no way he was interfering with play. Fortunately, the rules were different back then, the goal was disallowed and we scored a second to win 2–0. We went up, level on points with Portsmouth but with a goal difference of 79. They went into the play-offs with a goal difference of 78, and fell at the first hurdle to Leicester City, having finished twelve points clear of them. It was tough on Jim.

Our first season in the Premier League was hard. In fact, if we hadn't sold Julian Dicks to Liverpool, I don't think we would have survived. My philosophy is this: if you've got Lionel Messi, he's priceless, but a special few aside, I'd always rather have three good players, rather than one top individual, particularly if the team is struggling. If you've got one good guy, the opposition can make plans for him. Even Robin van Persie would not be the same player in an ordinary team, because a good coach would find a way of shutting him out of the game. That won't work against Manchester United at present, because by concentrating on Van Persie, space is then left for Wayne Rooney, Danny Welbeck, Shinji Kagawa or Javier Hernández. The worth of having several good players rather than one superstar becomes even more apparent if your best man is not a match winner. At West Ham that season our outstanding talent was Julian Dicks, a left-back. Stuart Pearce is remembered as the best full-back of that era, and understandably so, but on his day as a pure footballer Julian was every bit as good. He was also a complete nightmare to manage and his temperament could be a liability.

I don't think I ever came across a more disruptive dressing-room influence. Julian was a powerful character, and he had a great hold over his easily led little crew. If Julian didn't want to train, none of them wanted to train. And that was a problem because Julian hated training. He could be dangerous, too. Our big signing that summer was Simon Webster, a central defender, from Charlton for £525,000, and Billy planned to make him captain. He lasted four weeks in pre-season for us before Julian broke his leg in training. Simon had suffered the same injury at Sheffield United, a double fracture, and Julian repeated it. He didn't even think it was a bad tackle, saying he went for the ball, and without the benefit of replays I wouldn't like to come down on either side with certainty. What I would say is that Julian tackled in training the way he tackled in a match, and that wasn't always right or helpful. Simon was never the same after that and barely played another twenty matches before retiring in 1995. That was Julian's style. He slid in and caught

Simon the way he did a lot of people, except that day the damage could not be run off. He never changed. If you pulled at him as he went past, the elbow would come out and – bam. And it didn't matter whether we were at Old Trafford or playing a five-a-side at Chadwell Heath. I think Lou Macari might even have copped one of those from Julian when he was West Ham's manager. And when Julian wasn't booting our own players up in the air or elbowing the staff, he was arguing with Billy over having to train at all.

He wouldn't stretch, he wouldn't run. If we played a game and Billy said the ball had gone out for a corner, he would argue it was a goal-kick. And then he'd get the hump and walk off. And when Julian had the hump you knew about it because if he could be persuaded to stay, he'd start going into tackles even harder. As a coach, you'd almost want to look away as it happened. You couldn't mess about with Julian, you couldn't kid to him. Yet he had an aura and he was such a good player that the rest of the lads all respected him. So he carried the first team and then they all caused trouble. 'We're wearing suits to the match tomorrow,' Billy would say. 'Why can't we wear tracksuits?' Julian would shoot back. And then the lot of them would join in – Bishop, Morley, Martin Allen – it was impossible to get anything done some days. We'd start the warm-up jog and Julian would be lagging fifty yards behind and, slowly, three or four would join him. Another day he would start hoofing balls out of the training ground into the adjoining gardens, or skulk around at the back as everyone was doing their exercises, muttering, 'What a load of bollocks.' It got so bad that we had to invent drills just to get him to run. We'd line up cones for him to dribble around – real basic kid's stuff – but it seemed to keep him happy. And because he was top dog, if he was happy the rest of them stayed happy, too. They followed his lead like little puppies.

Yet, despite all this, what a player. With a better temperament he would have won fifty caps for England, easy. His hero was Mark Dennis, another nutcase left-back, and Julian reminded me a lot of Mark. Dennis could have been a real rival to Kenny Sansom, as Julian would have been to Pearce, but he was always getting into scrapes or getting sent off. But they were both good players. Fantastic, but hard work. We'd come into training, have a row, have a ruck, and then Julian would go out with the hump and start volleying balls from forty yards. Perfect, every time. No stretching, no warm-up, just take a loose ball and – bang – volley it straight on to the chest of a player across the other side of the pitch. It didn't matter if it was freezing cold, pouring with rain – he just had it, that natural ability that the best footballers possess. Drop the shoulder, put a cross in, always on the mark. You could have put your life on that left foot. He'd bend it, curl it, he could do anything with the ball. If we practised headers, he was the best at the club. The hardest tackler too, of course. Everyone hated playing against Julian – no wonder the fans loved him. He would have been the one of the finest footballers of his generation in England, if it wasn't for the flaws in his character.

In some ways the supporters brought the worst out of him. They loved his aggressive side and, even when he let us down badly, they could see no wrong in him. The season we won promotion, Julian was sent off three times, and Billy became so frustrated with his constant suspensions that he took the captaincy away from him. On one occasion he lasted fifteen minutes against Derby County before committing an absolute horror-show of a challenge on Ted

McMinn. I was seething about his irresponsibility, but the fans sung his name for the rest of the match. What they didn't understand was that if Julian hadn't been absent for so many games we might not have had to scramble over the line for promotion. The players had a good relationship with the fans after we went up, but for a while Julian was the only one they liked. The rest of the lads would be getting scary abuse, but they were always on side with Julian. We saw the high-maintenance cost, they saw the fantastic, committed player. Selling him was going to make us very unpopular.

So he was good, but he wasn't Messi. And when the next season began, and we won a single league game in our first seven, it was plain that we needed greater strength in depth rather than one talented but troublesome individual. Looking back, I still think if we hadn't done the deal for Julian, taking three Liverpool players in his place, we'd have gone back down again. I know I later bought Julian back to West Ham as a player – but at the time selling him was exactly the right thing to do.

We lost our first two matches – at home to Wimbledon and away to Leeds United – and the next day I went to see Jamie play for Liverpool at Queens Park Rangers. Graeme Souness was Liverpool's manager, and he could already sense we were in trouble. 'It's bad,' I told him. 'We're going to have to sell our best player to try to get a few in.'

'Who's your best player?' he asked.

'Julian Dicks,' I said. 'He's the only one who's worth good money.'

'What, the little fat left-back?' Graeme queried.

I could tell he respected my judgement. 'He's different class, Graeme,' I insisted, seriously. 'You'd love him. He's got the best left foot I've seen, he's great in the air, and as hard as fucking nails.'

Suddenly, he was listening. Then I clinched the deal. 'I'll tell you this,' I said, 'he'd kick fuck out of you in training.'

It was as if Graeme was up for the challenge. 'That good, is he?' he said. 'When are you playing next?' Coventry City, next Saturday, I told him. 'That'll do, we're playing Sunday,' said Graeme. 'I'll come and have a look.'

So along came Graeme and all was going well. We were leading 1–0 with five minutes to go before half-time and Julian was on top of his game. He took the ball, very smoothly, off their little winger Sean Flynn and began advancing up the left flank. Flynn, working admirably hard to recover, caught level with Julian and had a little tug at him. Instantly, we knew what was going to happen next. It was a like a trigger reaction, out came the arm and, wallop, right in the kisser. He laid Flynn out cold and carried on as if nothing had happened. 'That's it,' I thought. 'That's the Liverpool option off the table.' There was no way Souness hadn't seen it. In fact, luckily for Julian, I think the only person inside Highfield Road who didn't see it was the referee. The crowd went beserk, as did their players and the bench. The referee stopped the game for the injured player, but didn't have a clue what had happened. Meanwhile, the crowd were chanting 'off, off, off' and I was working out how we were going to reorganise to cope with ten men. Finally, after a two-minute conversation with the linesman, the referee showed Julian a yellow. Then it was half-time. Billy went mad at Julian in the dressing room and told him he could have cost us the game. Julian picked up his boots and threw them across the floor. We ended up drawing 1–1. And when I went to watch Liverpool again the next day, I was expecting to get no joy from Souness over our best player.

I couldn't have been more wrong. Graeme loved him, particularly the bit where he'd sploshed Sean Flynn. We were cursing Julian, but he was just Graeme's sort of man. 'I like him, Harry,' he said. 'He plays his fucking heart out. I'll have one more look, next week against Swindon, and then I'll make a decision.' I thought Julian had his worst game for us against Swindon. No drama, just a poor afternoon. But on the Monday, Graeme was on the phone wanting to get a deal done. We knew it wasn't going to be easy. We knew the truth from behind the scenes: Julian was a leader, but not in a positive way, and he had a lot of followers. Much of the misbehaviour at the club stemmed from his influence. Against that, he was only 25, but he was already a legend with the fans. They were not going to be happy. We had to make it worth our while.

Trevor Morley was our only striker and needed support, so we paid £250,000 for Lee Chapman from Portsmouth, and took Mike Marsh and David Burrows from Graeme at Liverpool. That Saturday, we won away at Blackburn Rovers – who would finish runners-up to Manchester United that season – and Chapman scored. The signings turned our season around. We only lost two games in our next eleven, rose to ninth by the halfway stage and ended up finishing a creditable 13th. And no, Burrows was not as good a left-back as Dicks, and he wouldn't make any Greatest Ever West Ham Teams, unlike Julian. But he did a great job, and Chapman scored goals and Marsh got our midfield ticking, so the three together were worth more than one player. As for Julian, it did not work out for him at Liverpool, and I bought him back two years later a quieter and more manageable individual. By then, I was the boss of West Ham – a change of command that would cost me one of my oldest and dearest friends in football.

CHAPTER SEVEN

BILLY AND THE KIDS

Billy Bonds was the most fantastic player. What would West Ham United, or any club for that matter, give to have him now? He could play central midfield, centre-back, full-back; he was fearless in the tackle, he could run all day. I've known Bill since I was 16, when he was a youth player with Charlton Athletic and an England trialist. We were together at the Football Association's training centre at Lilleshall. He was one of my closest friends in football. But was Billy in love with being a football manager? I don't think so. I can understand that. Throughout the time I knew him, Bill's idea of a perfect day was to go down to Dorset, to Thomas Hardy country, and do a bit of bird watching. He is very frugal. He is the sort of bloke that could live on fifty quid a week and certainly wasn't a big one for going out and spending fortunes. And there's nothing wrong with that. I loved Bill to bits, he was a fantastic fella. But in the Premier League world of modern football, he was increasingly a man out of time.

In an era when man management was more important than ever before, with foreign internationals coming into the English game and wages soaring so that players no longer needed their weekly pay cheque, Bill wasn't really a people person. He loved the game, but didn't much care for footballers or their problems. He would get the hump with the ones who weren't as talented as him, or didn't work as hard, or didn't have the same attitude. That was always a problem. I think he looked at his players sometimes and they just got on his nerves. It didn't help that at the end of our first season in the Premier League we signed a player who was everything that Bill wasn't: Joey Beauchamp from Oxford United for £1.2 million. Billy had the hots for him because he remembered Joey giving Julian Dicks a chasing in one of the matches during our promotion season. He was a talented wide midfield player who could play on either left or right.

We had tried to get him earlier in the year, but without success. Oxford wanted to do the deal, but Joey didn't want to come. That should have been the clue. Who wouldn't want to leave Oxford for West Ham? Undaunted, we tried again. This time, we signed him, but the deal dragged on for ages, far longer than was normal when a player was moving from the third tier to the Premier League. What was wrong with him? We soon found out. His first day at the club, I walked in. 'Morning Joe, you all right?'

He just groaned. 'I should have gone to Swindon,' he said.

I thought he was talking about his route to work. 'No, Joe, you don't want to go to Swindon, that's down the M4,' I told him. 'You go in the opposite direction from Oxford to Swindon. Come down the M40 towards London, round the M25. That's the best way. If you come on the M4, follow signs to Newbury.'

'No,' he said. 'I should have signed for Swindon. Swindon Town. The football club.'

'You're at West Ham, in the Premier League, and you're telling me you should have gone to Swindon?' I asked him.

Swindon had been relegated from the Premier League the previous season, rock bottom, having conceded 100 goals.

'Yes,' he said. 'I've made a mistake.'

And it got worse each day from there. He didn't like the journey, he didn't like the club, he missed home, he missed his girlfriend; his attitude was a drain on all of us. One week we took the squad training to Eastbourne, jogging around the hills. Bill was at the front, the fittest of the lot, as ever – I was at the back, lagging behind as usual – and Joey, our new signing, was four hundred yards behind me. We played some pre-season games in Scotland and he spent all day on the phone to his girlfriend. It was pathetic for a grown man on a good salary to be so lacking in independence. He acted like an eight-year-old. He didn't want to run, he didn't want to play the matches. I know what I wanted to do – I wanted to slap him – but I was supposed to be the man-manager in our partnership. Stuff like that did Billy's head in. Joey just sulked all day. He wouldn't talk to us, wouldn't discuss his problems. It drove Bill crazy. He had bent over backwards in the negotiations, allowing him to live in Oxford and arranging a signing-on fee of £30,000. Now Joey was saying that he was too tired and stressed to come in because he had been sitting in traffic jams. He just wanted to be back home, playing for his local team and going dog racing. He liked the dogs. That's about all we had in common. Even when we finally decided to cut our losses and sell him to Swindon, he demanded £350,000 to leave the club. I wasn't having that. The deal had been dragging on all night when I told their manager John Gorman to put Joey on the phone. John was tearing his hair out because Joey was insisting he wouldn't sign until he got his money. 'What is fucking going on?' I shouted. 'Don't think you're coming back here. You've been nothing but fucking aggravation since you arrived and we don't want you. You didn't want to be here, you wanted to go Swindon. So stop being a greedy bastard, take what they are offering and fucking go to Swindon.'

Joey changed his mind and signed, but problems like that took a toll on Bill. He was so straight as a player, so honest, that he couldn't stand the attitude of some in the modern game.

The drinking culture in football had not been eradicated, and there were a few at West Ham who were hard work. That definitely upset Billy. He hated being around them, and the lack of professionalism – the sport had changed beyond recognition since our own playing days – got him down. I think Bill's love of the game began and ended with pulling on his claret and blue shirt as a player, really. He loved football but when that final whistle blew, he'd be halfway through the Blackwall Tunnel and home before some of the lads were even out of the shower. Training was the same. There would still be people ambling off the pitch when Bill's tail-lights were disappearing out of the car park. So as a manager he was never going to be the sort of guy who was the last one out of the office at night, or away scouting five times a week. He was a home man, he loved his family, his wife – he didn't want to hang around the football club all day, he wasn't a great one for talking to other managers or any football people, at all. Was it the modern game that Bill disliked? It is hard to say. Even when he played he didn't have a great rapport with the rest of the team. We used to go greyhound racing and room together, so he was fine with me, but Bill wasn't a great mixer. One year, Ron Greenwood gave us the opportunity to go to America at the end of the season. It was an incredible trip, because nobody went there in those days. We were going to do five weeks in Baltimore, one more in Bermuda, and then home. Play a few matches, but nothing too serious. We all thought it was the opportunity of a lifetime, but Bill wouldn't go. Ron said that we all travelled or the trip was off, so we spent weeks pleading with Bill to change his mind. In the end, he flew out with the team, but came home early saying his aunt was ill. Bill never wanted to be too far from his garden.

So every day would start the same. I'd be in first, waiting for Billy, and then he'd arrive and issue instructions for the training or the match the next day. 'Shirt and tie tomorrow,' Bill would say. 'Bollocks to that,' Julian Dicks would reply, pick up a ball and boot it over the fence on to the railway line. You can imagine Bill's face in those moments.

I remember his absolute disgust before our first match in the Premier League, against Wimbledon. I got to Upton Park early and the groundsman told me that Sam Hammam, Wimbledon's owner, had gone into the away dressing room with a big pile of pens. 'He's been in there about forty-five minutes,' he said. 'I don't know what he's doing.' I told him to find out and come back and tell me. Neither of us could believe what we saw. There was graffiti all over the dressing-room walls. Filthy insults aimed at the Wimbledon players: stuff about Vinnie Jones, stuff about John Fashanu, calling them all wankers and worse. At that moment, Sam walked in. I was furious. 'What have you done?' I asked him. 'No, not me, you have done this,' he said, standing there with the pens in his hand. I told the groundsman to get a policeman. We used to take kids on a tour of Upton Park before match days. That was now ruined because they couldn't visit the dressing rooms and see this rubbish scrawled everywhere. Hammam then had the audacity to try to throw us out. 'This is our dressing room, you must leave,' he said. 'Get out, you have written this on our walls.'

We removed him in the end, but Billy was really upset when he arrived. It wasn't long after Bobby Moore had died. 'We've just buried Bobby,' he said, 'and this is what we've got to deal with.' He was all for going to the police and the Football Association with an official complaint, but the club must have talked him out of it. I thought Hammam was sick in the head at first, but then I realised it was merely a crude motivational tactic. He wanted his players to think we had insulted and demeaned them, so they could be wound up into a frenzy and would go out wanting to kill us. Apparently, the previous season, when Wimbledon played at Blackburn Rovers, he had got to Ewood Park early and thrown all their boots and the neatly laid-out kit into a freezing bath and written graffiti all over the walls there, too. Kenny Dalglish was holding a team meeting when half the Wimbledon team burst in threatening all sorts. Wimbledon came away with a point that day – they'd frightened the life out of them.

It was at those moments that I could really understand some of Bill's disdain for the modern game, so when a former chairman of Bournemouth, Geoffrey Hayward, called to offer me the opportunity to return to the club, I must say I was interested. Geoffrey lived around the corner from me, and his family had been involved with Bournemouth, off and on, for decades. He said he wanted to buy it again, but would only do so if I came back. I could have whatever title and job I liked, from manager to managing director. 'I'll give you the club, it's yours to run,' he said. It sounded a very appealing proposition. I was enjoying my time at West Ham professionally, but personally it was hard. I lived in a flat in Emerson Park, Romford, and only went home to Bournemouth and my family at weekends after the game. I thought that having helped the club win promotion, and consolidate in our first season in the Premier League, I could leave with head held high and no hard feelings. The news of Geoffrey's takeover was being announced by local newspapers the next day and as I was such a big part of it, I told Bill that I should come clean with the West Ham board. Bill knew how much this new job appealed to me. When I told him I wanted to go back to Bournemouth, his first reaction was, 'I don't blame you.'

We were in Scotland at the time on a pre-season tour, but Terry Brown, the chairman, and Peter Storrie, the managing director, were also staying at our hotel. We arranged a meeting and I explained my position, but Brown's reaction came as a shock. 'Why do you want to go back to Bournemouth?' he asked. 'Is it because you'd like to be a manager again?' I explained that wasn't the case. I wanted to go home to where my wife lived, and to a club where I had been very happy for most of my ten years. It wasn't about being a manager. The way Geoffrey had told it, I could be more than just the manager there anyway. 'Why don't you be our manager instead?' Brown continued. 'Bill can be the director of football – with a ten-year contract.' This wasn't what I expected and I felt very uncomfortable being offered Bill's job with him sat there in front of me. 'Bill's the manager,' I said. 'We didn't come in here for this. That's not the idea at all.' But Terry Brown had shown his hand.

'It's obvious you want Harry instead of me,' Bill interrupted. 'You think he's a better manager than me, and you want him to replace me.' There was an awkward pause. 'Right,' Bill continued. 'What does "director of football" mean, anyway?'

Brown began outlining the job. It seemed a very loose arrangement. Go to training when he liked, turn up on match days, and be the club ambassador. It was a job for life, too. Complete security and no pressure – I was beginning to wish they had offered it to me. Bill said he needed time to consider and we all parted company. It wasn't the meeting I had planned, the one in which I made a dignified exit to start anew at Bournemouth; and Bill was genuinely undecided, as well. We had dinner together that night, as usual, and there was not a squeak of difference between us. I told Billy I still wanted to go back to Bournemouth. 'I'm living in a flat, Bill,' I told him. 'Back home, we've got room, we're on the coast, my wife's there with our dogs. This doesn't suit me – I don't want to live this way any more.'

I don't know what the final straw was for Billy. Certainly, Joey Beauchamp turning up late for a friendly at Portsmouth that Saturday and not trying one leg did not help his mood greatly. I was torn as well. It still all hinged on his decision, though, and on the Monday Bill called me. 'I'm at the ground,' he said. 'I'm packing up.'

I drove down there as quickly as I could with Ronnie Boyce, our chief scout, but we couldn't talk him around. I even offered to stay as his number two, but he was set on resigning. He went in to see Terry Brown and quit.

Immediately, Terry called me in and asked if I would be manager.

I said I needed time to think it over. My head was spinning. A few days earlier I had decided to go back to Bournemouth, to be with Sandra and the family. Now I was going to be the manager of a Premier League club and more immersed and distanced than ever. I should have simply driven home and given myself time to think, but the club were eager to put on a united public face, and the biggest mistake I made, in hindsight, was agreeing to a press conference. The club wanted to make it appear that the loose end of Billy's resignation had been tied up, but I should never have agreed. I wasn't ready to be manager – I hadn't even made my own mind up yet, and I was so uncertain that I did not return to Upton Park for a week.

It wasn't until Frank Lampard Senior came to see me over the next weekend that I made my decision. 'I don't want Bill's job, Frank,' I told him. 'Why not?' he replied. 'Look, Harry, they clearly wished to make a change. Someone else is going to get offered this even if you turn it down. They wanted you – give them what they want.'

Peter Storrie kept calling asking for a decision, but I was still troubled by how Bill felt. It was only when we spoke that I felt content I was doing the right thing. 'Take it,' Billy said. 'It's a good job, well paid; you'd be a fool not to. Don't worry about me, I've been well looked after. Take it.'

Yet, even on the day I walked into West Ham as manager, I still felt most comfortable with the thought of returning to Bournemouth. People see me as a very ambitious person, but I'm not like that at all. If I'm happy with my life, that is good enough. All week, I kept telling Peter Storrie that I didn't want to be manager of West Ham, and it wasn't until Frank came down to see me that I began to open my mind. What I did not expect, though, was to lose Bill's friendship over the decision. All these years later, that still hurts – and I would swap having Billy as a mate for all of my seven years as manager at Upton Park.

Let me get this straight: I didn't push Billy Bonds out of West Ham. In fact, for the two weeks after I took the job we continued to speak. Yet each conversation grew more stilted and, in the end, I could tell it wasn't right. I knew what was happening. People were mixing it for us. That always happens when a manager leaves a club. There is always someone who can't wait to tell you what is being said, or what was going on behind your back. It happened when I left Bournemouth. Tony Pulis said this; Tony Pulis did that. The same at Tottenham with Tim Sherwood, who everyone said had the ear of Daniel Levy, the chairman. There is always a story, that is how it is in football, and probably Billy heard too many stories about me. The difference was that he believed them. I asked him to have his photograph taken with me, to show there were no hard feelings, but he refused. I realised then that it was over, and that it was always going to be difficult between us.

That is what happens when people stir the pot. Tony Gale was a terrific centre-half for West Ham, but in 1994 we let him go on a free transfer to Blackburn. Tony always blamed me – although it worked out well for him, because he got a championship winner's medal up there the following season – and he's barely had a good word to say about me since. But it was Bill who wanted Tony out of the club. Tony used to spend the summer working at a holiday camp owned by our chairman, Terry Brown, and Bill was convinced he was telling him our business.

Looking back, from the club's perspective, it could have been handled better. I think the way that Terry Brown sprung the director of football position on Bill was silly. Terry knew I had overseen the sale of Julian Dicks to Liverpool, and probably thought I was more into being a manager than Billy. In that respect, he was right. Bill often gave the impression that he found the job exhausting and if it had been broached differently, I think he might have enjoyed his ambassadorial role. It could have been a great job for him. I certainly wouldn't have turned it down had the positions been reversed. A job for life? I'd have said, 'Thanks very much, Mr Chairman,' and they wouldn't have had to ask twice. Bill would have been a perfect director of football for the club, and I genuinely think Terry Brown was trying to find a solution that would make Bill happy. In Terry's eyes, I was more of a manager than Bill at the time. I'd done well at Bournemouth, I liked scouting and coaching and mixing with players, and Billy just wasn't into that. With better management, I think Billy could still be there now, the one constant through the many changes of ownership.

So it was his decision to leave and, knowing that, I have been disappointed with some of what has subsequently been said. Billy clearly feels I overstepped the mark as his assistant. He says I gave interviews before matches on Sky discussing tactics, but that is certainly not my recollection of it. I may have sat in our meeting room and had a cup of tea with Andy Gray, but I don't remember doing anything for the cameras. Yes, I was direct in my approach at times, but it was Billy who asked for my help. Once I had accepted that invitation I wasn't in the business of being relegated. I was at West Ham to have a proper go. I still do not understand why Bill would take that personally. It was as if he wanted me to do a job, and then when I did that job and it got noticed, he didn't like it. The headline in the *Sun* from that time said I stabbed him in the back, but there is not a chance I would do that, not a prayer.

Bill has made his feelings clear, and that is up to him. I am loath to revisit the subject even now, because I don't want to kick up another war of words, but anyone who knows him will confirm he is not always the easiest guy to deal with. His family is what he loves and he doesn't seek much contact with anybody else. If the owners felt that Bill didn't want to be the manager that is merely because it was the vibe he gave off at times. He was much more comfortable playing than dealing with managerial issues. Yet West Ham was Terry Brown's business, so he probably looked at that and thought Bill would be better off in the directors' box and I would be more use on the training field. It was handled badly, obviously, but I can't blame them for reaching that conclusion. They tried to look after Bill and, in different circumstances, I don't think he would have been too upset with the offer; it just unfolded awkwardly for all of us.

I've heard all sorts of stories since. Some people even say that the fall-out with Billy cost me the England job, because Sir Trevor Brooking has never forgiven me over it – but I can't see that. Trevor wasn't around West Ham at that time, and I would be surprised if he had harboured a grudge all these years without confronting me about it. I was one of a handful of footballers that were invited to, and attended, Trevor's wedding. He has come to family occasions of mine. I don't see him as the spiteful sort. Yet though twenty years have passed since Bill and I spoke, the break-up of our friendship still hurts. Not the rumours, not the innuendo, not the gossip from people who were not there and wouldn't have a clue what went on behind the scenes. All that gets distorted by those who want to cause problems for you. What pains me is the fact that I no longer have Bill as a friend, because I loved him to bits and there is no way on earth I would have hurt him. I would give anything today to see him and just have a cup of tea together.

Back then, though, my only choice was to get on with it, and it wasn't an easy job at all. My first decision was to bring Frank Lampard Senior with me. Frank was my brother-in-law and an old friend, but he knew the club – he knew football, and for years he had been coaching the kids at West Ham on a Tuesday and Thursday night for free. Frank was ideal. He talks nothing but common sense about football, and I resented the criticism that it was an old pals' act. If that was my priority, I would have kept Ronnie Boyce on the staff. Ronnie was at West Ham when I arrived as a teenager, and was still there when I returned a second time. He had been a member of the coaching staff since 1973 and in 1991 he was made chief scout. I liked Ronnie but he seemed too much a part of the furniture, a long-standing member of the cosy little club that was the worst of West Ham. 'He'll be there when you've gone,' Bobby Moore had said to me. 'What does he give you?' He had a point.

Ronnie was a nice man, but if you showed him Lionel Messi, he wouldn't be able to make his mind up on whether to sign him or not. You rarely got a hard, firm opinion from him, and that's no use in a scout. This may seem harsh, but there is a great temptation in football to keep people on for old time's sake. When I brought Jimmy Hampson in, full-time, it was hard replacing Jimmy Neighbour: I had known him for a long time, took him to America, brought him to Bournemouth on loan. But we preferred Jimmy Hampson and, of course, before long, we had six young players in the England team. Much of that was down to Jimmy Hampson, the man who changed the club. I've heard all sorts of people getting credit for producing West Ham's golden generation, but the club hadn't produced a player for ten years before this batch came along. Tony Carr nets a lot of the glory, but he didn't suddenly unearth some genius method of finding footballers. All that altered was Jimmy Hampson started bringing us some of the best kids in London. And one, in particular, that I will never forget.

I first saw Joe Cole when he was 12. It didn't take much to make him a player. The daftest bloke in the world could have spotted Joe was a star in the making. I remember standing there with Frank, Alan Sealey and Peter Brabrook, and none of us had seen a kid like it in our lives. It must have been like watching Messi for the first time at that age. We were playing Norwich City's under-13 team. It was a 2 p.m. game, middle of winter and ankle-deep in mud at Chadwell Heath. After ten minutes we were all looking at each other. 'Who is this kid?' He was playing a year up from his age, the smallest on the pitch, all these big lads from Norfolk towering over him and he was getting the ball, spinning, beating three or four of them – and goal. Then he'd do it again – and goal. Don't get too excited, I was told. One of our staff had walked in behind Joe's dad, George, and had overheard a conversation. George was wearing bright red shoes, so he stood out a mile, and had been telling his mates on the way in that there was no way Joe was coming to West Ham. But he was the best player for his age that I have ever seen, and Jimmy grafted every day with George to make sure Joe kept coming back to our club. I would travel to Chadwell Heath to watch under-13 games just to keep in contact, too. We played Arsenal, won 3–1, Joe scored a hat-trick. We played Tottenham, it didn't matter who they had, Joe murdered them.

By now, every club knew about him. Sir Alex Ferguson sent him a Manchester United kit with COLE 10 written on the back. 'This is what your shirt will look like when you play for Manchester

United,' read the message. Alex was desperate to get him. He even invited him to travel on the team bus when United got to an FA Cup final. Arsenal were into him, Chelsea were into him, but I knew Joe was happiest playing for West Ham. So I gave him some space. When George said Joe had been invited up to train for two weeks with Manchester United, I let him go. I could have got annoyed, said that he had signed schoolboy forms with us and threatened to report United, but what good would that have done? It would just have antagonised George and we'd have lost the player. 'Great, George,' I told him. 'Let Joe go, let him have a look around, but never forget, we'd love him here. He's going to be in the first team in no time, you know. But Manchester United? What a great experience. Tell him to enjoy himself.' So we'd lose Joe for two weeks, but he wouldn't have as much fun as he did at West Ham where he knew everybody and got on with all the boys, so he'd come back more in love with our place than ever.

One Friday morning, we were preparing to play Everton away and Joe came over and trained with the first team. We ended up playing nine-a-side, his team won 4–2 and Joe scored three. He was still in our under-15 team and I can remember David Unsworth asking if he could play the next day. He was deadly serious. That is how good he was.

I tried to get Joe back at Queens Park Rangers, but he chose to return to West Ham. Looking at our league position at the time, and the pull to return to his former club, I could understand his decision. I wouldn't hold a grudge against Joe at all. He has always been a lovely lad. When Peter Brabrook needed a knee operation a few years back, Joe paid for it, because he remembered all the years Peter spent coaching him as teenager. That's class.

Meanwhile, at the same time, Rio Ferdinand was coming through our academy courtesy of Jimmy. He had arranged a game against a district team from south London at Chadwell Heath. They had some good boys and Frank and I started chatting up the chap who ran the team, Dave Goodwin. We said that if he ever saw one that he thought would benefit West Ham, we would reward him for the information. Every club has a whole roster of youth scouts that are paid for a good tip on a boy. It wasn't long before Dave phoned to tell us about one who had just attended his trials. 'He's different class, fantastic, the best I've seen in years,' he said, 'and he's only just started playing football.' That was Rio. He came over and, clearly, Dave was spot on. Rio was a natural.

Later that season, 1994–95, we played Chelsea in the South-East Counties Cup final. The first leg was at home in front of a good crowd, nearly 10,000, but we lost 4–2. The return was at Stamford Bridge and clashed with a first-team game. At the end of the match, the first call I got was from my dad. He had been over to Chelsea to watch the youth team and he was raving. 'What a game,' he said. 'It was fantastic – you won!' I couldn't believe it. We had turned the tie around and smashed Chelsea by four or five. 'I've seen a kid playing for you tonight,' Dad continued, 'he's the best I've seen for years. A midfielder – what a player.'

I thought he meant Frank Lampard.

'No,' he said. 'His name is Ferdinand.'

I didn't believe him. 'Rio Ferdinand, Dad?' I quizzed. 'It can't be him. He's not a youth player yet, he's a schoolboy.'

'Rio Ferdinand – that was it,' the old man said. 'I've seen nothing like it. He kept picking the ball up, running fifty yards, drifting by people, they couldn't get near him. What a player.'

Next on the telephone was Tony Carr. 'We played fantastic,' he said. 'And Rio Ferdinand was unbelievable. You've got to watch him again, Harry. I've never seen one like him.'

From there, we knew we had to get Rio on the fast track – and keep him at West Ham. Frank Senior was brilliant with that. Rio didn't really have a football background and when Millwall came in for him, because he was a Peckham boy and it was close to home, he couldn't make his mind up. Frank spent ages around his house, talking to Rio, talking to his mum, explaining the difference between the clubs. Dave Goodwin was grafting for us as well, to be fair, and in the end between the three of us we persuaded him to sign. The next step was to get him out on loan, so I recommended him to Mel Machin, who was then the manager of Bournemouth. He hadn't seen him play but he took my word and he went straight into the first team after a few training sessions. And that's how we nearly lost him.

Not long after the loan began, Mel came on the phone to tell me he had just received a call from Martin Edwards, the chairman of Manchester United, wanting to buy Rio. 'He thought he was our player, Harry,' said Mel. 'I told him to speak to you.'

Someone had clearly seen Rio in action and alerted Martin. I thought it was strange that he was conducting the business, not Alex Ferguson. Even so, I waited for his call. About half an hour later, it came. 'I've been speaking to Mel Machin about the boy Ferdinand,' Martin said. 'He's a bit of a player, isn't he?'

'He's fantastic, Mr Edwards. He'll be the best defender in Europe one day.'

'That's some statement, Harry,' Martin replied. 'How much is he?'

I told him Rio wasn't for sale.

'He must have a price,' he insisted.

'Not this boy,' I said. 'No price.'

'Would you take £1 million, or good money adding up to it?' he asked.

'Mr Edwards, you could not buy this boy, he's that good,' I told him.

Eventually, he backed off. It eventually cost Manchester United £30 million to buy Rio from Leeds United in 2002. And he was still worth every penny.

Michael Carrick also ended up having a fantastic career at Manchester United, and he was another of Jimmy Hampson's discoveries. Jimmy got him down from the north-east and he was a prospect, but a late developer. I suppose that was lucky for us, because if he had shown his true potential at a young age Newcastle United would have snapped him up. But Michael was one of those kids who had a sudden growth spurt. He went from 5 feet 2 inches to 6 feet 2 inches in about six months, went from being a kid to a man, and it gave him a disorder called Osgood–Schlatter disease, which is common in sporty adolescents whose bodies struggle to adapt to their rapid growth. Michael was stick thin and certainly no schoolboy superstar – if he had a bad game he could look like Bambi on ice – but you always knew that if he got stronger and moved around the pitch a bit quicker, there was a lovely footballer trying to get free. Eventually, we started seeing that side of him, and I loaned him out to Swindon Town for experience. It definitely worked because soon after John Francome, the former National Hunt jockey, was on the phone: 'Harry, I saw a player at Swindon last night, he's the best since Glenn Hoddle,' he said. 'Your boy

Carrick. I've never seen anyone pass a ball like he did. He was fantastic.' And John wasn't a bad judge, of horses or footballers, because, from there, Michael never looked back.

Around that time it seemed every week Jimmy would come in with a new player. Using his south London connections, he managed to smuggle Jermain Defoe away from Charlton. We had to pay compensation and they were furious, but it was worth it. We could see he was scoring goals every week in the South-East Counties League. When Sean O'Driscoll of Bournemouth came on, desperate for a striker, it seemed a perfect fit. 'I'll let you have Jermain Defoe on loan,' I said. 'He's a terrific player and he needs the experience.'

'How old is he,' asked Sean. I told him 17. 'That's no use,' he said. 'We can't score goals, Harry, and you know what this league is like. Kids are no good for me. I need a man.'

Loans were also limited in the lower divisions and I could tell Sean didn't fancy making a commitment. 'Trust me, Sean, he'll be great for you,' I insisted. 'He's different class.'

'Is he a big 'un?' he asked.

'No, he's a little titch,' I replied, and I could almost hear the sigh down the telephone line. 'Sean, I'll tell you what I'll do: take him for a week,' I said. 'We won't make it a loan. Just take him and let him train and if at the end of that you don't want him then you haven't used your loan up. But you'll see that I'm right.'

It took Jermain one training session to make his mark. First day, I got another call from Sean. 'We had a practice match today and he scored five goals,' he said. 'My God, Harry, he's the best we've had down here.' Jermain was a phenomenon at Bournemouth. He scored five goals in four games for them, didn't score in a match against Dover Athletic, and then scored eight in seven. Between 28 October 2000 and 23 January 2001, he scored in every League and FA Cup game he played.

I've taken Jermain with me since to Portsmouth and Tottenham. His mum isn't exactly his agent, but she exerts a strong influence. When we did the deal at Portsmouth, I left the room while the contract was being negotiated. Peter Storrie was in there and Milan Mandaric, Jermain and his mum. I was having a cup of tea next door when Peter burst in. 'You'd better come through,' he said. 'We've got a problem.' It turns out Jermain's mum was insisting on a goal bonus. That's right, for a striker. I couldn't believe what I was hearing. I thought it was a joke. 'Mrs Defoe,' I said. 'Jermain is costing us £12 million and he will be earning £50,000 a week. What do you think we're paying him for? To effin' miss 'em?'

'I thought it would encourage him to score,' she said.

'We were rather hoping the fifty grand would do that,' I replied. Anyway, Jermain signed his contract – without his goal bonus.

And then there was the player who arguably became the pick of the bunch. Frank. Junior, not Senior. His attitude was amazing, the best I have seen from any young player. But I know his secret: parental influence. The only professional I have known who came close to his commitment was his dad. Like father like son is genuinely true in this case. If anyone ever marvelled at Frank Junior's dedication, I simply told them what I knew about Frank Senior. In my playing days at West Ham he was the best trainer at the club, and he made a career from the game when others would have just given up.

I remember Frank as a 17-year-old left-back with the pace of a three-legged carthorse. He was a lovely footballer, but he couldn't run. We all knew it. One day Ron Greenwood walked into the dressing room and told Frank in front of everybody that he had fixed him up with a loan to Torquay United. There were a few ex-West Ham people down there at the time: Frank O'Farrell was the manager and he had taken John Bond and Ken Brown, with Malcolm Musgrove as his assistant. 'They will have you on loan,' Ron said, 'and if you do well, they would like to keep you.'

Frank was adamant. 'I don't want to play for Torquay,' he said. 'I want to play for West Ham. What's wrong with me? Why don't you ever tell me? What do I have to do to play for West Ham?'

We were all looking at the floor, because young players – or old ones – just didn't speak to Mr Greenwood like that. There was silence.

'What do I need to work on?' Frank said.

'Your speed,' said Ron. 'You're not quick enough, Frank. Work on your passing a bit, too, but it is your speed that is the problem.'

'I'll show you,' Frank shot back. 'I ain't going to Torquay. I'll play for West Ham and I'll show you.'

Everyone thought he was mad. Speed was considered a natural attribute in those days. You were just born fast – or you weren't. Nobody was going to get quicker simply by running. Yet Frank showed them, all right. He bought a pair of running spikes and came back every day after training – and I mean every day. As we were leaving, we would see Frank out on his own: run, jump, jockey, turn, jockey, jockey; run fifteen yards, turn, come back; run to a ball, turn and jockey. He would be out there for hours, working on these short sprints. And gradually, he got quicker.

He used to ask me back sometimes to help him, because I was a quick winger. At first, if I pushed the ball past him, I could give him five yards start and still meet it first. Ron was right – he couldn't run. Yet the more he got those spikes working, the quicker he got, and by the end he would take me on in a proper race. And when he had finished his hour or so at the training ground, he would get home and run again. He'd put a sweat suit on and go on a four-mile run. Sometimes he wore a sweat suit for his sprints, too. And he never missed a day. I can picture him now, walking out from the changing room with his spikes, in the opposite direction to the rest of the players, who were coming in. Typical footballers, they all took the mickey. 'Look at him, who is he trying to impress …' But Frank did not give a monkey's about any of them. He had a determination that was unbelievable. You got in his way, and he would trample all over you. And his boy was exactly the same.

I remember when he came to the club. Just like his dad: technically a good little player, but a bit dumpy, and not quick. The next time I saw him, he had spikes on. It was like watching old Frank all over again. He would practise for two hours like that every day. And what an athlete he became. Recently a clip of an old fans' forum at West Ham surfaced on YouTube. There was a supporter taking me to task for picking Frank Junior. It made interesting viewing with the benefit of hindsight:

Fan: I'd like to ask Harry if the publicity he has given young Frank here warrants it because, personally, I don't think he's quite good enough yet. In the last couple of years you've let some good midfielders go for peanuts, like Matt Holland and Scott Canham.

Harry: No, they definitely weren't good enough. He is good enough, and he definitely will be good enough. I let Scott Canham go, he was a good kid and worked very hard; he's gone to Brentford and he can't get in Brentford's team. He's 21 and I let him go because young Frank is 17 or 18, and he's miles in front of him.

Fan: Well, that ain't really true.

Harry: That is true. That's my opinion and that's why I get paid to make judgements on players. It's a game of opinions. You've got a right to your opinion, but I've also got a right to my opinion. I keep the players I want to keep. Young Matt Holland – yes, I think he may bounce back and may be First Division. He's a decent player – and young Scott Canham is a decent player, don't get me wrong. He's a decent young player, we offered him a two-year contract and he didn't want to stay. But we can sit here in front of all these people and I'll tell you now without any shadow of a doubt, there will be no comparison between what Frank Lampard will achieve in football and what Scott Canham will achieve in football.

Fan: But you're giving him the opportunity.

Harry: I don't give him the opportunity. There is no favouritism; in fact, I'm probably holding him back more because I'll tell you what—

Fan: You played him at Arsenal when he clearly wasn't ready to play.

Harry: I don't think he did badly at Arsenal: I think he came into the side and I felt the kid did well. But I'm telling you now, and I didn't want to say this in front of him, but he will go right to the very top, right to the very top, because he's got everything that's needed to become a top-class midfield player. His attitude is first class, he's got strength, he can pass it, he can play and he can score goals.

Fan: Well, I do go to reserve games, so I do know.

Harry: I'm not saying you don't. It's your opinion. It's fine, but this is my opinion and I couldn't feel more strongly.

I should be a fortune-teller, eh? I know I come across forcefully there, but I had absolute certainty in my opinions. It wasn't even an argument, really. Those fans who had it in for Frank hadn't seen how hard his dad worked to get to the top, so didn't know I had identified exactly the same qualities in his son. By then, we had all noticed how outstanding Frank's attitude was. He loved football, he wanted to be a player, and he had that essential determination. Rio Ferdinand was very similar. Early on in his time at the club, I remember sitting down with him and his little group at the training ground, with Rio quizzing me on what the players ate before matches, what boots they wore; he wanted to know it all. 'What does Paolo Di Canio eat, Harry?' I remember he was fascinated by the way Di Canio stayed so fit. I just sat there talking to those lads for hours, with Rio leading the way, asking about everything. 'What was Bobby Moore like, Harry?' He'd seen a big picture of Bobby on the wall, then gone off and read about him. That group was great to deal with. Rio and Frank were mates, and they drove each other on; they were both excellent trainers, both good influences.

Certainly, Frank's attitude would have inspired a lot of boys at the time, because I've never seen anyone work harder. There wasn't a day when he wouldn't do extra. I remember one week he went away to play for the England under-18 team. It was quite a long journey across Europe and they didn't get home until about 3 a.m. The next morning, the first one in at Chadwell Heath was Frank Junior. Very impressive. Then, later in the afternoon, when everybody had gone home after training, I looked out of the window and I could see a lonely figure, as far away across the field as possible. By then it was lashing down with rain, and I couldn't make out who it was. I thought some local kid had climbed over the fence to do a bit of practice. Running with the ball, and sprints. An hour later, he was still there in the rain, this nutter. I looked again, more closely the second time. It was Frank. Home in the small hours, first in, last out. Spikes on, just like his dad. An amazing talent.

I feel very upset about the way Frank is treated by West Ham supporters now. After Joe Cole left he would return to a standing ovation – the same with Rio Ferdinand – but the abuse they used to give Frank was merciless. I have never understood what he is supposed to have done wrong. When they got rid of me in 2001, they kicked Frank Senior out as well and, unsurprisingly, having seen his dad and uncle sacked, Frank Junior didn't want to be there. Glenn Roeder, the new manager, saw it could be difficult and was happy to let him go. The club got good money from Chelsea for him. What was the problem? I think people were often suspicious, resentful or just plain jealous of Frank. Even when he was playing well, I would sometimes have the oddest conversations about him. I can remember one match at home, when we were just hanging on to a 2–1 lead, and I introduced him late to give us some energy and keep the ball, which he did. It was an important game, a big win for us, but afterwards Terry Brown accused me of only playing Frank to get him some appearance money. I was furious. Frank Senior was coming up the stairs as the row broke out, but he could do nothing to calm me down.

'That's right,' I told Terry. 'His dad's got two hundred houses. When we were playing snooker at 17, he was out buying houses; he's got a fucking property empire – he probably owns half of the East End of London, but I thought, "I'll bring Frank on – he probably needs a hundred quid." I didn't care that the people behind me were giving me grief like you've never heard, or that I'd get absolutely fucking slaughtered if we drew the game, I just thought, "No, what matters is that Frank comes on for fifteen minutes and cops a hundred quid." Are you sure, Terry? Or are you mad? Because if that's really what you think we should book you in with a psychiatrist, because I don't think you're right in the fucking head.'

And that's still the polite version of the conversation. Frank said he couldn't believe I was talking to the chairman like that, but I had lost it. So if that was the attitude of the board, no wonder young Frank got such horrific abuse from the fans. I would have expected people inside the club to have thought more sensibly about him, though.

I certainly have never enjoyed having him on the other side. Box to box, box to box, that's what you get from Frank. When I was at Portsmouth we played against him at Stamford Bridge. He headed a corner out of Chelsea's penalty area, then ran ninety yards to get on the end of a cross. The ball came into our box, and who was there to put it in? Frank. And I'm told he is the same now as he was as a kid. Practice, practice, practice. Always determined, always the last to leave the training field, according to his managers. Take the ball to the left of a cone – bang. Take it to the right of a cone – bang. Left-foot shot, right-foot shot, twenty-five yards, then thirty yards. Take a cross down and hit it. Still doing his sprints; every day he's got his spikes on. He is his father's son, except with greater natural talent; and he has made himself into an unbelievable player, among the best in the world. I'd say there is no one like him – but there was one bloke.

CHAPTER EIGHT

FOREIGN AFFAIRS

I am proud of my seven years at West Ham, but it wasn't always easy. The game was changing and the days of sending out eleven boys from the East End – or eleven British players at least – were over. This was never going to be an issue for the manager of Bournemouth, but as a Premier League boss, I had to learn how to blend the different nationalities, and learn fast. I inherited a club that could never be sure of its place in the top division from one year to the next. We were down the bottom of the league most seasons and couldn't always afford to play the best football. The domestic market, at that time, had grown ludicrously expensive. It wasn't like going into Tottenham Hotspur fourteen years later and looking around the dressing room to see Luka Modrić and Aaron Lennon, players that could change a match. We had Trevor Morley as our striker, often on his own. The youth system was great, eventually, but no manager, not even Sir Alex Ferguson, could send out eleven kids and hope to win – no matter how good they were.

You can't simply walk into a failing club and turn it around with the same group. I knew I had to buy and I know, looking back, that some of those buys were controversial, but what was our alternative? I could either hold fast in the arrogant belief that I was some super coach who could turn rubbish into a good team, or I could do something about it. At various times, I decided I had to take drastic action to improve the team and, if I hadn't, West Ham would have gone down.

If I had to pick out one favourite signing from my time at West Ham it would be Paolo Di Canio; and getting him to rub along with the extremes of football culture in England was one of the biggest challenges of my career. I took him in 1999, after he had served an eleven-match ban for pushing over referee Paul Alcock. Paolo was cheap at £1.7 million, but a lot of people thought I was mad. One newspaper wrote that I was walking a tightrope without a safety net – but I couldn't understand the fuss. The way I saw it, we were getting a great footballer for a bargain price – there was no down side. And Paolo was a great player for West Ham, so much so that they still have a function room named after him at Upton Park. Yet was he easy to deal with? You've seen him – what do you think? Paolo couldn't understand why some of the British players, like our central defender Neil Ruddock, for instance, did not share his approach.

He had such a focused outlook that even the slightest disturbance on the training field would send him into a rage. He would come storming off. 'Hey, fucking gaffer, hey boss! We are warming up, we are supposed to be stretching. Razor Ruddock, he is talking about drinking last night, he is talking about shagging – how can this be right? This is not right. Johnny Moncur, he is fucking laughing, he is meant to be concentrating. What is going on?'

And out I'd go. 'All right, Paolo, I'll sort it.'

He was high maintenance, but I told the young lads to watch and learn. Paolo was as fit as a fiddle, a fanatic about conditioning. He used to come in every Sunday to work with his personal fitness coach, and stay for at least two hours. He wasn't a drinker – just the occasional glass of wine – and he ate all the right foods. That was what the best foreign footballers brought to this country: a serious athletic approach. Before that, there was just a drinking culture, from the bottom up. You would meet 16-year-old kids, who had not even played a game, and who thought football was about putting away as much lager as you could handle all week and then having a match on the Saturday. Players like Paolo stopped that, they helped others make the change. So, while taking him was a gamble, he soon showed he was an amazing talent and a great influence.

Something had to alter because English football could not carry on like it had. The rest of Europe had adopted a more professional approach, but we were still stuck in the old ways. If anything, things had moved on from a few lagers on the train home: at one time there was a spell when West Ham's players would smuggle hard alcohol on to the team bus, with bottles of brandy being passed around at the back. The smarter ones would mix up concoctions in plastic bottles and pretend they were only having soft drinks, but inside was brandy or vodka, with Coke. One night we took a team down to play a testimonial at Dorchester Town, a club in the Conference South. We stayed at a hotel, and when we made to leave at 5 p.m. several of the team were missing – Iain Dowie, John Moncur, Don Hutchison – all nowhere to be seen. We didn't have a clue where they were until they turned up about thirty minutes before kick-off, absolutely legless. I couldn't do anything then, but when the game had finished we had murders. Sure, it was only a testimonial, but a lot of people had turned out to see West Ham play, and what they did showed no respect. It should have been a great night; instead, I hired a driver and sent them all home. Football was a different game by then, and we couldn't have players on the booze – the supporters expected more.

Dale Gordon organised the players' Christmas party in 1994. We were near the bottom of the league at the time, and I can remember listening with mounting astonishment as he set out the plans for the day. They were going to get an open-top bus from our training ground in Chadwell Heath, with a jazz band on the top deck, and take it through the East End, down Green Street, past Upton Park and on to a nightclub in the West End. We were bottom of the league and they were going to drive a glorified disco past where our fans lived, with all the players hanging out the windows getting absolutely plastered. 'Dale, all of those people that pay your wages, they'll be watching,' I told him. 'There'll be blokes digging the road, people working hard in shops to make ends meet, and you're going by with a jazz band, and an open-top bus. They'll aim house bricks at you, Dale. They'll abuse you. And you know what? You'll deserve it for being so stupid. An open-top bus, son? You should be hiding. You're not going. Cancel it.'

But they still had their Christmas party: cancelled the band, the bus, and hired minivans instead. That caused more aggravation because Jeroen Boere – a Dutch striker Billy Bonds had bought from Go Ahead Eagles – set fire to the seats. He was a strange guy, Jeroen. I was in Spain with Sandra a number of years later, and a man came up, smartly dressed in a suit, and introduced himself in a 'remember me?' sort of way. I didn't recognise him. It was Jeroen, but he only had one eye. Apparently he had been stabbed in the face by two men, in the Roppongi district of Tokyo some years earlier. The next I heard, in 2007, he had died. There were conflicting reports – a car crash, suicide, in his home in Marbella, on the road in Ibiza; some people said he had got involved with drugs. He was only 39.

So Jeroen set fire to the seats, for which we had to pay compensation, and, frankly, the evidence of hooligan behaviour was beginning to mount. That testimonial in Dorchester was the gift that kept giving because we then got a bill from the Dormy hotel in Bournemouth. It transpired that while the players were getting drunk they had managed to knock a pint of beer over the snooker table and also rip the baize. We received a letter of complaint from the manager. Another golf trip, to Ferndown, where I play, ended up with a minor riot in the bar, which was personally embarrassing. I'd had enough. I think those early years at West Ham helped push me in the direction of recruiting more foreign players. We needed discipline. We needed good examples for the youngsters. It couldn't carry on like this. The high jinks were going to come at a cost.

The final straw came when Dale Gordon broke his leg on a pre-season golf trip. We had gone away down to Devon to train and the players had an afternoon off; Dale was driving a buggy, and it tipped over and landed on his leg, trapping him. I don't know if he was messing about at the time but, when he returned, the bone hadn't knitted properly and he walked with a slight limp. He barely played again, after that.

So, while Paolo may have been a challenge, it was a least a positive challenge for a manager. Some days he'd have the hump, other times he would be in a great mood. You never knew what you would get with him, but I'd have paid to watch him train, let alone play. He was a genius, with such fantastic ability. You always felt you had a chance of winning with Paolo on the pitch. He could get the ball and change the game; he could hurt any team, any defence, even Manchester United. Score a great goal, make a great goal, you were always involved. At home, in particular, he was our match-winner.

I don't think anyone who played with Paolo ever forgot the experience. Certainly not our goalkeeper, Shaka Hislop. He was a giant, Shaka, but the most amiable, lovely guy in the world. He ended up playing in the World Cup with Trinidad and Tobago and it is no surprise that he has since made a successful career in retirement as a summariser on American television. He was a very smart man. We were playing away at Birmingham City in the League Cup in 1999; it was 1–1 just before half-time when they got a free-kick outside our area. Paolo's job was always to line the wall up, but he didn't get it right and Martin Grainger scored. Shaka came into the dressing room and, obviously, he was upset, but being Shaka he wasn't about to rant and rave. 'Paolo, man,' he said in his deep Caribbean drawl, 'you supposed to line up the wall, man. You didn't line the wall up.' The reaction he got was extreme even by Paolo's standards. 'Fuck you!' he shouted 'You blame me for the goal? *Argh!* Fuck you!' And he marched across the dressing room and picked up this giant barrel of the sports drink Gatorade. It was a ridiculous sight. The container was huge and he could barely lift it. His knees were buckling like a weightlifter when he has taken too much on, and at first we all stayed seated, merely curious as to what would happen next. Then, somehow, Paolo got it over his head, full with gallons and gallons of thick, sticky orange liquid and that's when we knew we were in trouble. He was walking around the dressing room with it, shouting and screaming, his legs trembling with the strain. 'Fuck you! My fault? Fuck you!' All the players were diving for cover under the benches; I had a brand new suit on, so I scarpered quicker than most, under the table in the middle of the room. And from there I heard it – whoosh. He threw it. We all watched it, as if in slow motion, sail through the air until it landed on Shaka's lovely white linen suit, which took the brunt, but there was plenty of collateral damage.

Even then Shaka wasn't fazed. He just stared at him. 'Paolo, man, why did you do that?' he said, as the rest of us surveyed the wreckage of our flooded dressing room.

'Fuck you! I don't play no more. You blame me. Fucking hell,' Paolo screamed. He took his boots off, his socks off, and sat with his arms folded, sulking like a kid. Oh dear. What the hell were we going to do?

'Paolo,' I said. 'You're out of order. Come on, get your gear on, get your boots on.'

'No, fuck off, I don't play. He blame me.'

'No, he didn't blame you. He just said you should have lined the wall up. Look, it's a big game, let's just get on with it. We need a result.'

In the end, he put his boots on and went out. We didn't even have time to talk about the second-half plan. We scored two goals in the last three minutes and won 3–2 and, after the match, Paolo came in as if nothing had happened: no apology, no mention of his previous behaviour at all. He didn't think there was anything to discuss, so we carried on from there.

Goalkeepers seemed a special nuisance for Paolo. Another day he took against our number two, Stephen Bywater, and wanted to bash him up, as big as he was. Once the fuse had been lit he really didn't care who he was up against. I remember Steve Lomas, who was a really tough boy from Northern Ireland, having a go at him one day, and Paolo chased him into the shower for a fight. Nobody messed with Steve, but Paolo didn't care. Once he had lost it, nothing was going to stop him, and the lads had to pull the pair of them apart.

The only thing that scared him was flying. He didn't like it at the best of times, but when we turned up at Stansted Airport one afternoon to discover there was a problem with the plane, that was the final straw. We were flying up to play Bradford City, but Paolo decided he was staying behind. As the lads sat patiently waiting for the mechanical fault to be fixed, Paolo raged on: 'I don't like this plane. It is shit, this plane. Harry, why are we on this shit plane?'

'It's OK, Paolo,' I told him. 'The plane is fine. It's a tiny problem and then we'll be on our way. We can't get there by road now, it's too late.'

At that point a van pulled up and two skinheads got out. They were the mechanics, come to fix the fault: shaved barnets, shorts, big ear-rings, tattoos everywhere, up their legs, down their arms. Paolo was frantic. 'Fucking hell, boss, look at these two! I fucking told you boss. This plane is shit. They couldn't fix my kid's bike let alone an aeroplane! I don't want to die, I have children. I get off.'

'Calm down, Paolo,' I said. 'They wouldn't put us on a plane that is going to crash.' By now, looking at these mechanics, I was coming round to his way of thinking. But we had a game to play and a plane to catch. 'Look, none of us want to die, Paolo,' I soothed. 'I've got a wife and children, too.' Eventually we took off

– with Paolo complaining at every bump all the way up to Leeds Bradford Airport.

We won 2–1 but when we came to go home there had been heavy snow in the West Yorkshire area. The nearer we got to the airport the worse it got, and the forecast was very poor. As we checked in we received the bad news. 'You've got ten minutes to get on the plane otherwise the airport will close,' said an official. So now we started running to get out in time. You can imagine the state of Paolo. 'I don't get on this fucking plane. We're all going to die.' I didn't have time for it anymore. 'Paolo,' I told him, 'we just want to get home. Whether you want to come or not is up to you.' I turned to Paul Aldridge, the club secretary. 'Fuck him,' I said. 'Let's go.' Paolo stayed behind and got a car to drive him home. It wasn't the most pleasant journey back. All the way down I was thinking of the headlines: Entire West Ham team killed – 'I told you so, you stupid bastards,' says Paolo Di Canio.

But I loved working with him most times. He was a character, he was fun; and every day was different when he was around. Mind you, he was lucky to survive the afternoon he caught the ball at Everton. I thought Stuart Pearce was going to kill him. If he thought the plane to Bradford was a near-death experience, he should have seen Stuart rampaging around the dressing room in frustration. It has gone down as one of the most famous examples of fair play in modern sport, yet anyone who had been in earshot after it happened wouldn't have known that. The players were ready to strangle Paolo. They thought he had been conned, good and proper.

We were at Goodison Park, 16 December 2000. The score was tied 1–1 when Paul Gerrard, their goalkeeper, came out of the penalty box to collect a ball over the top under pressure but succeeded only in clearing it straight to Trevor Sinclair on the wing. Gerrard was stranded, halfway to the corner flag. He appeared to have been injured trying to make the save and had collapsed to the ground. Sinclair crossed to Paolo who had the goal at his mercy – but caught the ball so Gerrard could receive treatment instead. It wasn't the open goal people remember – he would still have had to volley the ball in from around twenty yards and there were two Everton defenders nearby, but it was certainly a very sporting gesture. Unfortunately, in the heat of the moment, it was hard to see it that way. Pearce was first into our dressing room. 'Don't let me near him,' he said. 'I'll kill him, I'll kill him.' I wasn't in much better humour. I think my first words to Paolo were, 'What the fuck were you doing?' Then it was time to go on television.

'Fantastic sportsmanship,' said the interviewer. 'Yes,' I lied, 'that's brilliant, really. Great to see. It's what the game's all about.'

Meanwhile, in the dressing room, Paolo was surrounded by angry teammates telling him he could have won us the game. They didn't give a monkey's about good sportsmanship. Being Paolo, he couldn't care less, either. He had made his decision and he wasn't backing down. He ended up winning a FIFA Fair Play Award, but I would rather have had the extra two points. How often do West Ham go to Everton and win?

Another time, we were playing Bradford at home and losing 4–2. Bywater was our goalkeeper and he hadn't stopped one. Under his body, through his legs, every time Bradford had a shot it was in the net. At the other end, Paolo had three blatant penalty shouts rejected. The last one tipped him over the brink. He looked at the bench, shrugged, pouted and made the rolling hand gesture to signify that he wanted to come off. I ignored him. Next, he walked over to the touchline. I wouldn't look at him. 'Boss, I no play,' he said. 'I come off.' Now I had to do something. 'Paolo, just get on with it,' I told him. With that, he sat down, on the pitch, arms folded. Then he put his head in his hands. 'I don't play no more,' he said. 'I finished.' It was getting embarrassing. 'Paolo,' I hissed. 'We're losing 4–2 to Bradford. Everyone's looking. Get up, Paolo. Get up, quick.' With that the play came over to our side and started going on around us. Bradford dribbled past him, charged up our end, and Dean Saunders missed the sitter of the season to make it five.

Incredibly, Paolo could do no wrong with the fans, though, and they started singing his name. That was it: suddenly, he was up and off down the wing. He won the penalty. Frank Lampard went over to take it. Now Paolo wanted the ball. The pair of them were having a tug of war for about a minute until Frank realised he was never going to win. Paolo ran up like he was going to break the net, the goalkeeper dived so far he nearly knocked himself unconscious on a post, and Paolo chipped it down the middle: 4–3. Then he beat about four players and set up Joe Cole: 4–4. Finally, Frank scored our winner with seven minutes to go. Paolo left the field with the fans still singing his name. He was certainly unique.

Sir Alex Ferguson was very close to taking him to Manchester United and I think he would have been magnificent there, perhaps another Eric Cantona. Against Wimbledon, on 16 March 2000, he scored the Goal of the Season. Marc-Vivien Foé played the ball across field to the right, Sinclair centred and Paolo at the far post hit a right-foot volley while completely airborne that went in like a missile. I went to present him with the award at the restaurant San

Lorenzo's, but we had one further surprise lined up. The Kemp brothers from Spandau Ballet. A little secret: Paolo is the biggest Spandau Ballet fan in the world, and his face when they walked in was a picture. He was up, singing all the songs, telling them how he saw their concert in Rome and got beaten up by a policeman because he tried to sneak into the second night without a ticket. It was as if he had won the lottery. I've never seen him so excited. But that was Paolo, full of surprises. You could come in one day and he'd be buzzing; the next day he'd be in a mood because he didn't like the new kit.

We got an all navy blue away strip and he thought it looked like Wimbledon. I told him if he could reimburse the club for the twenty thousand replicas that were already on sale, they would change it. Yet Paolo, like Julian Dicks, has ended up a West Ham hero. I am sometimes asked to compare the two. They were both fantastic players, both had incredible skill, both would get very close to any all-time West Ham XI – and both could drive a manager mad. The difference, I think, is that at the end, when the craziness had subsided, you could have a laugh with Paolo – and that wasn't always the case with Julian, or some of his teammates.

Football was changing in the 1990s. The influx of foreign players made our game richer and more professional, but it created a new challenge for clubs and managers, and we did not always deal with it adequately. Too often, we bought players in and dumped them in a house somewhere, gave them a car and expected them to get on with life. The lovely homes and other perks were all very nice, but if the wife does not speak a word of English and she is suddenly dropped in the middle of nowhere with no family or friends, and her husband disappearing on a pre-season tour for two weeks, no wonder things go awry. Some of the foreign players who failed to settle attracted a lot of criticism, but I think we simply expected too much of them, not just as footballers, but as human beings.

Probably the best example of this was Javier Margas, the captain of Chile. I first saw him in a friendly against England at Wembley, in the build-up to the 1998 World Cup. Michael Owen would go on to be one of the stars of that tournament, but Margas didn't give him a kick that night. Chile won 2–0. I was impressed. I checked him out again in the tournament that summer and he did nothing to undermine that good first impression. It wasn't hard to get him out of his Chilean club, Universidad Católica, for around £1 million, and he arrived that summer. Fantastic. We gave him a house, we gave him a car; someone drove him home the first day to show him where everything was, and that was it. We left him and his wife to get on with it. The following day, he got in his car, got lost, and ended up at Stansted Airport. Eventually he found his way to Chadwell Heath but, on the way back, going down some little country lane, the car got a puncture. He didn't know who to call, he didn't know what to do. And it just got worse from there.

Javier's wife came from a very wealthy family in Chile who owned a chain of hotels. She was very close to her sisters, and enjoyed a lovely life. Money, success, husband a famous footballer. Suddenly, she was in a foreign country, didn't know anyone, didn't even know where she was, really. She didn't know how to get here, or there, to do the most basic activity, like go to the shops. She couldn't even watch the television for company because she didn't know what anybody was saying. Javier would come in and tell me, through his interpreter, that his wife was unhappy, wanted to go home, and was crying all the time. So in the end she left. And then the problem transferred to us because, with his wife back in Chile, Javier's head had gone. His wife wasn't with him, his kids were on a different continent, he was in the house on his own: didn't know what to do, couldn't concentrate, couldn't focus. All he wanted to do from that moment was to go back to Chile to be with her. He ended up staying in a hotel off the M25 at Waltham Abbey, and that was where things came to a head.

I had arranged a meeting – Javier, me and our managing director, Peter Storrie. We arrived at the hotel. 'Could you put us through to Mr Margas's room, please?' No answer. He's definitely in his room, we were told, but still no reply. We kept ringing and ringing – in the end we asked to be shown to his room. He'd jumped out of the window – from one floor up – left all his clothes behind, his boots and all his kit; took his passport, his money, one small overnight bag and legged it. Never came back. While we were on our way to the meeting, he was on his way to the airport. He was a wealthy boy and could afford to put his family first. I picture him now, looking out of his hotel room at that nice patch of soft grass, and weighing up his chances. Peter went out to Chile after him, but he wouldn't return without his wife, and there was no way she was coming back, so we had no choice but to try to sell him back to his old club. Knowing the situation, they had us by the cobblers. I can't remember what they paid but it wasn't £1 million.

It's a different world now. Every club has player-liaison officers for all nationalities, who look after the new players and make sure that they are OK and that their families are settling in. I think that's why you get some foreign players, like Carlos Tevez, who have been here six years now but still seem to struggle with the language. They are so protected they can live as if they are still in their own country. Fans might think they are mollycoddled but I feel that is how it should be done. The players still get the house and the car, but their wives are cared for, their kids are set up in the best schools and everything is done properly. Back then, they were lucky if someone bothered to tell them we drive on the left side of the road. 'Here's your car, son, now get on with it.' And we expected these guys to hit top form straight away and walk into the team on Saturday. Can you imagine how different Universidad Católica is to West Ham and the Premier League? It is no surprise it takes players so long to fit in.

The problem for West Ham during my seven years there was that we were gambling. Prices in the domestic market had spiralled and there really wasn't the value at home. We would call about a striker who was scoring a few in the third division and get asked for £2 million. Then an agent would come on offering a foreign player who had made fifty international appearances and cost half that. Yet there was invariably a reason these players were being offered to West Ham, not Manchester United. There was often an element of risk. Their last move had been a disaster, or they were pushing 30 or had been picking up a few injuries. A boy might be the top goalscorer at the club, but had been sent off three times in one season. So you had to weigh it all up. The other problem with British players involved the transfer conditions: full VAT, 50 per cent up front, and the rest within twelve months. It wasn't the same for foreign players. So we gambled.

Some came off, some didn't, but we were all learning. One of the players that everybody remembers is Florin Răducioiu, who had a brilliant World Cup for Romania in 1994, scoring four goals. We took him two years later, after the 1996 European Championships when he had scored Romania's only goal in the tournament. He was second only to Gheorghe Hagi for his country. I thought he would be brilliant in the Premier League.

I was very harsh on Florin at the time but, looking back, perhaps I was as much to blame for his failure. He came from a very different culture, a very different style of football, and maybe I didn't have as much patience with him as I should have. Everything he did irritated me, right from the start when we met to discuss the transfer and he kept asking about the quarantine arrangements for his dog. I wondered why he wasn't as interested in our ambitions for West Ham. Yet if his wife loved the dog, as he said, why shouldn't he be concerned? I think a lot of managers were feeling their way through this new era at the time. It wasn't like dealing with Stuart Pearce or Ian Wright. The players were coming to a new country and they were unsure, too. If I had a player like Răducioiu now, I would handle him differently.

I think I had lost interest in him almost before the season started. We were playing Torquay United in a friendly and they had a centre-half called Jon Gittens who had been around a lot of the south coast and West Country clubs. He was known as a hard man and at half-time Răducioiu came in, practically crying. 'They are kicking me, hurting me, they are kicking me from behind,' he wailed. 'Florin,' I said, 'wait until you come up against Tony Adams. This guy's nothing.' But he looked as if he didn't want to go back out. He obviously decided to take Gittens on at his own game, but it was a pitiful effort. He aimed a kick at him, but it was half-hearted and ineffectual, and the next challenge Gittens got his own back, properly. He hit Florin with an elbow to the face – bam.

Poor Florin was on the floor, yelling and rolling around. I knew from there we would have a problem. He was the same at a friendly against Luton Town the following week, and our relationship went downhill from there. Perhaps I had such high expectations that I could only be disappointed. I stopped believing in him, and didn't get the best out of him for that reason. When I see film of him playing now, I am sure my original instinct was right, and he could have been a great player in the Premier League. Maybe I was on his case too much and didn't give him enough time to adapt. I know I wasn't alone in my frustration. Even Paulo Futre poked him in the chest and called him a big girl one day, and when he didn't turn up for our Coca-Cola Cup game at Stockport County, that was the final straw. He went back to Espanyol soon after.

Some of the risks were extreme. After being asked what I thought was a ridiculous amount by Bristol Rovers for a striker called Marcus Stewart in 1995, we went with Marco Boogers of Sparta Rotterdam, having only watched him on video. Other managers had bought on taped evidence but that had never been my way. Yet we were running out of time, the season was about to start, Boogers looked good, and would cost half of what Rovers wanted for Stewart. What the tapes never show, however, is what a player is like as a trainer, or a person. Boogers was hard work. The players didn't like him, and he was a lazy worker. He got one kick in our second game of the season at Old Trafford, but it was on Gary Neville, and he was shown a red card. This caused him to become depressed, he claimed, and he returned to Holland. Very soon, we made that arrangement permanent.

Some of the foreign players just had different priorities. For Paulo Futre – Sporting Lisbon, Porto, Atlético Madrid, Benfica,

Marseille, AC Milan – it was the number 10 shirt. Futre was another great player that came as damaged goods. He had been an international footballer since the age of 17 and a superstar of the European game, but he had suffered a succession of knee injuries and was available on a free transfer. He came to us in the summer of 1996 and his ability was simply remarkable. Training would stop just to watch him take free-kicks – I'd put him in the top-ten players I have seen. Our first game was at Arsenal and the team-sheets had already gone in when Eddie Gillam, our trainer, told me there was a problem with Paulo. Eddie had handed him his shirt, number 16, and got it thrown back in his face. Next thing, Paulo was in my face, too. 'Futre 10, not 16,' he said. 'Eusebio 10, Maradona 10, Pelé 10; Futre 10, not fucking 16.'

By this point, there were forty-five minutes to kick-off. 'It's changed now, Paulo,' I explained, as gently as I could. 'We've got squad numbers and your number is 16. We didn't choose that number. When you came, all the numbers were gone, so Eddie gave you number 16.'

'Number 10,' he insisted. 'Futre 10. Number 10. Milan, Atlético Madrid, Porto, Benfica, Sporting – Futre 10.'

'OK, OK, Paulo,' I said. 'Look, just get on with it today, we can't do anything now, play today and on Monday we try to change. But it's difficult, we need permission from the league.'

Still, no compromise. 'No fucking 16,' he insisted.

Now it was getting desperate. I tried to be firm. 'Paulo, put your shirt on, get changed, please, we have a big game.' That was it. The shirt was thrown to the ground, his boots aimed at the wall. 'No fucking 16.'

'Right, if you don't want to wear it, Paulo, off you go,' I said. And he did. Put his gear on and left. But the team-sheet was already in, so I had to knock on the referee's door with a good excuse. 'You won't believe this, ref,' I said, 'but Frank Lampard's done the team-sheet and he's filled it in wrong. He put Paulo Futre down and he's not even here, he's getting treatment in Portugal.' The ref said that if Arsène Wenger gave us permission to change it it would not be a problem, and, being a nice man, he did. We still got beat 2–0, though.

The following Monday, Paulo came back in with his team of lawyers to negotiate for the number 10 shirt. At first we tried to tell him that we had sold so many replicas with 'Futre 16' on the back that it would be impossible to change, but he called our bluff. 'How many?' he asked. 'I will pay £100,000.' And that was when I knew this was an argument we could not win. Futre was willing to spend £100,000 just to be number 10. In the end, he got it a lot cheaper. John Moncur, the number 10, agreed to swap, and Paulo let him have two weeks in his villa in the Algarve, which is about the best one there, on the cliffs overlooking the best golf course. Do you know what number it is? Have a guess.

I wouldn't want people to think every foreign venture ended in disaster or conflict, though. Quite the opposite. We got some great players out of it: Marc Rieper, Marc-Vivien Foé, Eyal Berkovic, and some of the Croatian lads, like Slaven Bilić and Igor Štimac, were outstanding. They did as much as anyone to change the drinking culture at the club. Guys like Slaven, Paolo Di Canio or Marc-Vivien, they would never have thought of going out on a bender. They influenced the younger players and gradually the atmosphere at West Ham, and throughout the rest of English football, changed.

Slaven would rather have a pint of milk than a pint of beer. He was a bright man, a qualified lawyer, spoke several languages and came from an intellectual family. Strangely, though, he made a big mistake when signing his contract, which allowed us to stop him going to Tottenham Hotspur after just six months.

We broke the club record to sign Slaven – £1.3 million – after he impressed us on trial from Karlsruher in Germany. We'd seen enough after the first day. He was a beautiful defender: aggressive but cultured and strong in the air. He was outstanding from the start and, at the end of his first season, we knew Tottenham wanted him. He came back from his holiday and he wasn't the same boy. His mind was elsewhere, probably at White Hart Lane. His agent, Leon Angel, was very well connected there and was no doubt driving the move. Slaven said he wanted to leave and had a clause in his contract: if a club came up with £3.5 million, he could go. But that wasn't quite correct. The contract had been worded poorly and the clause actually said that if a bid of £3.5 million came in, and West Ham wished to sell, he could go. The clause was meaningless. It might as well have put his price at a tenner. Unless we wanted to sell, Slaven was a West Ham player. You should have seen his face when I told him. 'You bastard,' he said. To be fair, we gave him another deal, with a release clause of £4.5 million, properly worded. Everton triggered it a year later – but at least we got another season out of him. Slaven was a good character, like all the Croatian boys. Štimac was a hard worker, too. The only one who didn't work out was Davor Šuker, who was past his best when we signed him – but it wasn't for want of trying on his part.

It always felt good to get one over on Tottenham, or one of our bigger London rivals. We were the poor relations at the time.

Alan Sugar, the chairman of Tottenham, was so confident his club would get Berkovic, being a good Jewish boy, that he started bragging about it even before the deal was done. We were due to meet Berkovic with Pini Zahavi, his agent, at Heathrow Airport. 'Why are you wasting your time?' Sugar goaded Peter Storrie. 'Why would he go to West Ham, when he can come to us?'

Yet we had one advantage over Spurs. I knew where I wanted Eyal to play and told him at our meeting, 'I will use you free off the front. I just want you to get on the ball and make us play. Everything will come through you.'

Eyal then sat down with Sugar and Gerry Francis, the manager of Tottenham. 'I can't guarantee you a place in the team, but you'll definitely be in the squad,' said Gerry, and the deal swung instantly in West Ham's favour. Sugar couldn't believe it – an Israeli international turning down Tottenham – but Gerry missed a trick. Eyal could have walked into Tottenham's team. He was an amazing player, a great little footballer. He was another that would never have contributed to the drinking culture – Eyal was a loner. He certainly wouldn't have been in big John Hartson's gang. Not after what happened between them, anyway. John was very lucky he did not cause lasting damage that day.

It is hard to imagine two more different characters than John and Eyal but no matter the appalling nature of John's attack on his fellow teammate, I still cannot bring myself to think badly of him. With Paul Kitson, he kept us up in the 1996–97 season, but my affection cuts deeper than that. I thought he was a top bloke and, for sure, if I'd been a player at that time I'd have wanted to be his mate.

I can remember going to the chairman that Christmas and announcing that unless we got two strikers, we wouldn't stay up.

On 1 February we were 18th and Southampton, two points behind us, had a game in hand. We found £5.5 million from somewhere, bought Hartson and Kitson and never looked back. John was on the fringes of the Arsenal team, Paul was going nowhere with Newcastle United, so it was a gamble, but they turned it around. They played fourteen matches together that year and scored thirteen goals – one or the other always got on the scoresheet and from 12 March to 6 May we lost one game.

The next season John, in particular, was even better. When he was fit and on form he was close to unbeatable. He was one of those strikers that would just bash defenders up. He was a dream to work with – powerful, aggressive and hungry. He could play back to goal, he could get on the end of crosses, and his leap put him in the clouds. There wasn't a centre-half in the country that could handle him, even the great ones, like Sol Campbell, and you knew goalkeepers didn't fancy coming off their line when he was about. John was old school. Even the best still got battered by him, and it was fantastic to have a striker like that at the club, giving us variation in our approach to goal. John's touch wasn't bad, either. He had scored seventeen goals by 3 December, a crazy amount for West Ham. He just tore the league to pieces.

I like Danny Baker, but I'll never forget listening to his radio show at the time we signed John. 'West Ham have bought a donkey,' he said. 'John Hartson – what a waste of money. West Ham fans, get down there on Saturday and make donkey noises.' Yet John changed everything about the team in that first year.

And then, in one summer, everything changed. John came back for pre-season and he had just blown up – he was way, way, way overweight. He had battled it throughout his career, but this was the beginning of a serious problem. He was going through a very bad time in his life. He was drinking, he was gambling heavily, and it was catching up with him as a player. Plus, he was big pals with Vinnie Jones, and he probably enjoyed the celebrity life a bit too much. He always liked his food, but he just couldn't keep the pounds off. He was going downhill fast. He came back for preseason training two stone overweight. Frank Lampard Senior used to take him running over Epping Forest to try to get him fit, but it was no use. 'I'm going at fifty-year-old man pace, and he can't keep up, Harry,' Frank said. 'I look round and he's collapsed on a log. He can't do it.' In the middle of this personal crisis, he took all his frustration out on little Eyal Berkovic.

It was a familiar story, to those who remembered the Julian Dicks era. John made a crunching tackle, to which Eyal objected, and while he was trying to help Eyal up, Eyal punched him in the leg. I don't know what John was thinking to make him lose control so badly, but he just kicked Eyal, full force, in the face. His jaw was so badly damaged he could not eat for two days. Physical confrontations have always happened between players on the training ground, but this was different. This was the worst I have seen between teammates. It wasn't even a fair fight: a tiny little fella versus big John, as hard as nails and a monster of a man. It was a total mismatch. I'm sure John felt like a horrible bully after he'd done it. I hope he did.

What made it even more difficult was that the whole thing was captured by a fan on a video camera, and he turned the film over to a national newspaper. Sky television had been at the training ground but had agreed not to run their footage, although once the story was out, they as good as put it on a loop. Any hope we had of keeping the problem in-house ended. It was all over the back pages and shown repeatedly on television news programmes. I was under real pressure to sack John – to sling him out of the club. Eyal, understandably, felt strongly about it, too. Yet there was never any heat from the directors and I did not consider terminating John's contract for one second. I know some people won't like me saying this, but he was simply too valuable an asset to discard. People ask why I stuck with John, the way they ask why Liverpool stuck with Luis Suárez. The reason is that football managers are pragmatists. If a great player and a crap player commit the same crime, the club finds a reason to keep the great player, and uses the transgression as an excuse to sack the crap one. Sorry, but it's true. We sold John to Wimbledon later and doubled our money. How could West Ham have afforded to just write off that amount? There was never a discussion about cancelling John's contract. We fined him £10,000, two weeks' wages, which went straight to a leukaemia charity, and John apologised to Eyal, first in public and then at a private dinner we held. I have no doubt he meant it, and that the apology was accepted. John knew he had made a huge mistake, one that proved hard to live down. And it left a stain on us all. Eyal departed soon after, and we had to start rebuilding again. Only at West Ham could we lose a great partnership like Hartson and Berkovic over a training-ground spat.

To be fair, there had been an early sign that John had to be handled very carefully. One day I got a call from some local businessmen who were starting up a betting shop in Ilford. They wanted me to be a guest at the grand opening. I didn't fancy it, so they asked if John would go in my place. I knew he liked a bet, like me, and I couldn't see the harm in it. 'We'll pay him,' I was told.

'Tell him, we'll give him an account with £5,000 in it.' So off John went and I never gave it another thought until about three months later when the same people called again. 'It's about John Hartson,' they said. 'He owes us £100,000.' I managed to get them all to do a deal for about a third of that – but I knew from that moment that I couldn't treat John like any other player.

After the Berkovic incident it was obvious that he was on his way out of the club, but first I had to get him fit. I took him to a Frenchman, a big bull of a trainer who had worked with Arsène Wenger at Arsenal. We met at Sopwell House hotel near St Albans, and he didn't mess about. He turned to John. 'You want to get fit?' he asked. 'Don't waste my time. I don't have time to waste on an idiot like you. If you want to work, you work. If you want to get fit, I get you fit. But don't waste my time. You understand?'

He took John back to France with him, got him up at six in the morning, did four punishing fitness sessions each day, made him stay at his house. In ten days, he knocked him back into shape. I've never seen results like it. John came back as happy as I'd seen him. He realised the mistake he had made and was delighted to be fit again – but I was worried that, back in London, he would fall into bad habits again.

John was very friendly with Joe Kinnear, the Wimbledon manager, through Vinnie Jones, and they came up with a £7 million bid for him. I jumped at it. I knew we'd had the best of John, and it seemed a fantastic deal for our club. He was a wonderful talent, but I suspected his personal weaknesses meant he wouldn't fulfil his potential – and I was right.

You might imagine from this that I bear a grudge against John for letting such an opportunity slip away. Not one bit. I could never stay angry at John for long, and he remains one of my favourite players. He was honest, he was good company; he wanted to be mates. I'll admit, I cared about him as a fella and wanted to help him in any way I could. I still do. What he has been through since with his illness, overcoming cancer, says everything about him. I'm sure lots of people wouldn't have beaten it as he did. He's a survivor, and I've got so much time for him. You couldn't meet a lovelier bloke, despite what happened between him and Eyal, and, from my experience, his actions that day were completely out of character. I went up to a charity match for John recently, and he knows he only has to pick up the phone to me. I'd do anything for him.

It is easy to look at the incident between John and Eyal Berkovic as a black and white issue, a straightforward example of right and wrong. Certainly I would never attempt to defend John's actions and, I'm sure, neither would he. Yet it also came at a time when English football was volatile, when there was a clash of cultures. Not that all English players were thugs and all foreign players soft, more a meeting of different attitudes and beliefs. As a manager I saw that collision every day on the training field. To Di Canio, fitness was everything, and even a light-hearted remark during a stretching exercise could send him into a fit of anger. British players like Dicks and Hartson, meanwhile, were not averse to a full-blooded tackle in training when, to a player like Berkovic, such physicality seemed ridiculous. In the middle was the manager, trying to marry and make sense of these different principles. It wasn't easy, but I learned a lot.

The foreign legion at West Ham taught the players new standards of professionalism, but they improved the man-management techniques of English coaches, too. I also came to understand that if you have too many players from a particular group or country you risk a clique developing, and I have tried to avoid this since. If you have too many French or African players, they will separate from the rest and the camp will become easily divided. That can even apply to having too many players who are under one agent, and I'd like to think I have become more adept at the difficult challenge of developing team spirit at a modern football club as I have got older. Towards the end at West Ham, I think cliques became more of a problem. Players get very close to others of the same nationality – and then if one isn't playing he starts to chip away at his friend. That is one of the big changes from my playing days. It didn't used to be like that. We all grew up as kids in the East End and we got on with our lives and careers. We all felt for a mate who was going through a rough time, but we didn't rely on each other the same way. Now, a group from France will all stick together and if one's not having it off, then two are not having it off, the other two are dragged down with them and soon you've got a core of players who are dissatisfied in the dressing room, destabilising the rest. That was the biggest lesson to me at West Ham.

And then there was Stuart Pearce. A one-off, he bridged the gap. He had the professionalism of the foreign players but the ferocious attitude of the British. He was 37 when I took him, he played two seasons for us and ended up as the Hammer of the Year in 2001. He was some guy – the only player I've seen turn out with a broken ankle.

It was his second season at the club, we played Chelsea on a Wednesday in March and Stuart went over awkwardly after eleven minutes, and had to come off. We knew it was a bad one because of the way the injury swelled up. I've not seen an ankle go like it. The physiotherapist said, straight away, that he would be out for six to eight weeks. He gave me a list of problems: ligament damage, muscle damage, bone damage. We had Tottenham in an FA Cup quarter-final on the Sunday. It was a huge blow to be without Stuart. By Thursday evening, we had the doctor's report. He agreed with the physio – anything up to two months. The next morning, I saw Stuart at the training ground. 'I think I'll be all right Sunday,' he said. I told him about the physio's verdict. 'I don't give a fuck what the physio reckons,' said Stuart. 'I'll see how I feel tomorrow.'

Saturday came and Stuart was straight in to see me in my office. 'Don't do any team work yet,' he said. 'Just give me half an hour. I'll go and have a fitness test over the back. I'll take one of the young kids to work with me and get back to you.' His ankle was so swollen that he had cut his boot down the side to get his foot in. Our physio, John Green, was going mad. 'There's no way he can play,' he said. 'He's talking rubbish. He's out for six weeks, minimum.' Yet in the distance, I could see him. The kid was running at Stuart with the ball, Stuart was smashing into him, knocking him six feet in the air. He saw me looking over and gave me the thumbs-up. He had injections on both sides of his ankle before that Tottenham game, and it was still killing him, so he had them again at half-time. Joe Cole walked off the back post for a Tottenham set-piece and the ball trickled into the goal behind him. We lost 3–2. Our man of the match? Stuart Pearce.

Yet of all the players I used at West Ham, there was one that would probably have given even Stuart Pearce a run for his money for pure commitment. You won't find him in any record books or on any squad list. His name wasn't even in the programme, but he did play, and score, for West Ham against Oxford City, on 28 July 1994. His name was Steve Davies – and he was in the crowd.

I was still assistant to Billy Bonds at the time and we had two pre-season friendlies arranged on the same night. One team went to play Billericay, and I took another group to play my old club, Oxford City. It was a beautiful summer evening and we were opening their new ground and floodlights, at the invitation of the secretary, John Shepherd. It was one of those nights when you can really enjoy being a football manager. No pressure, back among friends – just get out and play and have a good time.

We took a small squad, not many substitutes, but the minute the match started this bloke next to the dug-out started giving me earache. He wasn't nasty. There was no foul language or abuse, but he did look a picture. He had a T-shirt on and a pair of shorts, and every spare inch of him was covered in West Ham tattoos. He had two Hammers up his legs, more on his arms and it quickly became apparent he didn't fancy Lee Chapman, our striker, one little bit. 'We ain't got him up front again, Chapman, have we, Harry? Please don't pick him again, Harry, he's a donkey. He's useless, that Chapman, Harry.' On it went, all the way through the first half. Chapman. Chapman. He wouldn't leave me alone. I made two substitutions at half-time, and one early in the second half, and now we just had the bare eleven. With that, we got an injury. I had no other option. I turned round to big mouth. 'You've got some old bunny,' I said. 'Can you play as good as you talk?'

'I'm better than Chapman,' he said.

'Right,' I told him. 'Get your gear on, let's have a look at you.' Now he went quiet. He thought I was joking. 'Quick as you can, mate, you're on,' I said.

'What do you mean?' he said.

'You're playing for West Ham,' I told him.

'But I ain't got any boots, Harry,' he protested.

'What size are you?' said Eddie, our kit man. He found him some size nines and took him to the dressing room to get changed. He came back, kitted up, and stood on the touchline next to me.

'Where do you play?' I asked.

'Up front,' he said. 'Right,' I told him, 'we'll soon see if you're better than Chapman.' And on he went.

Oxford's announcer came down and wanted to know who the substitute was. 'Didn't you watch the World Cup?' I asked. 'That's Tittishev of Bulgaria. He scored three goals.'

'Oh yes,' he said, nodding wisely. 'I thought it was him.'

Anyway, he scored. We couldn't believe it. He ran around the field like he had won the World Cup, jumping, shouting – we were killing ourselves laughing on the touchline. The stadium announcer must have wondered why a star of the 1994 World Cup was making such a fuss about scoring in a friendly against Oxford City. At the end of the match, the lads all signed his shirt and he was photographed in the papers the next day wearing it, with the biggest grin you've ever seen.

And he was right, by the way. That night, he was better than bloody Lee Chapman.

CHAPTER NINE

BIG MOUTH STRIKES AGAIN

They were good times at West Ham. So why did it all end so suddenly? Just two years before I left we had achieved what remains West Ham's highest finish in the Premier League, ahead of clubs like Liverpool and Tottenham Hotspur, with a squad that included Rio Ferdinand, Frank Lampard and Trevor Sinclair. We became an established Premier League club, we produced good young players and played open, attractive football. We qualified for the Intertoto Cup, won that, and went through to the 1999–2000 UEFA Cup – the first time West Ham had played in a major European tournament since reaching the Cup Winners' Cup in 1980–81. And then, by the spring of 2001, I was out of a job. We had slipped back down the league to a disappointing 15th place finish by then but, even so, on the morning of 9 May when I walked into Terry Brown's office to discuss a new contract, I had no idea I would be leaving it, unemployed, ten minutes later.

As I said, it was always an uphill struggle financially at West Ham and I think, in the end, that just placed me in conflict with the chairman on too many occasions. Looking back, I think I created a lot of my own problems there, too. I was out of order at times. I would argue with Terry and the other directors in a way most other managers wouldn't. If they uttered something in a board meeting that I thought was rubbish, I'd say so, and I was probably wrong to talk to them like that. It took me a while to learn to count to ten. Back then, if I didn't agree, I'd jump down the directors' throats. 'What do you know about football?' I'd tell them. 'You haven't got a clue.' But Terry was the chairman. And you can only say that so many times before the chairman gets the hump and lies in wait for you. When we were fifth in the league, Terry couldn't afford to lose me. But at 15th? 'Right, I'll show you what I know, mate. You're fired.'

The tension that came out at the end of the 2000–01 season had been building for some time. Things got so bad financially in 1996 that Peter Storrie, our managing director, admitted we were struggling to pay the wages. He came to me after an away game. 'Harry, you know a lot of people,' he said. 'Do you know anyone that would be interested in buying the club? We can't pay the players. It's desperate.'

I told him I knew of one bloke who was a West Ham fan and very wealthy: Michael Tabor, the racehorse owner. 'He's a West Ham man, but whether he'd want to get involved, I don't know,' I said.

Michael wasn't at all keen, at first. 'Harry, do I really need to sit up in that directors' box, with all the fans chanting to put more money in?' he said. 'I love watching my team on TV, I go to racing all over the world; I've got the best horses, I go to America, Paris, Barbados for two or three months a year. What do I need that for? Leave it with me, I'll have a think about it.'

But we were in real trouble. I rang him again and explained there would never be a better opportunity to buy the club. 'OK,' Michael said. 'Arrange a meeting.'

The first get-together was just with me and Peter Storrie, to explain the financial side of it. That went well and Michael stayed keen. We arranged a second meeting, at Cheltenham racecourse the following week, and this one was to involve Terry Brown, our chairman. We were guests in Michael Tabor's hospitality suite, the best on the course, three times the size of all the others and right on the finishing line. That day it was full of the top people from the world of racing and beyond. Famous owners, famous trainers like Vincent O'Brien, I think the Prime Minister of Ireland was there. We were all booked into a fabulous hotel nearby, the Lygon Arms in Broadway, for dinner and a talk, but first we would meet Michael and his partners at the races.

It soon became apparent that Terry Brown hadn't done his homework. He didn't know Michael Tabor from Adam. The box was full that day, but we were reserved places on Michael's table, waited on by his personal assistant, Terry, who is about 24 stone. He is a lovely man, who has worked for Michael for years. He used to own a big hotel, but now he arranges Michael's travel and looks after his guests; anything Michael wants, Terry does. He was the one who sat us down in our seats. 'You go there, Harry; Mr Brown sit there …' He brought us our drinks and when Michael wanted the food served, he gave Terry a sign. It was a crowded box and a nice, mild day. Terry was busying about in his blue shirt with braces, sweating like a lunatic. Michael sat opposite us and Terry disappeared to organise the waitresses for service. Terry Brown had been on the telephone the whole time. No sooner had his conversation ended when Michael's phone rang and he motioned his apologies and withdrew to take the call.

'Who's that chappy?' said Terry Brown.

'What chappy?' I asked.

'The one on the telephone,' he said.

'That's Michael Tabor,' I told him. 'That's the man you are here to meet.'

'Oh,' he said, 'I thought that was Michael.' And he gestured to Terry, wet through, bringing out plates of lobster, salmon, chicken and prawns for the starters. This was the bloke he was ready to open talks with over West Ham. He hadn't even bothered to find out what Michael Tabor looked like. The chairman was a fish out of water that day.

When the racing began and Michael and his crowd were putting on serious bets, Terry Brown became quite alarmed. 'Who are these chaps?' he asked. 'What do they do? Where do they get their money from?' He was suspicious, as if he was surrounded by drug dealers or gangsters, rather than wealthy businessmen with a passion for horse racing. He had clearly never met people who gambled in tens of thousands of pounds and thought, instinctively, that they must be up to no good. Still, he couldn't afford to be choosy with the club in such a precarious state, and we all ended up back at the Lygon Arms for the brass-tacks conversation. Dermot Desmond came with Michael and was very interested in the figures. They were well up for it by the end, and I really do believe it would have been good for the club.

Michael made an offer which Terry did not find acceptable, but before the usual rounds of brinkmanship could proceed much further, the Premier League signed its new contract with Sky for mega money. West Ham's crisis was over. The club could pay the wages and, suddenly, Terry didn't need Michael any more. It was just bad timing, particularly for me.

I was now in the middle of an attempted takeover, having brought Michael to the table. A war of words between the camps escalated and it began turning quite nasty. The fans, obviously, were behind Tabor because they saw him as a rich West Ham fan who would increase the transfer budget. They besieged the lobby at Upton Park after we lost to Arsenal on 29 January 1997, and the unrest and poisonous atmosphere took its toll on the players and we began sliding down the table. As I have mentioned before, Terry had accused me of nepotism when bringing on Frank Lampard, claiming I was trying to get his appearance money up. I was furious at the suggestion. I turned the air blue and told him he could stuff his job if he was going to question my motives. I still make no apologies for seeing the good in the Tabor bid. He is a genuinely wealthy man who loves his sport, loves his football, and is a great guy to be around. So, yes, I think he would have made an excellent owner of West Ham, and it was a shame his bid didn't get over the line. In the end, though, it wasn't all bad news.

I remain convinced that it was the upheaval caused by Tabor's interest that persuaded the chairman to buy John Hartson and Paul Kitson that winter. He wanted the fans off his back and, from not being able to pay the wages, he produced £5.5 million from nowhere – and those two players kept us up. But did my relationship with Terry Brown ever recover? Perhaps not.

The beginning of the end was the sale of Rio Ferdinand to Leeds United in November 2000. I didn't want him to go, and I told him that. I sat with him and Frank Lampard Senior in my office, the pair of us pleading with him to stay. I'm not saying we could have kept Rio at the club for ever, but we were building something there with young Frank, Joe Cole, Michael Carrick, Jermain Defoe and Glen Johnson all progressing. Rio was our Rolls-Royce. I know many were astonished that Leeds broke the British transfer record by paying £18 million, but I was more worried about the message it sent to the other clubs. Pretty soon it would be open season on our young stars – but I was gone by then.

I think, quite simply, that our chairman miscalculated. The Bosman ruling had been introduced in the European Union in 1995, meaning clubs could no longer charge transfer fees for players whose contracts had expired, and Terry thought it would spell the end of big-money moves. He thought every player would run down his agreement and leave for nothing, and an £18 million offer, like the one we had for Rio, would be a thing of the past. He thought the bid from Leeds was exceptional, the last of its kind, and that if we did not take it we would lose him for nothing anyway. 'Harry, you've got to understand,' he told me, 'nobody will ever see this transfer fee again.'

I couldn't guarantee that he was wrong, but I always believed Leeds was the wrong move for Rio. 'It's not Manchester United or Arsenal,' I told him. 'You don't need to go there. It's not a good move for you. Stay here with us, you need another year or two here to mature and we're building a great, young team. You'll be at the heart of it. No disrespect to Leeds, but we could get ahead of them if we stick together.'

It wasn't just talk – I truly felt that. Sadly, I think Rio got pressured into going. He knew the club wanted the deal to go through, and obviously there were middle men doing well out of it. It was a big payday for a lot of people. Like many transfers it was as good a move for the agent as the player. I knew Terry wouldn't be happy if he knew I was trying to kill the deal, so I asked Rio to keep our conversation secret. I didn't want it rebounding on me if he stayed but, in the end, the money talked.

There has been a lot of subsequent controversy over a payment I received from the Ferdinand transfer, but if I was money-motivated I wouldn't have fought so hard to keep him at Upton Park. My cut of transfer money was actually Terry's idea. I think he knew we had the best young players this side of Manchester United and, with his thoughts on the consequences of the Bosman ruling, was always going to cash in if big money came along. He knew I would object and try to block any sale. So, earlier in the year, he had offered me a ten per-cent cut of the fee for any home-grown player. It was a way of keeping me sweet and could have been worth a fortune, but I refused. 'I don't want it, Terry,' I told him. 'I'm not going to sell players just to make money.' And then he sold Rio anyway, completely against my wishes. I felt such a mug. Had I signed that deal Ferdinand's transfer would have been worth £1.8 million personally. I didn't want the money, I wanted the player – but in the end I got neither. In the circumstances, I thought I was due some compensation for being completely ignored. I never wanted that ten per cent – but if he was going to sell players behind my back anyway, I may as well have signed up and just taken the cash. In the end, Terry gave me a £300,000 bonus from Rio's transfer. He said my stubbornness had forced Leeds to up their original offer by £3 million, so I don't feel guilty for taking it. I could have collected six times that, if I was willing to sit back and say nothing while the club sold its crown jewels.

After Rio left, West Ham began going backwards and, trying to address the slide, I went back into the transfer market, with only partial success. I stand by some of the signings I made during that time. The Bulgarian striker Svetoslav Todorov moved on with me to Portsmouth, and was top scorer in Division One the season we won promotion to the Premier League. Technically, he was fantastic. He was another one of those strikers that, on his day, would just batter teams. Christian Dailly played 158 games for West Ham and the season after I left was on the field every minute of every league game. Other signings, I know, were a mistake. I'd heard very good reports of Rigobert Song and Titi Camara, the pair I took from Liverpool, but they were poor. Song's first game for us was at home to Sheffield Wednesday in the Worthington Cup. Later, he told his old teammates back at Liverpool how happy he was that I had him in his best position as part of a back three. The only problem was, he was meant to be full-back in a back four. No wonder we lost that night. He was a decent player, though, and I still think he would have settled in given more time. Camara was a bigger disappointment. They loved him up at Liverpool, but he was ordinary for us.

It is very easy to criticise the manager when a transfer doesn't come off, but people simply do not understand the difference between the top and bottom end of the market. With the money we had at West Ham at the time, there were no guarantees and no magic wands. You want to change the players because what you have is not good enough, but your available market isn't exactly brimming with talent, either. The fear is that an ordinary team gets in a rut. How often do we see a group dragged into a relegation battle from mid-table? Once that losing mentality sets in, it is contagious. You see it now with a club like Wolverhampton

234

Wanderers falling through two divisions. Taking over a club can be even harder, and it is sometimes impossible to revitalise a team that is fighting relegation, as I found at Queens Park Rangers, but there are many reasons why a group of players struggle. At West Ham that season, Rio's transfer had a demoralising effect and I sensed we had to change personnel or be in danger of relegation. The problem was we had sold an £18-million player – but we weren't in the market for one. We had waved one of the best central defenders in the world goodbye, and were trying to pick up half a team in his place. That is not like taking Robin van Persie from Arsenal.

When Sir Alex Ferguson did that, he was not gambling. Taking from the top drawer isn't hard. Every manager can tell you the certainties. I wasn't taking a chance bringing Rafael van der Vaart to Tottenham Hotspur, either. Every manager knows what these players will give. The reason there is such a fuss if, for instance, a Manchester United goalkeeper doesn't work out is because it is so unusual. Most times, money buys class.

Yet every player I bought with the money from Ferdinand had an asterisk next to his name – there was a reason they were in the market for a move to West Ham. Some proved they could do it in the Premier League, others failed. Put Ferguson or David Moyes in my place and they would have been gambling just the same. Even inside the elite every manager has a list of signings that haven't worked out – but the further down the league you go, the longer that list gets. I still don't think my later buys at West Ham were bad. Fredi Kanouté and Marc-Vivien Foé were sold on for a profit, Di Canio was a great buy. If West Ham had kept all of my players together, including the younger ones like Rio, I sincerely believe we would have ended up in the Champions League.

Ultimately, though, the end of my relationship with the chairman wasn't over anything as meaningful as league position of transfer policy – it was an interview I gave to a West Ham fanzine called *Over Land and Sea*. It was run by Gary Firmager, a typical West Ham nut and a bit of a lad. I used to speak to him once a year on the record, and was probably a bit more open than I would be with a national newspaper journalist. Gary was a fan, and he was writing for West Ham fans, and that made me more relaxed. I thought he deserved straight answers to straight questions. You can probably see where this is heading now.

Gary started quoting some figures given to him by the chairman about the amount of the Ferdinand money that had been spent. I thought they were misleading. Instead of taking in the simple transfer fee, Brown had included wages, signing-on fees, bonuses, cars, houses, agents' fees, every last penny of expense to make the deal seem as costly as possible. Fine – but then why not add the money saved on Rio's wages, bonuses and other sundry costs to his £18 million transfer. You can't have it both ways. As Gary reeled off these figures – and the chairman had said Davor Šuker's free transfer had cost as much as the gate receipts from East Stand – I didn't think Terry was being fair. I made a flippant comment. 'Calls himself an accountant,' I said. 'He can't fucking add up.' It's a mistake I certainly wouldn't make now.

Until that point, while my relationship with the chairman was hardly perfect, I had no clue this was to be my last season at West Ham. We had been talking about a new contract and all the signs were positive. I had two years left on my existing deal, but Brown wanted me to sign a four-year extension. He had been waiting for me to put pen to paper for six months. It was me that had been dragging my feet. Until we were mathematically assured of survival, I had more important things on my mind. Terry was OK with that, to be fair. Mick Maguire of the Professional Footballers' Association was doing the deal for me and he kept calling to say Terry had been on wanting to get the deal done, but I'd put him off. 'It's no problem, I've got two years left,' I'd tell him. 'Don't worry, I'm not going anywhere.' Shortly before the end of the season, I saw Terry in his office and we talked about the length of the contract. 'Four years and that'll finish me, Terry,' I told him. 'Another four years and I'm done.' 'Harry, I want you for ten years, not four,' he replied. He could not have been nicer.

Sadly, I had more pressing problems immediately after that. My mum, Violet, died the week before we played at Manchester City on 28 April, and everything else went by the wayside. We'd had a house built in the grounds of our place in Dorset for Mum and Dad, because I thought the sea air would be good for her, but she wouldn't move down. She died in Poplar, in the same place that we always lived.

As for the football, the way the league worked out, we were not mathematically safe until we defeated Southampton 3–0 on 5 May, the penultimate game of the season. Now was the time to clear my head and sort out my future at West Ham. I thought we would need a substantial investment again in the summer and I was going to talk it all through with Terry before the final game of the season at Middlesbrough. I was going to get that contract signed while I was in there, too.

On the Monday after the Southampton win, I was on my way home from training. Kevin Bond and Ted Pearce, our chief scout, were in the car and I was on my way back to Bournemouth. I had stopped to refuel at a petrol station in Chigwell when the phone rang. It was Mick Maguire. 'Hello, Harry,' he said. 'What you done? I've just spoken to Terry Brown about coming tomorrow to do the contract properly and he's gone all the other way. Every time I speak to him it's always, "Harry this, Harry that, Harry's great, Harry's the best." Now he's saying he doesn't know if he wants to do the contract at all. He wouldn't tell me why. He just says he's not happy with you. What's up?'

I told him I hadn't a clue.

'I think you'd better find out,' said Mick.

'Don't worry, I'll go and see him in the morning,' I said. Mick offered to accompany me, but I refused. Whatever the problem was, I thought, it wouldn't be anything that we couldn't resolve.

I was wrong about that. In the time between the ten-year contract talk and Mick's conversation, that month's edition of *Over Land and Sea* had dropped, with my interview all over it. Terry read that stuff religiously. He didn't like some of the language I used, and he certainly didn't like being told he couldn't add up. When I walked into his office, he had his speech prepared. 'I'm not happy with one or two things,' he said. 'I think it's time to call it a day.'

And that was it. Do I regret giving that interview now? Absolutely. It did for me, I am sure of that. Nothing else had changed between our two conversations other than the publication of some rather rash comments on my part. I don't think Gary Firmager tried to trick me, either, I just believe it is very easy to fall into conversation sometimes, and not realise how different those words will appear in black and white. I didn't mean anything by it – I was just defending my corner against what I saw as a rather unfair appraisal of my record in the transfer market. I didn't think Terry would take it personally, but that was me at the time – I always had to bite, I couldn't let it pass.

It was a bolt from the blue, but I think I was most upset when Terry told me that he wanted Frank to leave, too. 'What are you talking about?' I asked. 'He's more West Ham than you'll ever be.' Managers get the sack, we all know that, but few give a thought for the staff, who are often shown the door having done nothing wrong. That was the case with Frank. As I said, he loved West Ham so much he used to work with the kids for nothing before becoming my assistant. If Terry was upset with me, fair enough, but what had Frank said or done to get the sack?

Terry got rid of Les Sealey, the goalkeeping coach, too, and that really saddened me. Les was one of the best characters you could hope to meet: trained with the reserve team, trained with the kids, trained Tuesday and Thursday night with the academy – absolutely lived for the club. His uncle, Alan, played for West Ham, as did Les. He was a club man to his boots and absolutely fantastic at his job. I'll tell you the sort of boy he was. One night we were playing Aston Villa and I had two mates up from Bournemouth. I planned to take them home after the game, but we lost. I'm horrible when we lose: I don't want to talk, I don't want to socialise, I don't want to do anything. I just wanted to go back to my flat up the road and shut the door. My pals were stranded. The last trains were gone and they were facing a night in a hotel. Les offered to take them home. He only lived up the road in Essex, yet he drove all the way to Bournemouth, and all the way back. That was Les. Just a great guy who would do anything for you. I couldn't believe that West Ham got rid of him. He was the life and soul of the dressing room and it hurt him terribly. I could have cried when he called me up and told me the news. He died of a heart attack, four months later, at the age of 43. His death came as a terrible shock.

Looking back, of course, Terry already had my replacement lined up – and just like with Tony Pulis at Bournemouth it was someone I had brought to the club. I had met Glenn Roeder at a dinner to honour Kenny Dalglish in London one Sunday night. He was a player I knew well. 'What have you been up to?' I asked.

'Nothing,' he said, morosely. 'I've been out of the game for two years, Harry. It's driving me mad. I don't think I've got any option but to look for work outside football.'

'Where do you live?' I asked, thinking of some scouting work.

'About five minutes from your training ground,' he said.

'Right,' I told him, 'come in tomorrow, bring your boots, you can do a little bit with some of the kids.'

We had a group – Jimmy Bullard and a few other teenagers who couldn't get in the first team – that we called the development squad. 'Come in and take them,' I told Glenn. 'We can't pay you, but it'll get you out of the house. Come to my office afterwards, we'll have a cup of tea. See how we go from there.'

The next day, when Glenn arrived, Tony Carr and Peter Brabrook, our youth coaches, were straight over. 'What you brought him here for?' Peter said. 'We're doing well with the kids. Bloody hell, Harry, he'll be after our jobs, won't he?'

'Don't worry,' I assured him, 'he's not after anyone's job. The fella's just sitting at home, nothing to do, so I said he could come in and work with us. Trust me, he's a nice guy. He's just going to take the little group that needs a bit of individual attention. He was a good player, maybe he can help them.'

Amazing, isn't it? The job he ended up taking was mine.

After that, I got Glenn doing a bit of scouting so he could earn some money, then more coaching with the youth team, and we had a great year. We went on and won the FA Youth Cup and, as Glenn was a part of that, at the end of the season he received a full-time contract. Terry Brown was delighted with the appointment. Just how delighted, I later found out.

Yet Glenn could never replicate what we had at West Ham, and his second season in charge ended in relegation. He was sacked early in the next campaign after losing away at Rotherham United.

I felt for my friends, like Frank and Les, but I don't hold any grudges against Terry Brown. He paid me every last penny of the two years that remained on my contract and, a number of years later, when I went to Southampton, their chairman Rupert Lowe said that Terry had given me a fantastic reference. I know there have been all sorts of dark rumours about the real reason I left Upton Park, but I think, in the end, it was just one argument too many. If I had done anything seriously wrong, the chairman would not have paid me up. It was a clash of personalities, nothing more sinister than that.

I do regret leaving the way I did. I was happy there, we had some great years, I worked with some finest players and loved it. Years later, the young players at Portsmouth and Southampton would ask me about coaching Rio Ferdinand, Joe Cole and young Frank, the way those players used to ask me about playing with Bobby Moore or Geoff Hurst. And while we had a bad year that last season, we had hung on, survived, and I think we could have moved forward again had I stayed. In the end, the way I spoke about Terry, in that interview and at other times, was wrong. I took liberties, I pushed him too far, and I shouldn't have done that. Even now, he's not a popular figure at West Ham, but when I've seen him we've always shook hands and he's been fine with me.

So how do I see my time at West Ham now? Well, looking at their fortunes since, first and most importantly, we were never relegated. They went down under John Lyall, under Billy Bonds before I arrived, and they have gone down twice since then – and some would argue were lucky not to go down in 2007, too, the year of the Carlos Tevez transfer. But West Ham were not a yo-yo club while I was in charge. We established ourselves as a strong Premier League team with ambitions to play in Europe. I always looked to sign guys who could play, like Paolo Di Canio, and the youngsters we brought through the club were players that people would pay to watch all day. There were times when we would just destroy teams, or win against the odds, like we did against Manchester United at Old Trafford in the FA Cup. We finished above Tottenham three years on the spin from 1997–98 to 1999–2000 and the team that went down two years later wouldn't have ended up relegated had I been in charge, I'm sure of that.

We came fifth in 1997–98. Which doesn't sound much compared to the achievements of Sir Alex Ferguson, but then we weren't Manchester United. I wish West Ham well in their move to the Olympic Stadium but, even if they can fill a 50,000 seater arena, unless someone comes in with mega money to buy the club, I think my Premier League record finish is safe for a long time yet.

CHAPTER TEN

GOING UP

I first met Milan Mandaric during my time in America. New York Cosmos had the star players but Milan had the highest profile of any owner. To the Americans, who didn't know much about football, he was as famous as Pelé or Franz Beckenbauer. The fans had been told those guys were big stars – but Milan was one of their own. A big hitter in business – his computer component company pioneered the boom that led to the creation of Silicon Valley – and a big personality in soccer. His first franchise was the San Jose Earthquakes and he built a team around good technical players from his homeland, then called Yugoslavia, and a scattering of well-known players from elsewhere: George Best, Jimmy Johnstone, Colin Bell and Vince Hilaire all played for San Jose while Milan was in charge, and it was always a great place to go.

They didn't get huge crowds, less than 20,000, but it was a small ground so it never looked empty, the football was good and the atmosphere was very different. Milan had a guy called Crazy George who would come on to the pitch before the game with a tiger on a leash, or a bear, warming the crowd up. He would jump on your dug-out and start banging it with a drum or beating the drum right in front of you. It was all good fun, and quite mad, but it made Milan the biggest noise in the North American Soccer League and people wanted to work for him. My friend Jimmy Gabriel was manager of San Jose while George Best was there, but it didn't last.

Now Milan was chairman of Portsmouth, via Charleroi in Belgium and OGC Nice in France. Coincidentally, I met him when he was taking over the club. I was still manager of West Ham and had arranged to play a testimonial for the old Portsmouth kit man, who had been there fifty years. It was the week after the end of the season and, typical West Ham, I remember it causing a massive row with the players because they were all looking to get away and start their holidays. In the end, we sent a good team – Ian Wright, Frank Lampard, Rio Ferdinand – but the situation down at Portsmouth was desperate. They were close to shutting the gates on the club, I was told on the night. That was when I met Milan. Bob McNab, the old Arsenal player, had brought him over. 'How are you going, Harry?' he said. 'I'm thinking of buying this club – what do you think?'

'It's a fantastic club in terms of tradition,' I told him. 'They had a great team after the war, with Jimmy Dickinson. If you could get it going again, they love their football team down here.' I don't know if that influenced his decision, but he ended up buying Portsmouth and saving it from administration.

Three years later and I hadn't long left West Ham when he got in touch with an interesting offer. The call came from David Deacon, whose family used to own the club. He was very polite. 'Harry, I hope you don't mind me ringing, but Milan Mandaric is looking for a director of football and would like you to meet him,' said David. I told him I didn't really know what a director of football was. When Terry Brown offered the role to Billy Bonds, I took it to mean more a club ambassador than a role with a defined duty. 'Would you just come to the meeting and Milan will explain?' Deacon pressed.

We arranged to meet for lunch the next day at Chewton Glen hotel in the New Forest. And it was lovely. We hit it off straight away. We talked football, he was very charming and he offered me the job that afternoon. He had interviewed another three or four managers, but in our brief time together he made his mind up. 'Harry, I want you to take the job,' he said.

I was still uncertain. 'I don't know, Milan,' I told him. 'What is it that I actually do?'

'Your main responsibility will be to find players,' he explained. That was something I knew I could do.

'I can't pay you the sort of money you were earning at West Ham; I cannot get anywhere near that,' he continued. 'But I'll pay you a reasonable basic salary and ten per cent of any transfer profit we make from a player you have brought in.'

'OK,' I said. 'We'll see how it goes.'

He was right about Portsmouth's status. The club was certainly no West Ham. To be blunt, it was a dump. Fratton Park was old and decrepit, the training ground was horrible, and they were only getting about 10,000 fans to matches. The money wasn't a huge issue for me, though, because Terry Brown had paid up my West Ham contract in full, and at least this way I stayed involved in the game.

Graham Rix was the manager and, understandably, my arrival put him on edge. His initial reaction, and again I understand this, was that I wasn't welcome at the training ground, but that didn't bother me: I didn't see going there as part of my role anyway. What I became, basically, was Milan's mate and his driver – a shoulder to lean on because he had spent millions saving Portsmouth from administration and, frankly, the place was going nowhere. Graham was a good lad and, I'm told, a good coach, but it wasn't reflected in the results. Portsmouth had finished 20th in Division One (now the Championship) in 2000–01, a point above the relegated clubs. The next season wasn't much better. After a promising start the club went steadily downhill and lost 4–1 at home to Leyton Orient in the FA Cup, having already been knocked out of the League Cup by Colchester United. At those times, my job, as well as chauffeur, was to keep Milan in check. I remember one game at West Bromwich Albion, when we were 5–0 down at half-time. 'Right, Harry,' said Milan, 'we are going home.'

I told him we couldn't go home. 'You've got to go to the boardroom,' I said. 'We can't all just walk out. It's bad manners.'

'I can't,' he said. 'I am ashamed.'

'Look, Milan, we're losing, we're getting killed, I know that,' I reasoned. 'But West Brom are a good team and you've just got to accept it.'

In the end, I persuaded him not to lead the entire Portsmouth board in a walkout after 45 minutes and we stayed. Fortunately, West Brom lost interest in beating us up further and the score stayed at five. Even so, we didn't hang around too long. Milan's relationship with Graham was only heading one way.

I should have borrowed Bobby Moore's old chauffeur's cap, because that's all I was in the early days. I would drive Milan, his friend Fred Dinenage – who used to present the television programme *How* – and another pal, Terry Brady (Karren's dad) around the country to games. One Saturday, Milan was away on business, Terry couldn't make it and Fred fell ill, and I ended up driving Mrs Dinenage, just the two of us, from the south coast to Rotherham United and back. This was not my idea of directing football. Directing traffic, maybe.

Indeed, I had only been at Portsmouth a few months when I was given the opportunity to escape and return to football as a manager. Leicester City had sacked Peter Taylor and they wanted me to replace him. There were four or five candidates, but I met John Elsom, the chairman, and he offered me the job. I had even agreed the appointment of backroom staff. I was taking Frank Lampard and the former Wimbledon manager Dave Bassett with me as assistants, and they had agreed their deals.

And then, when I drove home from Leicester on the Friday night, it took me five hours to get back to Dorset. All the way, stuck on the M1, I was thinking, 'I don't fancy this. We love where we live. We've got the grandchildren, we've got the dogs, I'm never going to see anybody. I'll be up in Leicester all week, I'll never get home.' It was a journey and a half. And getting up the M1 is as bad as coming down. It was a nightmare, I had been told. I spoke to John Elsom again. He assured me it must be a bad day for traffic and that it would normally only take, at most, three and a half hours. Oh blimey. 'Don't worry,' Mr Elsom said. 'Martin O'Neill was our manager and he didn't used to come in much at all. If we saw Martin at training through the week we thought he had got lost, but on Friday and Saturday when he picked the team he did fantastic things.'

John loved Martin, but I knew I wasn't the same kind of boss. If I was Leicester manager, I was going to be there every day. I changed my mind and turned down the position. I rang the chairman the next day, thanked him for the offer, but declined. Dave Bassett ended up taking it instead, had a complete nightmare, and got sacked the same season. For my sanity's sake, I probably made the right move. Imagine five hours on the motorway after every defeat.

Yet in between driving Milan and friends around, I did find some good players for Portsmouth. Peter Crouch is the most famous one, for obvious reasons, but we also brought in Svetoslav Todorov from West Ham, Alessandro Zamperini from Roma and Robert Prosinečki, the great Croatian international. He was Milan's best signing. What a fantastic player. He was in a different class to anything in that league. He might have been coming to the end of his career but I would have paid to watch Portsmouth every week, just for him. He reminded me of Paolo Di Canio in the way he could do things with the ball. He was a man apart, with frightening talent. We played at Barnsley one night, won 4–1, and the home supporters gave him a standing ovation as he came off with six minutes to go. I don't care what the level of the opposition was, it remains one of the best individual performances I have seen. He was a genius. He'd make out to cross, jump, come back this way, the defender would stick his boot in, and he'd be gone. If you look at his record, he played for all the great clubs in Yugoslavia, plus Barcelona and Real Madrid. How he ended up with us, I'll never know.

One scouting trip I do remember took me to Japan to watch a goalkeeper, Yoshi Kawaguchi. It was a long flight. I arrived exhausted, got straight on to a train, another hour and a half to the hotel, and then another train to get to the match in Yokohama. I didn't know where I was by the end. The game started, and I fell asleep. I was completely wiped out. I kept trying to open my eyes but it was no use: I was gone. The agent was with me, and every now and then, he'd nudge me and say, 'That was good save, Mr Redknapp,' and I'd say, 'Oh yeah, good save,' and pretend I had seen it, but in 90 minutes I don't think I remember him touching the ball. I was fighting to keep my eyes open but whenever I did he wasn't in the game. His team won easily, 3–0. After the match, I met him for dinner and quickly realised I was in the presence of a bona fide Japanese superstar. He was a nice kid, a good-looking boy as well, and everybody in the restaurant was all over him. They all wanted pictures with Yoshi. I could see why Milan had the hots for him straight away. He thought Portsmouth would make a fortune commercially in the Japanese market with Yoshi on the books. Some years later, he ended up the captain of Japan.

Back in England I told Milan it was hard to make a judgement because Yoshi wasn't involved in much action. I didn't have the heart to tell him the Rip Van Redknapp story. 'He hasn't touched the ball,' I said. 'The only thing we can do is get him over on trial.'

So we did, and he worked with our goalkeeping coach, Alan Knight, who wasn't keen. Milan, however, wasn't looking for a goalkeeper as much as a business proposition, and we ended up paying £1.8 million for him, which was a club record at the time. Sadly, Yoshi never settled in to English football. It was too physical for him and he eventually played most of his career in Japan, where I'm sure he is still a hero.

The rest of my time as director of football was spent listening to Milan moan about Graham Rix. We'd sit in the directors' box together and, if the team didn't win, Milan would stomp back inside and slaughter Graham, sometimes to his face. Graham would just sit there and take it, but I would have to move away, embarrassed. I didn't want to be involved in that but, from the other end of the room, I could still hear Milan going off. 'This is rubbish, why am I paying for this rubbish?' I thought Crouch would help us – he was a player Graham liked, too – but although he did well, the team continued to struggle. Portsmouth were second after seven games, but with twelve matches to go had fallen to 17th and Milan was genuinely concerned we would go down. He was putting considerable pressure on me to get involved.

It was the last thing I wanted. Having managed in the Premier League with West Ham for seven years, why would I want to go back into management with Portsmouth? I had already turned down a better job at Leicester. I liked being on the south coast with my family, and I liked being with Milan, who had become a pal, but I certainly wasn't itching to take on a relegation scrap in a lower division. I did everything I could to keep Graham at the club that season. If Milan had had his way, he would have been gone sooner.

All the urgency to get me in at the training ground came from Milan. His insistence had been growing since the FA Cup defeat by Leyton Orient, but I had resisted. 'You've got to get involved with Graham,' he would say.

'It's difficult for me, Milan,' I told him. 'I don't want to get under his feet. I've been in his position – he won't want me around.'

But the situation was worsening. 'I spoke with Graham, he said he really wants you to help,' Milan told me one day.

So I spoke to Graham, too. 'Milan's got the hump,' I told him. 'You need to start showing him some improvement.'

I felt sorry for Graham. He was a good coach but parts of the manager's job were too much for him at this stage of his career. I took Graham to Bristol Rovers one night, tried to show him specifically what I looked for in a player, or the way a team was set out. We got on fine and I thought the atmosphere was improving, but then we lost at home to Wimbledon and Milan wanted Graham replaced again.

We would go around in circles. 'You've got to be the manager.' 'I don't want to be the manager.' I even spoke to Dennis Roach, Graham's agent, to warn him of the mood and see if he could get Milan to turn the heat down. In the end, I think Graham got a two-match stay of execution. We drew away at Crewe Alexandra and at home to Sheffield Wednesday, and that was it for Milan. He changed tack. Now it wasn't Graham who was going – he was going. 'I'm going to pack up, Harry,' he said. 'I've had it. I'm resigning. Unless you take over for the last five games, I'm leaving. I've given Graham the chance and we're going down.'

So I took over for the last five games of the season.

Managing Portsmouth wasn't something I ever saw as part of my future and those final five games did little to change my opinion. We didn't win once. We got a draw against Burnley and another point away to Birmingham City, and stayed up by four points, meaning Graham could have remained in charge. We wouldn't have gone down anyway, even if we had lost every game, as we already had enough points to survive – although Milan wasn't to know that. Still, it wasn't a great start, and I still had ambitions of managing in the Premier League.

'I've enjoyed it here, Milan,' I told him, when he offered me the job permanently, 'but it's not what I want to do.' He can be a very persuasive chap, though, and I did enjoy his company. We got on very well – as tight as I have been with any chairman. We went out for another dinner at Chewton Glen, Milan and his wife, me and Sandra, and by the end of it I was the new manager of Portsmouth. 'I'll give it a go,' I told him. 'I'll do a year and see how I feel.'

It is fair to say it went better than either of us could have expected. We won the league by six points the following season. Incredible, really, given the circumstances. We didn't even have a proper training ground: we used somewhere in Portsmouth when Graham was in charge, but the facilities were appalling. There was a big oak tree in the middle of the pitch and the changing rooms were derelict, and what remained had been vandalised by kids. There was an old hut that had been there since the war, which doubled as the dressing room, and the kids used to get in there at night and smoke. It was filthy. We would clean it out the best we could, but it was cold – no hot water there and no food, so we had to bring sandwiches or soup over from the club at lunch-time if we were going to train all day. I can remember driving around that summer looking for an alternative, and finding the Wellington Sports Ground, just by Southampton Airport. It was Southampton's old training ground, not perfect, but better than what we had. I drove over there and saw the groundsman. He said it had been mainly used by Southampton university since the football club built their own facility. That was all the encouragement I needed. The university weren't keen at first, but they were struggling for money, so we struck a deal. We had to be off there by 11 a.m. on Wednesdays, out of the building and gone because it was needed for hockey, and there was a cricket square in the middle that couldn't be touched. Sometimes we had to start training at 8.45 a.m. to accommodate the university, and the space we did have wasn't big enough to mark out a full-size pitch, but what alternative was there?

Yet the players never complained. Steve Stone was an England international, yet he suffered it without a murmur. Do you think he had to put up with that at Aston Villa or Nottingham Forest? He could easily have moaned yet, like the rest, he was too professional. We had a fantastic spirit at the club. Every morning we'd mark out the little areas that we could use and, when it wasn't raining, it was at least a good surface. Different when it was wet, mind you. The rain used to come pouring off the side of the hill and flood it completely. As for the changing rooms, they were stone cold with no heating at all. It was like playing in kid's football again. If anything, the dressing rooms we used to get changed in over at Goresbrook Park in Dagenham were better than this.

There was no manager's office at the training ground, and no secretary; all we had was a little canteen upstairs where we used to go and have a cup of tea. Eventually we got a Portakabin in the corner and one member of staff, and that was it. We had an old settee with all the springs sticking out of it, and that was where we would gather in the morning and discuss what we were going to do.

For the first six months we didn't even have hot water in the showers because the university had trouble paying the bills, but it helped forge a fantastic camaraderie, with experienced guys like Steve or Shaka Hislop just shrugging it off. If they could handle it, I reasoned, the rest would follow suit. The Portsmouth team that came up were all good lads – not a minute's problem to handle, any of them.

We turned the promotion-winning team around in one summer. I took Arjan de Zeeuw from Wigan Athletic on a free transfer, and he was a fantastic player for me. He's a doctor now, specialising in forensic detective work. A clever man, very well educated, but as hard as nails: a proper, old-school, centre-half. I got Shaka from West Ham, so we had a good goalkeeper; but the biggest signing was Paul Merson from Aston Villa. Steve Kutner, his agent, called me to ask whether I would fancy taking Paul on loan. I said there was no way he would come to Portsmouth. 'Well, he's got to get away from Villa, Harry,' he told me. 'He's got problems and he's not happy there.'

'We can't afford his wages, Steve,' I explained.

'Not an issue,' he replied. 'They'll pay nearly all his wages.'

I think we ended up giving Merson about £5,000 a week – and Villa were paying him £20,000. As soon as he walked in the dressing room, he had an effect. Linvoy Primus said to me, 'I was three seasons at Barnet, Harry. I never in all my life thought I'd be walking out in the same team as Paul Merson.' He was a great player for Portsmouth. He lifted everybody. The players just loved being on his side and I played him in a position, in behind the front, with wing-backs, so he was with two strikers and it freed him to play, to score goals, to make goals, to make passes that no one else could see. He was a different class.

He was another one of those guys that needed handling on the training ground but would be terrific every Saturday. The rest of the time, Paul would always be moaning about something.

'We're playing two-touch.'

'Why can't we play all in?'

'We're playing all in.'

'Why can't we play two-touch?'

I loved him, though, even if he did nearly get me killed one afternoon at Millwall. He came into the dressing room that day with a big, brown bag full of readies. 'Would you look after this for me, gaffer?' he asked.

'What is it?' I said.

'It's thirty grand,' he said. 'It's for a bookmaker, an Irish mob. They're after me and I've got to meet them after the game. Will you look after it for me until then?'

'Why don't you leave it in your pocket?' I asked.

'I can't,' he said. 'It's Millwall. I can't leave thirty grand lying about here. I spoke to their manager, Ray Harford, and he said they had a robbery last week. Nicked all the money out of the players' jackets. If that happens today, I'm in big trouble.' So I was lumbered. Couldn't leave it in the changing room, didn't know how I could keep it on me. I almost always wear a suit on the touchline, but that day I changed. I put a tracksuit on so there was more room to conceal these readies. I stuffed them down my trousers, I stuffed them down my pants until nothing was showing, and then I walked out for the game. We made a good start, Yakubu scored, but after about 20 minutes I needed to hand out some instructions, so I sprung up from my seat on the touchline. As I did, I felt something move. As I was trying to get a message to the players I could feel Merson's thirty grand making its way south along my trouser leg. I looked down and the notes were coming out the bottom of my trousers, all wrapped up individually because there was no way I could stuff one big envelope down there. I had £50 wads bound with elastic bands about to fall out of my trouser leg on to the track – at Millwall, of all places. There was going to be a riot. I edged back to my seat like a bloke who needed the toilet quickly. The staff were very concerned. 'Are you all right, Harry?' I was virtually doubled up, as if in pain. I slid into my seat and didn't move, stuck in this awkward position in case the money moved again. What option did I have? I could hardly stick my hands down the front of my trousers and start sorting things out. Not with everyone watching. The staff kept asking if I needed to see the doctor, and I kept telling them it was nothing, I was fine, I just needed to be left alone. But I was rooted to the spot. We ended up winning 5–0 and Merson got cheered off by the Millwall punters, he was that good. It wasn't the only result he had that day. He told me afterwards that the money he owed was nearer £100,000 than £30,000 but the bookmakers had decided to cut their losses.

Another time, Paul came to see me before we played a game at Brighton and Hove Albion. He said he needed to visit Tony Adams's clinic for addicts, Sporting Chance. We had been knocked out of the FA Cup by Manchester United and didn't have a match for thirteen days. 'I've got a problem with the drinking and gambling again, gaffer,' he said. 'I need help. I think if I could get to the clinic I could sort myself out.'

If he insisted it helped him, how could I disagree? I was desperate to have him fit and firing for our promotion run-in. Paul said he would be back the Monday before our next game, against Grimsby Town, so I gave him my blessing. Milan thought it would be good if I could get a few days to clear my head, too, so Sandra and I flew to Michael Tabor's house in Barbados, near the famous Sandy Lane hotel. Michael had been asking me to go for a while and it is such a beautiful place – even better than the five-star accommodation down the road. We spent the days sitting by the pool looking out across the beach, or having a game of golf or tennis. Fabulous.

And then one lunchtime, when Michael had a few friends over, a chap I'd never met before introduced himself. 'Hello, Harry,' he said, genially. 'I've just seen one of your players, up the beach there, walking with his wife and kids. He must be on holiday, too.'

As far as I knew, most of the players were still in for training.

'Who's that?' I asked. 'Paul Merson,' he said.

'Merson? No, it can't be,' I insisted. 'He's back in England.'

'No, it was definitely him,' the man said. 'I'm a big Arsenal fan. We even had a chat. Amazing, isn't it? I don't meet any footballers and then I see two in one day.'

The following Monday I was waiting at the training ground, and in walked Merson, one shade lighter than Linvoy Primus – I've never seen a white man so brown. It was the middle of January, he was meant to have been at a clinic in Hampshire, and here he was looking like he'd spent two months in Benidorm.

'All right, Merse?'

'Yeah, I feel a lot better, gaffer.'

I thought, 'I bet you fucking do.' But I had two choices: either have a big row with our best player, just as we reached a critical part of the season, or let it lie and see if his unscheduled break had caused a problem. We beat Grimsby 3–0 and Paul was absolutely outstanding. 'I'm glad you're feeling better,' I told him after the game. I did let him know what I knew eventually – but not until our title-winning season was over.

There was great quality in that team, but we patched it together, really. Steve Stone left Aston Villa on a similar deal to Merson, and I spotted Matt Taylor playing for Luton Town. I thought he would make a great wing-back, he could run all day, and ended up playing close to 200 games for the club. Yakubu had been scoring plenty of goals in the Israeli league, and we took him in the transfer window, through his agent Pini Zahavi. He had been on trial at Derby County but there was a problem securing a work permit. Suddenly, he had met this nice girl and got married, and his employment circumstances had changed. Now he had a work permit, a new wife, and went on to have a superb career in English football.

A week before the season began, however, I made what might have been my most important signing – and it wasn't even a player. Bringing Jim Smith on to my staff as assistant manager was as shrewd a move as I have ever made. He was a hero at Portsmouth, having taken the club to the FA Cup semi-finals, where they were unlucky to lose a replay to Liverpool on a penalty shoot-out, and the fans warmed to our partnership straight away. His contribution was invaluable. He was one of those guys that could make you laugh and put you at ease, but he knew the game and would talk common sense all day when we needed to get serious. Jim was just a great man to have on your team, really, and with Kevin Bond I had a very strong staff.

Jim was a blunt speaker, no messing. He certainly wasn't a yes man. We had Jason Roberts on loan in our first season in the Premier League, and he was going through a rough time. 'Is his real name Unlucky Jase?' Jim asked.

I look at him quizzically.

'I'm only thinking,' he said, 'because whenever he plays all I hear you say is, "Unlucky Jase, unlucky Jase ..." unlucky fucking Jase.' Jim claimed he had an idea to build up Jason's confidence. 'I've done it before,' he said. 'Shooting practice, but without a goalkeeper.' He took Jason, and Teddy Sheringham, so it didn't look as if Jason was being singled out as a duffer, and a big net of balls. He got one of the young lads to just clip crosses in from wide, and the strikers would finish into a gaping empty net. It was painful to watch. Teddy was scoring as easy as shelling peas, but Jason – the ball went through his legs, off the top of his head, over the bar, wide of the post. It turned out it wasn't the goalkeeper that was stopping Jason from scoring. He was managing that quite nicely on his own. 'Thanks for that, Jim,' I said after the session. 'You've ruined him.' Roberts has been around a few clubs since and done well. He's a handful, holds the ball up and looks the part, but for some reason that wasn't the case with us. I can remember one good game, his last, against Aston Villa, before we shipped him out to Wigan.

Jim was at his best on the Friday night before matches. We'd go out and have a meal: Jim, me, Kevin, Milan and maybe Terry Brady – find a good little Italian and a couple of bottles of Amarone later, have a row. Jim would usually start it, but it didn't take too much for me to join in. Kevin was always the quiet one. I don't think I've ever had a better time as a manager than those Friday nights.

It always ended in a ruck, but nothing was carried on the next day. Milan would say something, and I'd jump on it. 'What are you talking about, you haven't got a fucking clue.' And then Jim would join in, and Milan would say that he used to work with George Best and he knew more than fucking any of us, and it would go from there. I loved that company.

We'd argue about all sorts – league positions for one. Milan would go around the table asking for predictions of where we might finish.

One end of the table would be saying, 'all we need to do is stay up'. Then somebody else would wade in with, 'top half, easy'.

I would go nuts. 'What do you fucking know? We're going to finish ninth? Fucking hell!' The balloon would go up and there would be no stopping us. I remember when Joe Jordan first joined us on a Friday night. He just sat there, unable to believe his eyes, or ears. He thought he had signed up to work with a bunch of nutters. Maybe he had. But next day we were all mates again.

The biggest row I remember was over Papa Bouba Diop, a Senegalese midfield player we were trying to buy from the French club, Lens. He was known as the Wardrobe because he was so big, but Willie McKay was his agent and was touting him around for just £1 million. He had been down with us all week training and looked absolutely magnificent. On the first day he outjumped Arjan de Zeeuw to score from a cross, and that was enough for me. Nobody got the better of Arjan in the air like that. I was keen from the start, but now the deal was dragging on. I left the deal in the hands of the club and set off for the West Country, where we were staying for five days and playing a pre-season game. Milan phoned en route. 'Are we going out for dinner, Harry?'

'Absolutely, Milan. How many should I make it for? There's me and Jim here.'

'And I'm with Peter,' Milan said.

'Peter? What's Peter there for?' I asked. 'He's doing the deal for Diop.'

'He's left him in the hotel,' Milan explained. 'They're going to finish it Monday.'

'He won't be there Monday,' I said, agitated. 'The word's out about him. I know Willie – he'll take him elsewhere. We'll lose him.' I was furious. Peter and I had a big row. Sure enough, halfway through dinner, I got a call: Diop's at Fulham. By now I was raging at Peter. 'We could have doubled our money,' I told him. 'You've cost us millions – and a fantastic player.' Finally, Peter stormed out.

Milan, who had been laughing and ordering more wine, got straight on to Willie McKay to offer him more. Willie agreed, but I decided I wasn't being held to ransom. I grabbed the phone and called Willie every name under the sun. 'If you give him a penny more, you get a new manager,' I warned Milan. 'Willie don't ever bring another fucking player here again.' It was another lively dinner date for the Portsmouth fraternity and, sure enough, Diop was fantastic for Fulham. We had to wait another three years to get him, by which time my animosity towards Willie had cooled, although we didn't speak for eighteen months. Peter later told me that it was in fact Milan who had not wanted to buy Diop, but at the time Milan wouldn't allow Peter to tell me this as he was worried about the two of us falling out so close to the start of the season.

Yet whatever people think of Milan, I loved being with him. Deep down, he was just one of the guys. Plus, he had an aura about him, a bit of class. He had forty thousand employees and was the biggest name in American soccer when was he was only in his thirties. We genuinely liked each other, that was our secret. We had our fall-outs, but I've always maintained he was on my side.

I don't think Milan was ever sure about Jim, though. In October of our promotion season we were playing Preston North End at home and I was taken ill. I was driving to the training ground, suddenly went giddy and the next minute I was sick, all over the car, without any warning. I felt really rough. I managed to get home, but went straight to bed. There was no way I could be on the touchline for the match that night; Jim would take charge. I remember lying in bed, with the radio on, listening. We went 1–0 down, got it back to 1–1, 2–1 up, 3–1 up; Preston came back to 3–2 but we held on. 'Great game tonight at Fratton Park, great excitement,' said the commentator, and I went to sleep happy.

Jim went upstairs to see the directors after the game, thinking Milan would be delighted, but instead he appeared in a foul mood. 'What was that rubbish?' he stormed. 'That was the football we played last year. It wasn't like it is now. The quicker Harry gets back the better.' For once, Jim didn't know what to say. I could think of a few choice replies, but I don't think Jim wanted to make trouble for me. I thought it was very unfair on him, though. And the more popular Jim got with the fans, the more Milan seemed to resent it.

Those problems were in the future, though. As it was, the 2002–03 season simply could not have gone better for any of us at Portsmouth. We had the time of our lives, which I didn't see coming. Usually you can tell. The day I walked into Tottenham as manager I knew we would be all right, and I had pretty much the opposite feeling after a week or so at Queens Park Rangers. Portsmouth, I failed to predict. Yes, we had some stars, but we also had lads like Richard Hughes, whom I had signed for £50,000 from Bournemouth. How would he fare, jumping up two divisions? It was a hotchpotch team, really. We did some great deals, but it wasn't as if Milan was just throwing money about. He ran a very tight ship. We took good players, but often they were guys other clubs wanted out. There were no massive wages at Portsmouth then, either. We had Linvoy Primus, from Barnet, next to Gianluca Festa, who was a defender Middlesbrough had bought from Inter Milan, but had fallen out of favour with the club. Another bargain. They paid the bulk of his wages, we gave him £6,000. Middlesbrough just wanted him out of the building, but he suited us. It was that sort of team.

In fact, I cost a friend of mine a small fortune, by putting him off having a bet. He said we were 33-1 to win the league. 'Don't waste your money, Alan,' I told him. 'If we get top half, it'll be a miracle.' Shows you what I know.

There were some strong teams in the league that year – I particularly fancied Wolverhampton Wanderers and Sheffield United, and Leicester City who came up with us – but the fans just got behind the team and we took off. Our first game of the season was at home to Nottingham Forest: we won that and never looked back. We were top by the end of August and stayed there all the way through to May. Having been near the bottom for the last three seasons, the fans really responded. In November, we went to Wolves with no fit central defenders. They were a good team – Denis Irwin at left-back, Joleon Lescott in defence, Paul Ince running the midfield – and I ended up playing two lads that had never been in that position before and we drew 1–1. That was when I knew we were going to be all right. We led from the front all year.

The last game of the season was at Bradford City. We won 5–0. There was nothing on the game, we were already up as champions, and all the lads wore white boots, which was Festa's trademark. It must have inspired him because he scored the first goal, and we coasted. I decided to bring our Japanese heart-throb Yoshi on at half-time. He was such a nice guy, no trouble at all, despite not really being involved since having a nightmare against Leyton Orient in the FA Cup the previous season. I could sense the lads didn't think this was my best idea. It turns out they really fancied us to win and a little group had put money on a Portsmouth win. They needn't have worried. Todorov scored a hat-trick in the second half and we were never in danger.

I think it was probably the best season for Milan at the club. He must have been the most popular chairman in the country, and absolutely revelled in the attention. He only ever wanted to be loved. I remember during my time as director of football, we were playing at home to Crystal Palace, and Milan came into the boardroom very excited. 'Harry,' he said, 'there is a horse running in a big race today called Milan. Is it owned by a Portsmouth fan? Do you think they have named it after me?'

'No, Milan,' I told him. 'It belongs to a friend of mine, Michael Tabor. It's running in the St Leger at Doncaster. But it's a good horse.'

'Right,' he said, 'put £60 on it for me.' He gave me the money, but I decided to lay the bet myself. I fancied something else in the race. Sure enough, Milan won and I was out ninety quid. Our

Milan was delighted. We were beating Palace comfortably, which helped his mood, and he'd had it off on the St Leger. We were sitting together for the second half and our fans started singing, 'Milan, there's only one Milan ...'

'Are you jealous of that, Harry?' he asked. 'Do you hear them all singing to me?'

'They're not singing to you, Milan,' I told him. 'They've all had a few quid on that horse.'

He looked very crestfallen. 'Do you think so, Harry?' he said.

We didn't set the Premier League alight in our first season, but we stayed up, which was more than a lot of people expected. We weren't the size of Wolves or Leicester, but they both went straight back down again and we survived. I had doubts about some of the players, obviously. I wondered if guys like Linvoy Primus or Arjan de Zeeuw could handle the Premier League, but they were fantastic. The group that got us promoted kept going, and I added a bit of class with Teddy Sheringham and Tim Sherwood. Some people have found Teddy a bit aloof, but he was fine with me. He was a good pro, a good trainer and in top nick for his age. Milan had finally agreed to do the drainage at our training ground – the university had abandoned the cricket by then so we could get a proper pitch in – but he wouldn't make a commitment until promotion was guaranteed. So the work started late and by the time pre-season arrived we had nowhere to train. We ended up in the in the park over the road. It was like the old Bournemouth days, scuttling through the traffic and starting the session by clearing up dog's mess, but Teddy mucked in with it all. He had scored in a Champions League final four years earlier, but he didn't care. All the players just got on with it. Nobody moaned.

I don't think Milan was too sure about Teddy at first, but after he scored a hat-trick against Bolton Wanderers in August, he changed his mind. Not that it was all plain sailing. We had dropped into the bottom three by March, and there was a real fear of relegation, but a 1–0 win against our great rivals Southampton on 21 March turned our season around and we lost only one game between there and the end of the season. We finished 13th.

Yet, for some reason, all was not well. Milan had never taken to Jim Smith, and now he was angling to get rid of him. He hated that the fans sang 'Harry and Jim'. He was always going on about it. 'Why do they sing Harry and Jim?' he would ask me, thinking I would get wound up about it. 'Milan, I don't care if they sing Jim and Harry,' I would say, but he wouldn't let it drop. I don't even think he wanted them to sing Harry and Milan. It was more that he was protective of me, and thought I wasn't getting my due. Milan would say that I built the team and should be getting all the credit. 'They should sing Harry and Harry,' he said. He never understood that it didn't matter to me. What difference does it make what they sing? What's the problem? Yet it seemed to fuel his anger against Jim.

It was at the end of our first season in the Premier League that matters came to a head. Milan moved to sack Jim – and even went on radio claiming the whole plan was my idea. I was livid. I said if Jim went, so would I, Milan retreated, and that smoothed things over – but not for long. Milan was still scheming to move Jim out and in November of our second season in the Premier League, the row blew up again. There were just too many bust-ups now, and they were always over Jim. This time the pair of us went to see Milan and Peter Storrie. We had a huge row, which must have lasted a couple of hours. Jim didn't say a lot this time, I think he was just embarrassed to be the cause of so much trouble, but it certainly wasn't his fault. Milan had just taken against him. He wanted to bring another coach in, and Jim didn't fit the profile. Milan wanted a young, foreign coach, but I argued against having to work with someone we didn't know. How could we know the new man would fit in? What if we didn't agree on football? I thought I had got Milan to see sense. I left the meeting thinking we were all moving on. Jim had been great for me, and I was determined he was going to remain part of my staff. Yet as I drove home with, I thought, the situation resolved, I began to get some strange phone calls from newspaper men. 'Hello, Harry, I hear you're getting a new director of football ...'

It was the first I had heard of it. They kept mentioning the same name, a Croatian coach, Velimir Zajec. I knew him, of course. He had been the captain of Yugoslavia at the World Cup in 1982 and the 1984 European Championships. Yet I didn't really know him as a coach, and I certainly didn't know him as a person, the way one would hope to know a close colleague. He was definitely going to be Milan's man. I didn't like the sound of it at all. I started off telling the press guys that there was no chance the story was true. That I had just been talking to Milan and he hadn't mentioned it. But the calls kept coming. I began to feel I was out of the loop. So I called Milan. 'They are trying to cause problems between us, Harry,' he insisted. 'This is bullshit.'

'I'm glad you said that, Milan,' I told him, 'because I've got Jim with me, and he's got thirty years' experience in English football. We don't need any help.'

The next day, Zajec was there.

He didn't come to the training ground, but I knew he was at the club. From that moment, it was the end for me. If Zajec was coming in, I'd be going out, I could see that. Maybe not immediately, but soon. They tried to soft soap the appointment at first by saying he would develop a youth academy and be responsible for scouting in Europe, but I felt undermined. Milan obviously knew Zajec, and maybe he fancied making a change later that season. Either way, I wasn't going to hang around to find out. I'm sure Zajec had a good knowledge of European players, but I saw his appointment as stepping all over my position as manager, and there was no talking me down. I rang Peter Storrie and we met at the Little Chef in Ringwood, on the A31. 'I've just had enough of it,' I told him. 'I don't want to meet this fella, I just want to avoid him.' Peter did his best to stop me and eventually asked if I was sure. I said I was.

We put out a statement saying that the parting was amicable and that Milan and I remained friends, and I'm sure few people believed it – but I could never stay angry at him for long. He saved Portsmouth, never forget that. Long before their current troubles, the club was going out of business and he went in and rescued them. He certainly wasn't an absentee owner. He devoted more and more time to the project, bought an apartment on Gunwharf Quay in Portsmouth Harbour and was very hands-on – he was at the club almost every day. He brought in Storrie for some of the day-to-day executive duties but, make no mistake, Milan ran that club. Whatever money was spent, he knew about, and he did business properly. There was never a sign of Portsmouth getting back into financial trouble when Milan was around.

Mick Maguire went in the next day and agreed a settlement figure for me. Really, as I was the one that resigned, they didn't have to pay me a penny, but Mick pointed out that the board had caused this problem, and they offered £150,000 plus my car. Mick called me, very pleased. 'Don't sign anything until I ring you to say the money has been transferred,' he said.

'Mick, I don't want their money,' I insisted.

'You don't understand,' he said, 'they've agreed this and it will be there tomorrow.'

'Tell them, no thanks,' I said. 'Put it into the community pot or kids football in Portsmouth. I'm not interested.'

Mick thought I was mad, but that's what we did. He later stood up in court and told that story. Mick said he hadn't come across another manager that had acted in that way.

CHAPTER ELEVEN

....

GOING DOWN

I left Portsmouth on 24 November 2004, and I know what some people think. They believe that, on the day I resigned, I already knew where my next job would be. They think I was tapped up and used the appointment of Velimir Zajec as a means of extricating myself from Portsmouth. Nothing could be further from the truth. The day I walked away from Fratton Park, a return to football at Portsmouth's biggest rivals, Southampton, was not even on the horizon.

It was Dennis Roach, an agent, who first approached me about replacing Steve Wigley, twenty-seven miles along the south coast. I took the call while on my way to a funeral. I had been sitting at home for close to two weeks, watching football but hating not being involved, when Dennis phoned on behalf of Southampton chairman Rupert Lowe. Zajec was now the manager of Portsmouth, so there was no way back for me there, but I knew such a move would be controversial. 'No, I can't go there, Dennis,' I said. 'Sure you can,' Dennis replied. 'Southampton's a big club, it's got a great new stadium, a fantastic new training ground, but they've got to stay up. You're the man for the job. Rupert really wants to meet you.'

That last part was only half true: Rupert actually wanted his friend Glenn Hoddle to take the position, but could not persuade the rest of the board to back his decision. If I had known that, I might have thought twice. Mind you, if I had known a lot of things I would have run a mile that day. I had no idea of the hatred and bitterness my move would cause. I was supposed to be going on holiday to Dubai with Jim Smith and our wives, and Jim had already travelled. Instead, I postponed the trip to meet Rupert at his house in Cheltenham the next day, 7 December. I left there as the manager of Southampton. Looking back, I probably didn't think hard enough about the consequences. As usual, I dived in when I shouldn't have. I just didn't realise the pure hatred that existed between the clubs. We were rivals, yes, I understood that – but the level of anger and abuse that greeted my decision shocked me. It was a bad season anyway, but that made it worse – and so much harder.

On the day my appointment was announced, Wednesday 8 December, Southampton were 18th, two points from bottom club West Bromwich Albion. They had not won away from home all season, and had won only twice at their new stadium, St Mary's. Dennis was right, it was a lovely arena, but it wasn't intimidating like The Dell used to be. Southampton's old ground was their secret weapon, the ground where they once put six past Manchester United. I imagine opponents looked forward to coming to St Mary's.

As far as I was concerned, I had done nothing wrong making the switch. I didn't want to leave Portsmouth. I had done a good job there; it was Milan's decision to bring another man in, and chip away at my staff. It wasn't as if I had misled anybody. It wasn't as if I had pretended to be a Portsmouth fan or had given the impression I had always wanted to be manager there, and could not think of working for another club. I was an employee, there to fill a role. People go where the work is, and in any other walk of life if a man can find good employment near to home, he takes it. Southampton were the only other Premier League club within range of where Sandra and I lived – why shouldn't I work for them? Why should I have to move up the other end of the country? I had all these very reasonable thoughts in my head as I left my new chairman's house, and I thought enough people would see the logic with me. If I couldn't work for Portsmouth, this really was the next best thing. I was very, very wrong. The first day in I realised the backlash was going to be horrendous. The Portsmouth fans could not forget the past.

Southampton's training ground is at Marchwood, to the west of the city. To get to it, I had to drive down a long country lane to a T-junction, and turn right. As I approached that first morning, in the distance I could see substantial roadworks were taking place. There were what looked like signs, too – except they weren't signs. The nearer I got, I could see they were banners. JUDAS, SCUM, and a few other choice phrases. The contractors were Portsmouth boys, about ten of them, and they were there to welcome me every morning for months. They had plenty to say, too, and I had no option but to stop at the road every morning, to make sure no traffic was coming. I just kept my head down, but it wasn't the best way to start the day, cursed all the way into my office.

I know Alex McLeish also got abuse from Aston Villa fans when he took their manager's job having previously been at Birmingham

City, but there was no question of being shot by both sides. The Southampton fans were great with me. We managed to throw away a two-goal lead at home to Middlesbrough in my first match in charge, but they remained supportive. There was never any bad feeling, considering I had been so popular at Portsmouth, and their welcome was unbelievable. Seeing how badly the move had gone down with Portsmouth's supporters, I really didn't know what to expect at St Mary's, but there wasn't any problem. I think they were just pleased to see a manager they thought could dig them out of a hole. They knew I had done well at Portsmouth.

If Rupert Lowe anticipated the negative reaction from my old club, he did not say anything. He wasn't really a football person, so I don't think he properly understood, but, more than that, I truly don't think he much cared what fans said about him. His attitude would have been: take the abuse and get on with it. He was distanced from the pressure of it, too, living in Cheltenham. Jim Smith, who I took as my assistant, could also escape, with his home in Oxford. But situated very prominently on the south coast, there was no place for me to hide, and it was the same for my coach, Kevin Bond.

Even at home, there was no respite. We live on the sea, and a lot of Portsmouth boys go out fishing my way. I would be out in my garden and I would hear the unmistakable accents. 'You fucking scum, Redknapp.' Sandra would hear it, too. 'Oh my God, Harry, what have you done?' she would ask me. It was a real mess. The word got round about where I lived, so even staying inside didn't make much difference. I could hear the abuse every day ringing out from the boats, even from our kitchen. They don't hold back, the fishermen: they're a tough, tough group. And there seemed to be an awful lot of fishing going on that year. It was as if half of the city had set sail. They just thought, 'Let's go round there and give him some grief.' Wherever I went, there was always the chance of running into some nutcase from Portsmouth.

They don't get huge crowds at Fratton Park, but what they do get is fanatical. Portsmouth people are ferociously loyal to their city and their club. It is not one of those places where you see a load of Manchester United shirts; Portsmouth's colours are defiantly royal blue and on display everywhere. I suppose my time at Southampton taught me how much the club meant to Portsmouth fans – because when I left Southampton to go back to Portsmouth a year later, the reaction wasn't half as intense. There is nothing quite like Portsmouth people – if you aren't with them, you are the enemy. I had no choice but to get on with it, but sometimes it was hard. I was a guest at Sandown races one day and a chap in one of the boxes along from us spotted me. Suddenly, all this abuse was echoing around the racecourse. People were looking up, and they didn't have a clue what was going on. Racing just isn't like that, but this bloke didn't care. He was Portsmouth and he had just seen Harry Redknapp, and that was justification enough. If I ever met anyone from the city, I never knew which way it was going to go. There was a lot of anger, and it was tough not being able to answer back.

And then there were the phone calls. They started almost immediately. Someone posted my mobile telephone number on the internet and it would ring twenty-four hours a day with abuse. If I didn't answer it, messages were left until my box was full. It was non-stop. There would hardly be time to delete one message before the next one arrived. Wicked phone calls, horrible phone calls, real filth. 'I hope you crash your car and kill your wife; I hope you get cancer. I hope your wife gets cancer ...' I had to change my number in the end. It was too much. It was on me all day, every day. It got so bad that I wouldn't answer the phone because I knew what was coming. If it was a number I didn't recognise, or a withheld number, as 90 per cent of them were, it was just going to be another horrible message.

Kevin Bond used to get it, too. He told me there was one particular guy who kept ringing him all the time, when he was drunk in the pub with his mates. He would leave the most stinking messages, the worst, most disgusting abuse that you can imagine and, incredibly, he didn't even bother to hide his number. So Kevin rung him back. He waited until a time when he wouldn't be in the pub and full of bravado, and he called.

'Hello?'

'Hello mate, it's Kevin Bond.'

'Who?'

'Kevin Bond. Why do you keep ringing me and leaving such vile messages on my phone? You don't even know me. I left Portsmouth, I got offered a job at Southampton, I have to work. I've got a family like you; if you were offered another job, a better job, better pay, or if you were out of work and you were offered a job, you'd take it, wouldn't you?'

This guy went quiet as a mouse. He had no answer. He still kept ringing Kevin after that, but it was as if they were friends. 'Hello Kev, hello mate, how are you going?' It was a bully mentality, a mob mentality. People get together and they feel very brave, but when you meet them on their own it's not the same. I think if I could have put my point across to a lot of the

Portsmouth fans individually, they would have understood; but you rarely get that chance. All through that time, I would have loved the opportunity to just talk to some of these people and explain my position at Portsmouth.

Looking back, I think that maybe they liked me so much when I was there, that we had such a good relationship, that my leaving hurt far more intensely than the departure of another manager would. They treated me like God because we had gone from being nowhere, to being a Premier League team that had survived. We had the best year, winning the title to get promoted, and I don't think any of us felt we could top that. So when I went to Southampton, it was as if I had betrayed all that affection. They were too upset to step back from the situation and think, 'Harry got pushed out because they brought this other bloke in.' They would just look at it and think, 'He's gone to Southampton. He's scum.'

So I do understand the resentment, even if I don't agree with it. What I cannot understand, and what I will never understand, is the more extreme levels of abuse. It is often said that football people don't understand the fans, but I think that cuts both ways. Supporters have never been in our position, where we have to be loyal to a number of clubs through our careers. West Ham wanted me out as a player, and then as a manager. Portsmouth shunted me out as a manager, too. The majority of departures in football are like that. People don't go because they are disloyal, but because the club makes a decision – and we all know and accept that from day one. It would make life impossible if players thought like fans and could only care for one club all their lives. Most players once supported a team; but when a man enters professional football, he supports the team he plays for, and loses interest in the rest.

Supporting is kid's stuff – it was what we did before we started working. I was only 11 years old when I followed Arsenal and, sorry, but that means nothing to me now. I don't love the Gunners any more; I'm not interested in Arsenal, only in beating them. Apologies, but it's true. Once I went to West Ham, Arsenal were never again a part of my life. As a schoolboy I used to spend all week hoping they would win – no different from any fan – but how could I carry on doing that while playing for West Ham? Once a player signs professional forms, that is his team. I'd be a liar if I said I ever looked for Arsenal's results once I became a professional footballer. I look for the results that affect my team – Queens Park Rangers now. Before that Tottenham, before that Portsmouth or Bournemouth.

My dad was an Arsenal man, my uncle was an Arsenal man, I could have signed for Arsenal – but it was bottom of my list of clubs. You learn very early on that you can't make decisions with your heart. Jamie Carragher was a mad Everton fan, who has probably spent most of his adult life hoping they lose every week. As a Liverpool player, he's desperate to finish ahead of Everton. His old allegiance doesn't come into it. When I was at West Ham and Tottenham, I was desperate to see Arsenal lose, desperate to finish above them. They were our rivals. If I'm at Portsmouth, I want to beat Southampton; if I'm at Southampton, I want to beat Portsmouth. How could I look at it any other way? I have never met anyone in football who I would call a genuine fan: someone who fervently supports a club that is not his. They might still have supporters in the family, but even that changes. When I was manager of West Ham, if we played Arsenal, I know who my dad wanted to win. He's my dad, what do you expect?

The abuse aside, Southampton was as Dennis Roach told it: a good stadium, a good training ground, and a good club. Even the team was decent, really. I just felt we were we incredibly unlucky. That may sound glib, but it is not an explanation I trot out very often. I have been involved in good seasons and bad seasons and, usually, a team gets what it deserves. Yet it seemed as if we couldn't buy an even break at Southampton that season. We played Everton at home on 6 February and absolutely battered them. We went a goal down almost from the kick-off, but after that it was all us: Peter Crouch equalised before half-time, Henri Camara scored ten minutes into the second half, but we couldn't get that third goal. We had so many chances: Alan Stubbs cleared one off the line, David Weir handled the ball but the referee missed it, and our players were queuing up – Camara, Crouch, Rory Delap, Graeme Le Saux, they all could have scored. Then, in the second minute of injury time, Crouch got the ball and set off on a run downfield. Instead of taking it into the flag and eking the remaining time out of the game with a throw-in or a corner, he decided to go for glory, and have a shot. He hit it straight at their goalkeeper, who hoofed it up to Duncan Ferguson, out to Marcus Bent, past Calum Davenport, right foot, 2–2. And I never saw him score another goal like it. He wasn't a top player, Marcus Bent. Strong, big physique, but I can't remember him getting too many like that. It went off the underside of the bar at an angle and down like one of those goals Brazilians score at World Cups. We had barely kicked off when the referee blew the whistle. And that was typical of our season. And, of course, it's not all bad luck. If Peter doesn't have the shot, we win. Yet if we made a mistake, any mistake, it seemed we got spectacularly punished that year.

In my very first game, on 11 December, we were leading Middlesbrough 2–0 when the referee put the board up for time added on. Middlesbrough had a corner, they whipped one in to the near post, it skimmed off Danny Higginbotham's head and went in at the far corner, an own goal. Almost from the kick-off, Middlesbrough won the ball back and Stewart Downing scored an absolute corker from twenty yards. He didn't get another goal until 23 April. It was if they were saving them up for us. We were winning 2–0 against Aston Villa at home, and murdering them, when we lost our centre-half, Andreas Jakobsson, a big Swedish lad who hadn't given Carlton Cole a kick. We brought on Davenport and he just got bullied by him. We ended up losing 3–2. It was one of those years. In the penultimate game of the season, we went to Crystal Palace and got a point in the last minute, but Crouch was sent-off – so he would miss the last match. It was a big one. On the final day of the season, any three of four teams could have gone down.

'Survival Sunday' they called it on Sky. Norwich City had 33 points, Southampton and Crystal Palace had 32 points, West Bromwich Albion had 31, but we had the toughest game. Palace were away to their big south London rivals, Charlton Athletic, Norwich had to go to Fulham and West Brom were at home to Portsmouth. We were playing Manchester United. I wasn't expecting too many favours from Portsmouth, either – their fans turned up wearing West Brom shirts! We had two advantages – we were at home and Manchester United were playing Arsenal in the FA Cup final the following week. If Sir Alex Ferguson rested some of his big guns, as he often did before important matches, we might have a chance. The league was over from Manchester United's point of view, anyway. They were coming third. They couldn't catch Arsenal in second place, and couldn't be caught by Everton in fourth. And then I saw the team-sheet. Up front: Wayne Rooney and Ruud van Nistelrooy. Manchester United had played West Brom, managed by Old Trafford legend Bryan Robson, eight days before and neither man made the starting line-up. West Brom got an unlikely point away from home that night; Southampton weren't going to be so lucky.

West Brom moved from bottom to 17th place and safety on the last day. They were the only threatened team to win on 'Survival Sunday' and I'm sure the Portsmouth fans were delighted. Norwich got chinned by six at Fulham, Palace could only draw at Charlton, and we lost 2–1 to United. As was the story of our season, we went a goal up but couldn't hang on. Van Nistelrooy scored the winner with 27 minutes to go.

That was the most dispiriting day of my time at Southampton; but the most traumatic? Not by some distance. In the draw for the fourth round of the FA Cup we got paired with, of all teams, Portsmouth. Fortunately, it was at our place, because even in a minority, the Portsmouth fans could clearly be heard telling me exactly what they thought. We were two minutes into injury time, drawing 1–1, with a very uncomfortable replay beckoning when a cross from David Prutton struck Matt Taylor's arm. The referee, Steve Bennett, did not see it, but thank heavens a linesman did, and after what seemed an age of consultation – and silent prayers from me – he pointed to the spot. Peter Crouch was our third-choice penalty taker, but the first two were not on the pitch, and he stuck it away nicely. It was only a temporary reprieve, though. On 24 April we were due at Portsmouth in the league – and there could be no escaping that one.

By then, I was under no illusions about the nightmare I would be facing. The abuse from Portsmouth's end had not let up all season and, whether at Sandown races or in my back garden, there always seemed to be someone shouting at me. I'm sure those bloody workmen near the training ground had made the job last longer just so they could carry it on, too. Then the nearer it got to the Fratton Park game, the more poisonous the atmosphere became. Whatever had been said, however threatening, I never thought that anyone would physically hurt me. Suddenly, I wasn't so sure. The abusive messages became death threats, and now the police were involved. They said the match between Southampton and Portsmouth was always their busiest of the year. The previous year, when I was at Portsmouth and we won 1–0 at Fratton Park, there had been about eighty arrests made. My situation was only going to make it worse, they reckoned.

It had not crossed my mind before, but now I was afraid of some nutter running on and trying to do some damage. Going right back to that day with Bobby Moore in the Blind Begger, there is always some bloke out to make a name for himself. All week we were in consultation with the police and private security firms. Whatever was lying in wait for me in Portsmouth, at least I was going to be surrounded by some big powerful boys. The police were at the training ground keeping us informed of strategy. They said I would have two policemen with me on the bench, and a couple more behind the dug-out. They told me exactly what I had to do in the event of a goal or a Southampton win. 'If you score, don't jump up and start celebrating,' I was told. I assured them I had no intention of doing that. I wasn't mad.

As soon as we arrived at the training ground the police were waiting, and from that moment they never left my side. They even escorted my car safely back on to the motorway when our coach had returned at the end of the day. It was reassuring but at the same time unnerving. The fear of an attack wasn't all in my mind, then. Clearly, the police were worried about it, too. They were everywhere: on the bus, on the bench, outside the dressing-room door, and on every bridge from Southampton to Portsmouth. We had six ex-SAS man travelling with us just in case we were ambushed *en route*. The police stood patrol in case a lunatic tried to drop a paving slab on to our coach. We had two helicopters overhead all the way there keeping an eye on the surrounding roads. It was terrifying for the players. It wasn't like going to a football match – it was unreal. The police got us there and inside as quickly as they could, but just driving through the streets in Portsmouth, the abuse we were getting on the coach was scary. As we disembarked we could hear this furious reaction – without doubt the players were petrified, and I don't blame them at all for losing the game that day. It felt like we had driven into a war zone. It was a scary few hours and impossible for them to play their best football.

We felt protected in the dressing room, but the players could still detect the anger outside and a lot of them didn't want to go out for a warm-up, particularly those with connections to Portsmouth, like Nigel Quashie and Peter Crouch. They were also targets. Crouch was doubtful with a hamstring – we had been fighting to get him fit all week – and when he heard the abuse before the game, it definitely tightened up – along with a few other body parts, no doubt. The atmosphere felt alien, considering it was only a football match. I have never experienced anything like it and you could tell the players were frightened out of their lives.

My son, Jamie, was in our team that day and it was very hard for him to hear what was being said about me and stay focused. I know I found it difficult to concentrate. It was just a wall of hateful noise, and you were always on the alert for that lone nutter ready to go one stage further. Jamie knew what it was going to be like every time he touched the ball, but he was determined to see it through. 'Look, Dad, walk out with your head held high,' he told me before the game. 'Whatever they say, you've done nothing wrong.' But, hearing the reaction, I couldn't help but feel I had made a terrible mistake. I didn't need to put my family through this. How could I have got it so horribly wrong?

God knows what would have happened had we won, but there was precious little danger of that. Portsmouth were in a different class and I took no personal satisfaction that it was two of my players, Yakubu and Lomano LuaLua who bashed us up. It made it very difficult for me, but I'm sure for the police it came as something of a relief when Portsmouth surged ahead. To be fair, the Portsmouth players were fantastic. They all came up, wished me well and still called me gaffer. LuaLua was on fire, and I think he took pity on me, because they scored four goals in the first 27 minutes and a minute later he came off. I shudder to think what the score might have been had he played the whole game. He was ripping us to shreds. We did score, after 20 minutes, but there wasn't much danger of causing a riot with a spontaneous celebration because we were already 2–0 down by that time and I could see the way the game was going. Portsmouth were soon 4–1 up and I think it was at that point LuaLua decided enough was enough. We had always got on well and he didn't want to rub it in. The day was going to be difficult enough for me as it was. The people around me were nice, too, funnily enough. I'm sure there were some Portsmouth supporters who remembered the good times and were embarrassed by the worst of the chanting, because I didn't get much of the really revolting abuse in my ear. The bad guys kept their distance. At the final whistle, I looked up to the directors' box and I could see Milan Mandaric standing up applauding his players, so I gave him a little wave. He waved back and maybe that was the beginning of our *détente*. He was on his third manager of the season by then, Alain Perrin replacing Velimir Zajec at the start of April, and perhaps we were missing each other. I certainly didn't enjoy the same rapport with Rupert Lowe that I had with Milan, and he probably missed our weekly barney on a Friday night.

It didn't get much easier even after the game. To get to the press room for the post-match conference at Fratton Park, you have to go up the stairs past the hospitality boxes and, as you can imagine, there were a lot of Portsmouth punters lying in wait, who had been drinking all day. It wasn't pleasant. Some grounds shut the managers off from the public, but I had no such luck. It was pretty quiet on the coach on the way home. Guys like Jim Smith and Kevin Bond had been around a bit, but they had never been confronted by an atmosphere like that, either. I'm not particularly communicative after a defeat anyway, but this time my disappointment at losing was mixed with regret. Southampton was a poor choice.

I cannot blame myself completely, though. I keep coming back to a simple fact: it is supposed to be a game of football. I still think that, one on one, many of those hurling the abuse might have been different. I did meet the odd guy in that time who expressed his disappointment in a way that allowed us to talk, sensibly. 'Harry, we loved you at Portsmouth, why did you go?' If I fell into one of those conversations, I was always polite and I always explained as best I could. They might not have agreed, but at least they heard my side of the story.

It was a pity that Jamie had to go through all of that with me, too. It was the first time I had managed him since he was a youngster at Bournemouth, and I don't regret the signing, more the way it ended. That was Jamie's last season as a professional footballer and it ended in relegation. He didn't deserve that.

Jamie was one of those kids that just looked like a player from the start. Going all the way back to our time in America, he had a football with him wherever he went. He'd come in training with Bobby Moore in the morning, and in the afternoon, when we went to the lake, he'd spend all his time volleying footballs around with Mike England or Geoff Hurst. I can't remember a day when I didn't see him playing and then, when I was manager of Bournemouth, he would go to work with me just the same. I'd tell Sandra I was taking him to school, but let him stay in the car and go on to the training ground with me instead. He'd train with us and then put his school uniform back on and return home with me, as if I'd picked him up from a day of history, geography and maths. Sometimes he'd drop me in it. 'What did you do at school today?' 'I kept the ball up fifty times, Mum.' I did the same with Jamie's older brother Mark, too. He could have been a professional footballer as well – he was a big defender with a lovely touch – but a kid smashed his ankle to pieces playing for Bournemouth against

Cardiff City reserves. It was a horrendous tackle and the doctors couldn't repair it. I felt sick for him, he had so much promise. He ended up in non-league football with clubs like Bashley and Dorchester Town, but even then it would take him two days to walk properly after a match.

Jamie, though, flew through. He was on the books at Tottenham Hotspur as a young player and, by the age of 11, was having the odd session with the first team. At 12 he was taken away for a league game by the manager, Peter Shreeves, just to give him the experience of sitting in the dressing room with the top players. He was always going to be among them for real one day. The problem for Jamie was that Tottenham liked him more than he liked Tottenham. Later, under Terry Venables, Spurs were still very much a buying club, and Jamie didn't think he was going to get an opportunity. When he was up there, he had shared digs with Shaun Murray, who had been regarded as the brightest prospect in the country as a young teenager. He had even played for an older team as an England schoolboy, which is very unusual. Murray had signed for Tottenham with a big fanfare, but hadn't made a single appearance for them. He was from the north-east and went from being the next Bryan Robson to scraping a game in Tottenham's reserves. Jamie didn't want the same to happen to him. He had signed schoolboy forms but was adamant he wanted to leave. 'I won't get in the team at Tottenham, Dad,' he said. 'They're not giving kids a chance. I want to come to Bournemouth with you. If I'm good enough, you'll play me, won't you?'

Terry and I had a big fall-out over it. He said, 'We've signed fourteen kids this summer, and he's the only one we think is a certainty.'

'What can I do?' I asked him. 'He's my son, and he doesn't want to come. I've tried to talk him round, but I don't want to make him unhappy. He wants to play league football.'

'He could play league football here,' Terry insisted, but Jamie had made his mind up. I know Terry still thinks I just wanted him for Bournemouth, but it wasn't like that. If anything, being my son held him back at first.

It was 11 April 1990. We were playing away at West Ham and Shaun Brooks fell ill on the way to the game. Paul Miller, the former Tottenham centre-half, who was coming to the end of his career and had dropped down a division to play for us, asked if I was going to play Jamie. I said I wasn't. 'Why?' he asked. 'If he wasn't your son, you would play him. He's the best we've got.'

'Maybe,' I said, wavering.

'So you're wrong,' Paul continued. 'If the only reason not to play him is that he's your son, you're wrong.'

So I picked Jamie. It was a hard game and we lost 4–1, but Jamie was far from out of his depth. Not long after that, I met Kenny Dalglish at a function in London. He interrupted my dance with Sandra. 'Harry, they tell me your boy's a good player,' he said. I told Kenny he was doing OK. 'Ronnie Moran saw him play at Birmingham on Saturday, and loved him. Can we have him up to train with us for a week?' I knew Kenny really trusted the judgement of Ronnie Moran, a coach who had been at Liverpool for ever, and it was a fair sign that he would be given a chance. Even so, it would be difficult if Jamie wanted to play first-team football. 'West Ham, Arsenal, Tottenham, Chelsea, they've all been in for him, Kenny,' I explained. 'He just wants to play.' In the end, we agreed that Jamie and I should go up to watch Liverpool's FA Cup replay with

Blackburn Rovers that week. They made a real fuss of us and we finished up going out to eat with Kenny. He was very enthusiastic about Jamie's chances and I agreed to a one-week trial. Jamie had only been there a day when I came back to eight messages from Kenny. My first thought was that he had broken his leg. After what had happened to poor Mark I couldn't stand more terrible luck. I rang back immediately. Kenny picked up the phone full of the joys. 'Hello, Harry – have you got any more at home like him?'

'We've got to sign him,' Kenny continued. 'Just got to have him. He must come to Liverpool.'

'I warned you about this, Kenny,' I reminded. 'He wants to play first-team football, and he won't get that with you. He won't be in the team.'

'Trust me, Harry,' Kenny insisted. 'He will be in the team. He'll be in the team quicker than you can believe.'

So Jamie signed for Liverpool. I don't think Terry Venables has ever forgiven me.

As Liverpool manager, Kenny was fantastic with Jamie – for all of thirty-eight days. Jamie joined on 15 January, and on 22 February, following a 4–4 FA Cup replay with Everton, Kenny resigned. In that brief time, though, he had been a magnificent influence on Jamie's career – even letting him stay at his house so he would feel more at home than he could in digs. Jamie still idolises Kenny.

His next manager was Graeme Souness, and it felt very different. Graeme didn't know who he was and Jamie thought he had walked into the precise situation he was trying to avoid at Tottenham. I went up to see him play Wolverhampton Wanderers in the reserves one Tuesday and went back to his digs. They faced straight into the ground in what looked like a big, old haunted house. It was freezing cold and he was on the top floor. Mrs Sainsbury was the landlady and she was a lovely person, but the house was spooky. I'm not a religious person but there was a statue of the Virgin Mary on the wall with a big chip out of it, and you wouldn't want to walk past that every night. It was eerie and Jamie's room was so cold. Even the inside of his windows were frozen up, and I knew reserve-team football was getting to him. He was getting a bit emotional. 'The manager don't even know me, Dad,' he said. 'I've been here six months and he hasn't even spoken to me. I've got no chance with him.'

Not long after, I received another phone call, a little more excited this time. 'Dad, I think I'm playing tomorrow in the UEFA Cup against Auxerre,' he said. 'The manager's pulled me in and put me in the first team.' He never looked back after that. Graeme Souness loved him.

To be fair, Terry Venables didn't bear any grudges. He picked Jamie for England and played him at the 1996 European Championships. It was a pity that, against Scotland in the second group game, he broke his ankle landing after jumping for a ball. That became a big problem throughout his career. Jamie ended up having a bolt through his ankle to strengthen it. Long-term, that proved a mistake. He went back to see his specialist in London, to have the bolt out, and it was decided to let it be to add support. Jamie said he couldn't feel the presence of the bolt, but it made him run differently and, without knowing it, his gait changed and he began wearing his cartilages away. That was beginning of his knee problems, which were complicated by another unsuccessful op. The first guy that performed the operation was in Sheffield and, after it, Jamie's knee was still falling to pieces. Jamie should have gone to Dr Richard Steadman in Texas, who is the world leader in this area, but it was too late, the damage was done. He did end up with Steadman but by then all he could do was repair previous mistakes. By the time Jamie came to us at Southampton, it was close to the end. I knew he was what we needed, because he was still a classy midfield player, and he ran a couple of games, at home to Liverpool and Tottenham, just like the old days, but he was in a constant battle with knee injuries and, after we were relegated, he retired. He loved football as much as ever, but his body couldn't take it.

There was never a problem with Jamie in the side, though, never any resentment from the other players. They knew he was worth his place, and he's always been a popular guy with the group. I've managed teams that have included my son, and my nephew, Frank Lampard, and if your kid is a proper player I don't see the issue. If you keep picking your boy and he isn't any good – that's a problem. But I'm sure Paul Ince doesn't think twice about picking young Thomas at Blackpool, and it was very much like that with Jamie and Frank. I copped it over Frank at West Ham, but I think I was vindicated, and it never crossed my mind to duck out of bringing Jamie to Southampton, for that reason. Jamie was up for it, and I don't think he considered any potential for negative reaction. He certainly didn't come for the money – compared to his previous contracts, he was earning peanuts. It was just sad how it ended for him. Speaking as his dad, more than his manager, I just think it was a shame he didn't have the length of career available to other modern players, when you think that Ryan Giggs and Kevin Phillips were born in the same year, 1973.

Relegation invariably comes at a cost, and Southampton's, sadly, took a toll on my backroom staff. I didn't know whether the club would want to keep me but, following talks with Rupert Lowe, I stayed on. He was insistent, however, that we had to cut the number of coaches and that either Kevin Bond or Jim Smith would have to leave. Kevin, the younger man and the first-team coach, remained. Jim had only been given a six-month contract when we arrived and was coming up to his 65th birthday. My wages were cut back, too. The chairman was adamant that we could not exist on Premier League funding in what was then Division One. Jim and I parted amicably. He had been great for me.

I don't think either of the chairmen, Rupert Lowe or Milan, quite understood what Jim brought to the club. They just saw him as this old-school, bluff figure, maybe a bit confrontational; but he was so much more than that. It wasn't as if we were huge mates when I took him to Portsmouth in 2002. I had known Jim, obviously, as a contemporary in football management, but my first thought at Portsmouth was that he was a man who knew the game but equally knew the club, and would have an immediate bond with the fans and the people. He was ideal for all those reasons. Jim wasn't averse to steaming into the players, either, if he thought there was a problem. It took some of the pressure off me that I didn't always have to be the bad guy. A lot of managers work like that. Brian Clough did. If he thought the players looked unfit he would get Ronnie Fenton to have them running up and down the steps in the main stand, which they hated. After half an hour of this, he would suddenly emerge. 'Ronnie, what the bloody hell are you doing that for – come on, let's get the ball out, have a bit of fun.' And suddenly he was the good guy, and they wanted to play for him.

I think every manager needs someone like Jim. An assistant doesn't need to have Jim's experience, necessarily, but it is good to have a colleague on the same wavelength when you want to sound off. Jim wasn't a big presence coaching, he was there to talk to. He'd been a manager, he had been in all the same situations, and it can be a lonely job when results are not going well. Those long coach journeys after a defeat, you need a friend. It's horrible sometimes. A lot of clubs fly or take high-speed trains around the country these days but, believe me, there is nothing quite like the coach journey back from Newcastle, as a manager, if you've just got beat 3–0. You hear someone laugh at the back of the coach and straight away, you get the needle. I used to look round and think, 'What are you fucking laughing at?' The irony is, that when I was a player, I would be one of those up the back carrying on. I can see why it drove Ron Greenwood mad now. He was sitting there stewing, and we were all planning where we were going to go out on the Saturday night. You've lost, you feel so low – you can't bear to see anyone smiling. That's where Jim would come in. He'd start talking about next week's team, how we are going to win, what we should change, and by the end of the trip you almost had your team in mind for the following Saturday and the lousy result was gone. Suddenly, it wouldn't be about how bad we were that afternoon; we would be looking forward. 'We ought to bring him back in, and he hasn't done it, and what about if we play him there and him there?'

And Jim was a funny guy. He had these stories about working with Robert Maxwell that would crack me up. He said that when Maurice Evans was manager of Oxford United, first match of the season, a member of staff came out to see him: 'Mr Maxwell is on the telephone, he wants to speak to you,' he said.

'I can't speak to him now!' Maurice exclaimed. 'The game's going on. Tell him we'll speak afterwards.'

The man went away, then came back. 'Mr Maxwell insists he speaks with you. He says it's important. I think you'd better come.' So Maurice left the dug-out and took the call. 'It's the team photograph on Monday,' said Maxwell. 'Make sure the players wear the away kit – the *Daily Mirror* logo stands out better.'

Compared to that, maybe Rupert Lowe wasn't so bad, after all. If a young manager is lucky enough to have employment options, Sir Alex Ferguson always advises them to pick a chairman, not a club.

After Jim went, to cut costs, our chairman revealed another reason why he may have wished to clear the decks. He appointed Sir Clive Woodward, England's World Cup-winning rugby coach. Clive had announced his wish to work in football having achieved all he could in rugby, and Lowe had been considering the idea of involving him, even before I arrived. What I would say, though, is that for a club looking to save money, Clive's brand of expertise doesn't come cheap.

People have always made a big thing of it, but I didn't really have a problem with Clive. It would make a better story if I said we were arguing all the time, but it wasn't like that at all. We never had one minute's problem. We made a deal early on that we would never undermine each other, and we stuck to it throughout. In fact, he was a really interesting guy, and I had nothing but respect for him. It wasn't as if he came in and started telling me who to pick. We ended up sharing an office, a bit like *The Odd Couple*, but I certainly wasn't dismissive of Clive, and I hope he would back me up on that.

I admired him greatly as a rugby coach, because his England team had won the World Cup. I was preparing Portsmouth for a Monday game against Fulham that morning, and we put back Saturday training so we could watch it. I knew what Clive had achieved, but trying to transfer those ideas from rugby to football was complex and I don't think he received proper guidance from above on what they wanted him to be. He was left on his own, to just get on with it, with no outline of what we were to do with these ideas, how much was theory or what should be put into practice. There wasn't a clash of personalities, more a clash of cultures. Clive was feeling his way in football and thinking long term, meanwhile we had Saturday, Wednesday, Saturday, Wednesday matches to win. He might have had a good idea, but we didn't have the time to implement it.

Clive did all he could to help. He would come out and film the players striking the ball, looking at technique, because he had worked that way with Jonny Wilkinson and it was obviously successful. I think if we had been more open to his thinking, it would have worked at Southampton, too – but we didn't have the hours that Clive had with England to put his plans into action. Play Saturday, Sunday off, Monday, Tuesday training to prepare for a Wednesday game. We had to work on set pieces, team play, patterns of play, study the opposition. We didn't have a schedule that allowed players to sit down and go through two hours of volleying videotape with Clive. And even if we did, changing technique comprehensively is a long-term project. It could be counter-productive if the players were thinking about how they should strike a ball during a game, rather than acting instinctively. Yes, volley technique can be coached, and we all try to improve players' performance in training, but I got the impression Clive's ideas were bigger than a tweak here or there.

He couldn't understand why Rory Delap took all our long throw-ins. I could see his point, to some extent. If Delap has to make his way from left-back to the far right touchline, wipe the ball and then make his throw, the opposition has time to set up. Clive believed everyone at the club should be able to throw like Rory. He saw it as a matter of achieving upper body strength and working on technique. He thought that the moment the ball went off, any Southampton player should be able to launch it back on as Rory did, before the opposition had a chance to regroup. It's a good idea, obviously – except we had no time to put it into practice. We couldn't abandon proper training for months on end to teach this specific skill; and even if we could, it would not always be of use. It wasn't just the defenders that got into position for Rory's throws; our team needed time to get into the penalty box, too. A bit pointless the nearest player launching the ball Delap-style before our players could get on the end of it. In the end, all we could do is suggest Clive put the idea to the academy coaches to see if they wanted to develop it with the generation coming through. They had the time to work on throw-in technique – we didn't.

Clive and Rupert also thought they had found this wonder coach, called Simon Clifford, an ex-schoolteacher who taught a Brazilian method of training called *futebol de salão*, which was talked up as radical and new, but actually dates from South America before the Second World War. He seemed a nice enough guy and Clive had great belief in him, but when I watched one of his sessions there really wasn't much that was ground-breaking. He would put lots of different drills on, but he never seemed to correct

Above: Promotion with Pompey in 2003. I like a glass of bubbly as much as the next man, but a whole bottle was too much for me.

Above: All change as I
acknowledge the fans
at St Mary's alongside
chairman Rupert Lowe
in December 2004. But
this episode of my south
coast saga did not go
according to plan.

Left: Returning to
Fratton Park with
Southampton was one
of my hardest days as
a manager. There were
death threats, police
escorts and the ground
echoed to cries of Judas
and much worse. And
we lost 4–1.

Left: I brought in Dave Bassett at the start of my second season at Southampton to mix things up a bit, but by then things had already gone too far. I knew that it just wasn't working out.

Below: Celebrating with Jamie after a 2–0 victory over Liverpool. Southampton was the first time I'd managed him since he was a kid. I don't regret the signing but felt sad that his last season as a professional had to end in relegation.

Above: All change AGAIN! Back at Pompey as Milan's blue-eyed boy, but what would the fans say and how long would Mandaric be there? Either way, I couldn't resist a second bite.

Below: Staying up, staying up, staying up. Celebrating Premiership survival with the players after a win at the DW Stadium in April 2006.

Above: Announcing the signing of Peter Crouch with Peter Storrie. The Gaydamak money certainly helped us buy big, and they don't come any bigger than Crouchie.

Below: Celebrating Kanu's goal against Cardiff City in the FA Cup final. The biggest moment in Pompey's history. The secret of our success was pre-match karaoke.

Above: Celebrating back home in the obligatory open-top bus with the people of Portsmouth out on the streets in droves.

Above: A kickabout on the Wembley turf before the Community Shield with the next generation of Redknapp talent – in the form of my grandson Harry.

Above: Leading the teams out before kick-off at Wembley alongside Sir Alex.

Above: As you can see from my face, it was all a bit awkward receiving the Freedom of the City at the Portsmouth Guildhall just three days after I'd quit Pompey for Spurs. There were more than a few jeers and choice words from the assembled crowd when I arrived.

Walking out for the first time at the Lane. In truth, the club had fallen so low that climbing the league was a reasonably straightforward mission.

Above: The Champions League is the biggest stage of all and shortly after this press conference Gareth Bale lit up the San Siro with a stunning hat-trick against Inter that announced his arrival to the world.

Below: I know who I'd back in a straight fight. AC Milan's enforcer Gattuso loses his head and butts Joe Jordan – a man still capable of enforcing himself when pushed.

Above: There's some right old rubbish talked about me and Bale. Whatever faults I have, I do know a player and Gareth was in the first Spurs side I ever picked.

Below: He brought me to the club and eventually moved me on, but Daniel Levy and I had a good relationship, and got on as well as any manager and chairman.

Above and below: 'Not Guilty' – a feeling of sheer relief, but not like any I had experienced before. The emotional stress and turmoil of my long-running trial for tax evasion put the strains of football into perspective and I was glad to be able to finally put it behind me on 8 February 2012.

Above: Jamie was with me every day in court. I couldn't have done it without him.

Below: The passing away of his mother hit Frank Lampard and his dad hard, just as it did Sandra, her sister.

Above: 'Would you take the job Harry?' Within hours of the court case finishing my life was turned upside-down again as the media had me as the people's choice to step into Fabio Capello's shoes in the newly vacant job of England manager.

Below: After coming within a whisker of accepting the job of managing the Ukrainian national side, I was suddenly back in relegation scrap mode at QPR and it looked to be my hardest job yet.

Left: It wasn't long before I discovered QPR were in a bad way. The dressing room lacked confidence and spirit of any kind, and the squad had an attitude towards training that stank.

Below: Beating Chelsea, then champions of Europe, at Stamford Bridge was one of the few highlights of my first season at QPR. But whenever I thought we might have turned a corner and go on a bit of a run we reverted back to bad habits.

This page: I've made many good friends and come up against many great managers in football. I'll never forget what Kenny did for Jamie at Liverpool; I always enjoy a glass of wine and a chat about the horses with Sir Alex; and it's good to have Jose back in the Premiership.

Where I'm happiest – down the garden
with the dogs and the family around,
but my mind is never far from football.

what was going wrong. Players would be volleying the ball, but if it flew off awkwardly, he wouldn't step in and say, 'Bend this leg, fall away, get your foot up high.' There was no great technical instruction happening. Some of the stuff we had been doing with Ron Greenwood at West Ham in the sixties. In fact, if you look at the way young Frank Lampard strikes his volleys for Chelsea even now, you can see Ron's training techniques. We called it the West Ham volley. Ron taught it to Frank's dad, and he passed it on to his son. There is not a huge amount going on that is completely new, and it is useless having a million drills if the instruction isn't present. That's why it's called coaching. Clive thought Clifford was the best, and tried to get him involved in the youth team, but the youth coaches were not up for it, either. Simon left and tried to claim that his ideas were too progressive for us but, if anything, a lot of them were old hat. Visionaries are no use if the basics are not right. I heard all sorts of talk about offers he had received from Premier League clubs, but then took over as manager of Garforth Town. He said he would make them a Premier League club in twenty seasons. The last time I looked they had just been relegated to the Northern Counties East Football League. Rupert Lowe was the club chairman.

I didn't agree with Clive about Clifford, but that doesn't mean we were at loggerheads. Maybe some of the football people shut their minds when he spoke, but I didn't, and I found him eager to learn and very keen and willing to both give and take advice. I thought he had a lot to offer on the fitness side of the game. With the right people around him, bridging the gaps, I'm sure it would have worked. Given more time he could have added to the training plans, and he is a great organiser and facilitator. I think we all struggled with his role, and how it was meant to fit into the routines of a football club. What was he supposed to be doing? Was it about now or later? That was the problem – and I don't think Rupert Lowe knew what he wanted, either, to be frank. I was falling out with Rupert quite a lot by then. At first he didn't even make it plain whether Clive was on the staff, or just coming to gain experience. It was only later that I heard he was well rewarded.

But Clive certainly didn't cut across my position. I was the manager, and that was never in doubt. If anything, all I resent about his time with me at Southampton is the suggestion that I just wanted a cosy little cabal of coaching pals around me, and could not handle anyone who might challenge my opinions. Bottom line: I'm there to win football matches. If there are people that can help me do that, I will listen to them, and it doesn't matter who they are. I will bounce ideas off everybody, but at the end of the day I have to make my own mind up. It's not a case of feeling threatened by Clive or Velimir Zajec, more that a manager has to completely trust the opinions of those around him, and it takes time to build that relationship. You can't just parachute a guy in and the manager takes his word as gospel. He might not know what he is talking about.

Joe Jordan, who I worked with at Portsmouth and Tottenham Hotspur, was a manager; so was Jim Smith – and Dave Bassett, who came in at Southampton during the second season. At Queens Park Rangers, I brought in Steve Cotterill, who is a young coach with management experience. If I start losing, I'm going to get the sack anyway, and at Bournemouth, West Ham and Portsmouth I was replaced by a member of my staff, so the idea that I surround myself with unthreatening individuals is nonsense. I don't see

Arsène Wenger offering Pep Guardiola the assistant manager's job at Arsenal – and Guardiola isn't looking to be a number two anyway. That isn't how football works. I am prepared to work with players that are hard to handle, and my coaches are certainly not yes men.

I think part of the difficulty for Clive was that rugby was very much behind football in terms of technical progress. Some of the improvements that were considered quite radical in his old sport had been going on for years in his new one – specialist coaches, specialist training, some of the advances in fitness and nutrition. Guys like Sam Allardyce have been working with everything from acupuncturists and Chinese herbalists to sports psychologists for years, and football had been using specialist position coaches for decades. We didn't have goalkeeping coaches when I was a player – Ernie Gregory used to be a goalkeeper, but he never worked with them at West Ham – but that changed as the game progressed. Goalies didn't just go in goal during training. They went away with a great coach like Mike Kelly and worked on the specifics of their game. I cannot remember anyone saying a word to the goalkeeper at West Ham during my playing days, even if he let five through his legs – but football has moved on, just as English rugby did under Clive.

Clive left Southampton in August 2006, but by then I had already departed, too. A chance meeting between Frank Lampard Senior and Milan Mandaric in the directors' box at Fratton Park was about to get my south-coast roller-coaster ride moving again.

CHAPTER TWELVE

THE MAN WHO UNDERSTOOD THE DIAMOND FORMATION

26 November 2005. That was the day my return to Portsmouth became a reality. Chelsea came to Fratton Park and Frank Lampard Senior sat in the directors' box watching his son play. I think by then, both Milan Mandaric and I were regretting our decision to part the previous season. I had only been gone a year but he had already appointed, and sacked, two managers, and Joe Jordan was his caretaker. As for me, I hadn't been able to keep Southampton up and I knew I wasn't suited to another year with Rupert Lowe. We were increasingly falling out over even the smallest thing. Sure, I argued with Milan, too, but it felt different. We were mates and all forgotten the next day. The mood at Southampton just didn't feel right.

I had brought in Dave Bassett, the old Wimbledon manager, to start the new season. People might have seen the styles of our teams as very different, but I have always liked Dave. He's a common sense guy, someone who has strong opinions and isn't afraid to share them. I didn't want to change the way we played, but I thought Dave might be able to give us a bit more grit and organisation around our set plays. You need to mix it up a little more outside the Premier League, I think. Dave didn't really take much in the way of salary. He was happy to help out and he brought Dennis Wise, who was a class above in that division. I suppose Dave was more sceptical of Sir Clive and his ideas, though, which looking back wasn't helping harmony among the backroom staff.

After relegation, you look at everybody in a new light, to try to see what they will bring to the team in fresh circumstances – particularly players. A lad that looked out of his depth in Premier League football, might suddenly find his level and be very effective in the second tier. A physically strong player who lacked a little finesse, might now not be at a disadvantage. One guy we had our eye on was Kenwyne Jones. He had spent the previous season out on loan at Sheffield Wednesday and Stoke City, who were both outside the Premier League, and, at Wednesday in particular, had looked terrific. He had only played a handful of matches for us, and hadn't been too clever, but we thought perhaps this level would suit him.

We got our first shock in pre-season training when we did a bleep test and Kenwynne was beaten by Kevin Bond. Bleep tests are gruelling, but they are the best measurement of fitness. A player has to run between two points in a certain time – indicated by a bleep noise – speeding up as he gets more exhausted. It allows coaches to assess maximum oxygen intake. Kevin would have turned 50 the year he outran Kenwyne. He just pulled up, like a tired old racehorse. 'Keep going, Kenwyne, what have you stopped for?' I shouted.

'I'm tired, man,' he said.

'I know, Kenwyne,' I replied. 'That's the point of it. We have to find out how fit you are when you are tired.'

But there was no getting him going again. He'd just had enough. Later that summer we were playing Bournemouth in a pre-season friendly and he asked to come off.

'What's the problem, Kenwyne?' I said.

'It's too hot,' he said, shaking his head.

'Kenwyne,' I reminded him, as politely as I could in front of several thousand people. 'You're from Trinidad. This isn't even a warm day for you.'

He had all the tools – a great spring, good pace, and power in the air – but he was laid back to the point of semi-consciousness. He just looked like he would rather be on a beach somewhere. A lovely boy, very nice boy, but seemingly without any sort of drive. So am I surprised he went on to make a significant career as a Premier League footballer? Yes, you could say that.

Less of a shock was a young man who played his first game for me on 6 August 2005, as a 73rd-minute substitute against Wolverhampton Wanderers. Theo Walcott was only 16, but we knew even then he was going all the way. His success at Arsenal and with England did not surprise me at all.

I first came across Theo when he was about 12. Mike Osman, the comedian, got involved in setting up a television show that was going to take a few kids who were good footballers, and follow their progress over the next few years. He wanted me and Alan Ball to make guest appearances, doing some one-on-one coaching. He was a good judge, Mike, because two of the players were Theo Walcott and Adam Lallana, who has made over 200 appearances for Southampton. It would have been interesting had he seen the project through, but Mike is one of those chaps who gets good ideas but doesn't always take them to the end. So the show fell apart, and I next met Theo as a kid going through Southampton's youth ranks. He was on the right track even then – a smashing kid from a lovely family – and I had no worries at all introducing him to first-team football at such a young age. Southampton have always had a strong youth policy and had been working wonders with their academy, utilising a great talent scout called Malcolm Elias, who is now at Fulham. I had tracked the progress of that youth team all the way to the FA Youth Cup final, where they lost to Ipswich Town, despite being much the better side over two matches. Theo was on one wing, Nathan Dyer the other, and Gareth Bale, who was a year younger, was on the bench with Lallana. It was quite a team – there was a real conveyor belt of talent at Southampton, and there still is, by the sounds of it.

Theo's first start for us was at Leeds United, and it was Dave Bassett's idea to play him through the middle as a striker. He had always been a wide player in the youth team, and that was where I was going to use him, but Dave fancied him against their central defenders, and he was right. Theo was so good it was frightening. He scored after 25 minutes and could have had five – I haven't seen such a confident debut from a young man. One of their defenders was taken off because he was in such trouble against him. He absolutely ripped them to pieces. He came short, got it to feet and turned and ran at them. He spun in behind, and we played him in. He went past them like they had their legs tied together. He was unbelievable – you knew straight away that he had the ability to change the biggest games. People talk about him as if he hasn't got the football brain of a top player, but I think he's a very clever runner off the ball. He killed us with Arsenal in my last season at Tottenham Hotspur by bending his run, and I think he is a player who knows precisely what he is about. His final ball is sometimes not the best, but that often happens with a player who is exceptionally quick. Every left-back knows he is in for a game against him because he is so lightning quick.

Even with a talent like Theo, though, it was a struggle at Southampton. By the end of November we were mid-table. Nothing disastrous – a couple of wins and we would have been in the play-offs – but I was beginning to realise what I once had with Milan Mandaric. We didn't mix the same way at Southampton; we didn't have fun. And Portsmouth were in trouble, too. The fateful day they played Chelsea they were fourth from bottom, level on points with Everton, who everyone thought wouldn't be in that position for long. Soon, there was going to be a vacancy in the bottom three and Portsmouth were going to fill it. Milan was worried.

He had sacked his last manager, Alain Perrin, and the word was that Neil Warnock was going to get the job. I had been told Milan had as good as offered it and Neil had agreed. He was just waiting to finalise the contract. And then, that Saturday, Milan saw Frank at the Chelsea game. Portsmouth lost 2–0 and maybe he was feeling vulnerable. He began talking to Frank about me. Frank said he should ask me back. He said to Milan that I'd like that. 'I don't know,' said Milan. 'I'd like it too, but he'd never come back here now. We fell out. We don't talk any more. I think I'm finished here, Frank. We're going down. Unless you could persuade Harry to come back?'

So that night, Frank called me. I remember it, because we had played Wolverhampton Wanderers that day and Peter Knowles, who was my roommate on England Youth team trips many years before, had come over to see me. What an incredible life he'd had. Peter was a wonderfully gifted footballer, a forward with Wolves and prolific scorer, who had given it all up in 1969 at the age of 24 to be a Jehovah's Witness. Astonishing. Not least because in his playing days he was a lunatic. He was renowned for pranks. He drove me mad. I got stuck with him, really, because nobody else wanted to share his room. It was like being shacked up with Keith Moon from The Who. He was wild. Flash, too. He would sit on the ball, or beat his man and deliberately go back and beat him again. I remember him intentionally getting George Best sent off once, by tripping over his own feet. He had such talent, he would take the piss during matches. And then he went to Kansas City to play in a promotional league one summer, came back, and gave it all up for God. I hadn't seen him since, really. It was a nice surprise.

So that weekend, Frank called. He said he had been talking to Milan and Peter Storrie and they would like me to go back to Portsmouth. He said Milan thought I was the only person who could sort it out there. 'They'd love you back, Harry,' Frank told me.

I didn't have to think long about my reply. 'To be honest, I'd love to go back, Frank,' I told him. 'It hasn't really worked out at Southampton. It's difficult. Tell them to call me if they are interested.' Later that day, Peter Storrie made contact.

I arranged to meet Milan at his flat in Gunwharf Quay on Portsmouth Harbour. After all I had been through previously with the south coast clubs, the meeting was very hush-hush. Milan buzzed me in, and I parked my car underground, in the pitch black, and sneaked in up the lift at the back. 'I need an answer, Harry,' Milan told me, over a glass of wine. 'Because if you want the job, I've got to tell Neil Warnock that it's off.' I agreed in principle to go, but we still had to sort out my contract. Unfortunately, Milan trusted a friend of his, a newspaper man, with the secret, so the next day it was all over the papers. And that caused a fresh round of trouble.

Anyone who knows me understands what I am like with the public. Talk to me, and I'll talk back. I am not one of those people who is determined to be left alone. If we're in a lift, or a taxi, and you start the conversation, as long as it's polite or friendly, I won't ignore you. I meet football fans all the time. It doesn't matter what club they support, I'll always have a chat. Maybe that's why I hated all the confrontation around joining Southampton. It meant that when a person approached me in the street, I never knew whether there would be trouble. And I'm used to making friends. Now, I was being linked with a return to Portsmouth. What was I going to do? Lie? It was around that time that I was in an Italian restaurant with Sandra and bumped into Richard Hughes, who was a player at Portsmouth with me, and Eddie Howe, another pal, who is now the manager of Bournemouth. They came over for a chat and Richard asked me, straight out, if I was going back to Fratton Park. 'You never know, Richard,' I said. 'It's definitely a possibility. There's every chance.' That was enough. Richard likes a bet. Suddenly, there was money going on my return. I was 33-1, but the price came down quite sharply. And that was enough for the Football Association's compliance unit to get involved.

No bets traced back to me, but they did to Richard. I'm not going to deny what I told him that night. He's a friend. He asked me a straight question, I gave him a straight answer. What he then does with that information is his business. I certainly didn't tell him to put a bet on, and my friends know that I am as likely to change my mind as go through with any career move. On other occasions, I would have said there was every chance I was going to Leicester City, Newcastle United or Tottenham Hotspur (the first time I was asked) – yet I didn't take any of those jobs. Anyway, I like Richard a lot. Am I supposed to bury him, lead him up the garden path, tell him to get lost? I talk frankly to everybody. If a cabbie had asked me the same question that night, I wouldn't have lied.

If betting on managerial appointments is wrong, then ban it completely. Don't pretend it's fine unless you actually know the manager in question. Since when did having good information in a betting market become a crime? We all know people at football clubs or racing stables do it. The bookmakers quickly close the book if they suspect the punters know more than they do. Yet I ended up having to go before the FA, and Richard was quizzed as well. Milan was very supportive, but it dragged on far too long. In the end Brian Barwick, who was FA chairman at the time, got involved. He realised we had done nothing wrong.

Why did I go back to Portsmouth? I think, more than anything, I went back for Milan. We picked up where we left off, as if nothing had happened. I appreciated his faith in me, and he appreciated the gamble I was taking. 'You know there is going to be some aggro, Harry?' he told me. 'You know the fans are divided?'

I did. I knew I was hanging myself out to dry and there would be a group who would not accept me for going to Southampton, but I thought I could win them over with some good results. I always think that. 'I know the score, Milan,' I said. 'If I do no good, I'm dead. If I do no good, this is my last job in football.' Harry the gambler, that's me. I knew I was taking a big chance but I felt sure I could turn them round and get the fans off my back by keeping Portsmouth up. Fail, and I would get ten times the grief that would have been aimed at Neil Warnock in the same circumstances. I didn't mind that. They had loved me before, and they could love me again – as long as I got the results. Believe me, Saddam Hussein could have been a Premier League manager provided he kept winning. Had Milan given him the job, and he'd finished where I did that season, by the last match of the season the fans would have been singing, 'There's only one Saddam.'

I suppose my memories pushed me to take the risk and go back, too. I'd enjoyed my first time at Portsmouth so much – all but those last few weeks – that I just wanted a second bite. Portsmouth was nothing but ups for me, really. Winning the league to earn promotion, staying in the Premier League, working with great players; I had so many good feelings about the place, so much I was looking to rekindle.

Even so, I had put myself under real pressure, there was no doubt of that. It was only when I walked into the club that I realised the extent. The first day, Dejan Stefanović, a big Serbian centre-half who had been one of the last signings during my first spell, gave me the full rundown and told me he thought I was mad to return. 'This is not the team that you had before,' he said. 'This is the worst team that you will ever manage. All your players are gone. We've got nothing now. It's desperate.' He wasn't far wrong. In the year I had been away, the squad had changed hugely. From the last team I picked in November 2004, to the first I picked in December 2005, only five players started both games. I'd left a good team, I thought, but a lot of them had gone and been replaced by inferiors. My gut instinct was that we were in trouble.

Our first game was away at Tottenham Hotspur. It was strange, I can't deny that. Before, I could do no wrong: Milan had saved the club, but if we fell out, the fans were 100 per cent for me. Now, there were banners up branding me JUDAS, SCUM, along with a lot of abuse as I took my seat. Losing that first match 3–1 was certainly not a good start. As I walked away to boos and curses I knew this was the hardest job of my career.

The team wasn't good enough, and we had to do something about that fast. In the January transfer window, I bought Benjani for £4.1 million, Pedro Mendes, Sean Davis and Noé Pamarot from Tottenham for £7 million and took Wayne Routledge and Andrés D'Alessandro on loan. These weren't my first choices. We had originally tried to get Darren Anderton from Tottenham, but we couldn't match his contract. He had a deal that gave him parity with Tottenham's best paid player, meaning he had been getting rise after rise and was on an absolute fortune. I only wanted Mendes initially, but Daniel Levy drove his usual hard bargain, and they came as a job lot. Plus, Milan kept a typically tight budget – the only one we pushed out the boat for was Benjani.

The first game with our newly assembled squad was Everton at home. We lost 1–0. Next up, Birmingham City away. On the day of the game they were a point behind us with a match in hand. Birmingham won 5–0. It was scary. The three Tottenham men had barely played, and were so unfit they were going over with cramp early in the second half. This one couldn't run, that one ceased up. No matter how much a player trains, nothing prepares him for the sheer physicality of a match – but we had no time to ease them in.

I sat feeling powerless as Birmingham murdered us. They didn't have a bad team at all: Matthew Upson, Jermaine Pennant, Stan Lazaridis, Muzzy Izzet, Emile Heskey and Chris Sutton started; David Dunn and Mikael Forssell were on the bench. By the first week in March they were five points clear, still with a game in hand. We were struggling to gel. West Bromwich Albion were in 17th place and they were eight points ahead of us. We looked doomed. I had done all I could in the transfer window, but we needed ten players not five.

Milan had really pulled up for Benjani, who we had signed from Auxerre in France. He was a club record signing but couldn't score a goal if his life depended on it. His saving grace was that I have never seen a boy work so hard. He never stopped running. He would terrify defenders with his awesome athletic ability, but when it came to the fateful moment in front of goal he had more chance of finding the hot-dog stall outside than the net. I used to say that we had to alert Southampton Airport whenever we trained, but the joke was beginning to wear a little thin. I swear one morning we had more balls bobbling around the M27 than we did on the training pitch. Yet the fans loved him from the start. Sure, he couldn't score – but they could see the work he was putting in. They are grafters down in Portsmouth, and they like their players to be grafters, too.

Yet, suddenly, as can happen, it all clicked. Sometimes you just need that change in fortune to gain momentum, and on 11 March it happened. We were leading Manchester City at home, and playing reasonably well, when with seven minutes to go, Richard Dunne equalised. Typical. Here we go again. And then, with the last kick of the match in injury time, Pedro Mendes scored our winner from twenty-five yards. From there, our season changed: D'Alessandro hit form at the perfect time, Benjani was a nuisance, our Tottenham lads were fit and able, the remainder of my old Portsmouth team dug in. We scored seven goals in our next two away games, against West Ham United and Fulham, then we drew with Arsenal. It was tight, but we stayed up with a game to spare. We won at Wigan Athletic and Benjani scored, bringing to an end a run of fourteen goalless games for him. We were a goal down with 27 minutes to go, but then Benjani equalised and Matthew Taylor scored from the penalty spot. I remember looking up to Milan and Peter Storrie because Birmingham were at home to Newcastle United and could have taken it to the last day, when we were set to face Liverpool, but that match finished goalless and they gave me the thumbs-up. I went to the supporters and they were going wild. They were on my side again. It was a great day for us.

Birmingham, incredibly, with all that talent, went down. But, unbeknownst to me, Milan had secured a little survival bonus of his own that day – and after the summer Portsmouth would never be the same again.

Milan hadn't changed one bit. He was all over the running of the club, occasionally infuriatingly so, but always good company. I was Harry again, not Redknapp, as I'd been at Southampton. There were good days and bad days, but I don't think any manager and chairman had the rows, or the healthy relationship, that we did. I've heard Milan slaughter people at the club, and he would try that with me, too – the difference was that I'd give as good as I got. And then he'd forget the whole thing. 'Where are we going for dinner?' he'd say, and there would be more food, more wine, another row, and we'd start all over the next day as if nothing had happened. As close as we were, he kept one secret to himself, though – he was selling the club.

It was January, a month into my second term, when he told me. 'Harry, there are some people I need you to meet,' he said, 'they want to buy into Portsmouth.' There was no mention of a takeover at this stage. Milan made it sound as if they were just investors. I went along to the Marriott hotel in Portsmouth, and waited to be called into a room. When I entered, there was a party of Russian guys sitting around the table. Milan had told me to talk positively but, again, faced with a direct question, I wasn't going to lie. What did I think of the team, they asked. 'It's bad,' I told them. 'Actually, it's terrible. It's going to be very difficult to stay up.' Nobody could say the Gaydamak family were roped in under false pretenses the way I laid it on the line. I think I even told them that if we went down it would be very difficult to return. I certainly wasn't guaranteeing Premier League football next season. 'If they are coming in,' I thought, 'I want them to know that we need investment.' I hadn't met these people and I wasn't going to try to fool them. Deep down, I probably wanted to carry on the old way too, with Milan. My speech did not deter them, though, because within weeks Alexandre Gaydamak had bought 50 per cent of the club.

I can't say I was happy when Milan told me the long-term plan. I had basically gone back to work with him and here he was informing me that Sacha was going to be the new owner. The 50 per cent deal was only stage one. The Gaydamak family was going to buy the remaining half of the club in the summer. I wasn't sure I wanted to work for them at all. After one defeat, Sacha arrived at our training ground and fixed me with an accusing look. 'Mr Redknapp,' he said, 'why does this team not try hard?'

'They do try hard, Mr Gaydamak,' I replied, 'they're just not good enough. And you're insulting me if you say that my teams don't try.'

In the meantime, I heard they had been speaking to John Gregory about my job. An agent was touting John around and had been given quite a lot of encouragement by Portsmouth, apparently. Six weeks into my new job and I was already thinking I had made another error. Suddenly, the club was going to be sold and I would be working for strangers again. I felt in limbo. This was not what I had envisaged at all. Milan collected his bonus from the new owners when Portsmouth secured Premier League football, and left me to my fate.

That summer, I flew out to Tel Aviv in Israel with Peter Storrie to meet our new owners and discuss the future. 'I'd like you to bring a man to the club who understands the tactics of football,' Mr Gaydamak said. 'Very well,' I replied, 'but what do you think Tony Adams and Joe Jordan are doing here?' I had only just given Tony a job. He was a player and a leader that I greatly admired – very conscientious and I thought he would bring us a different coaching dynamic.

'I've got my own staff, Mr Gaydamak,' I insisted. 'I don't need anybody.'

'I would like you to meet this man,' he continued. 'He is a very clever man. He understands the diamond formation.'

'Well, that's very interesting,' I said. 'The diamond formation, eh? I think I saw an under-11 team playing that in the park last Sunday. It looked very complicated – are you sure our players will be able to cope?'

But heavy sarcasm was getting me nowhere. He was my boss now. It was an argument I was never going to win. So while

Gaydamak entered another round of meetings with Peter Storrie, I was driven to meet the man who understood the diamond formation. Avram Grant seemed a nice enough bloke, and he was clearly well connected. When I returned, Mr Gaydamak laid it on the line: 'Roman Abramovich is a very good friend of Mr Grant,' he said, 'and he would like him to have a job in England.'

'Well, if he's so keen, why doesn't he give him a job at Chelsea?' I asked.

'No,' said Gaydamak. 'He wants us to give him a job. He wants him to gain experience of English football. If we employ him, if we let Avram work at Portsmouth, he will let us take maybe one or two Chelsea players on loan. He has asked is if we want Glen Johnson. Do you like him?'

'I love him,' I said. 'If we can get Johnson, that's great. But what would Mr Grant do?'

'Mr Redknapp,' said Sacha, 'it doesn't matter what Mr Grant does. Do whatever you want with him, use him as you wish. Sit him in an office, take him to the training ground; it is up to you. But it helps me, and it helps the club, if we give him a job.'

So Avram joined the staff. And we had a great time together.

People won't believe me when I say that, but Avram Grant is a really good guy. He's funny, he's good company, and we have remained friends. Obviously, the way he came into English football is peculiar. I don't know what the link is, why he has the patronage of Abramovich, why Abramovich is so keen to help him find work – but Portsmouth were not the only club to be told there could be benefits in giving Avram a job. What's behind all that? I don't know. Maybe they're all just good friends. It wasn't a series of relationships that I could ever get close to understanding as an outsider – what was in it for them all. Sacha Gaydamak is not an easy man to get to know, so I just looked at Avram's appointment as a way of getting good loan players for Portsmouth – and Glen Johnson was a brilliant loan signing for us. There was no great hardship in having Avram on the staff because I never thought it would be anything beyond a short-term appointment. I always knew once he had gained a little knowledge of English football he would end up at Chelsea. I don't think anyone, other than family, is closer to Abramovich than Avram. He trusts him on football, completely, and when he went to Chelsea as director of football the following summer, I rather suspected it would not be long before he stepped into José Mourinho's shoes. I wasn't sorry to see him go because I never regarded him as a vital part of our operation, but, just like with Sir Clive Woodward, we never had a moment's disagreement. He made contributions, he never interfered, he was as good as gold. And, yes, he does understand the diamond formation.

I did not get close to Sacha Gaydamak, our new owner, but I was very aware of what people were saying about him. He was an extremely wealthy man, perhaps in the Abramovich league, and he certainly made it clear that he had big plans for Portsmouth. We were going to get a new stadium, based on the Allianz Arena in Munich, and the team would be getting an upgrade to fall in line with those ambitions. The message from the owner was that Portsmouth were in the big league and were going to have a go – so we had a go.

I often read that we spent fortunes in Gaydamak's first year at Portsmouth, but that isn't right. I think our biggest signing that first summer was Niko Kranjčar for £3.5 million. The rest were bargains: Sol Campbell was a free transfer and dropped £50,000 a week from what he was on at Arsenal; Kanu was a free from West Bromwich Albion, too. I think Andy Cole would have cost us £1 million in bonuses if we won the league, the World Cup and the Ashes; Lauren cost £500,000; David James £1.2 million – we improved the squad but we weren't in among the truly big spenders. And they were great value, those boys. I don't want to take anything away from the other players, but I have always maintained that David James won us the FA Cup in 2008. He was exceptional in every round – and without him we might not even have made it out of round three. He had an unbelievable game at Ipswich Town in our first game, when we should have lost but ended up winning 1–0. Then in the fifth round we got murdered at Preston North End, David saved a penalty, and we won through an own goal in the last minute. And no team wins away at Manchester United, as we did in the quarter-finals, without the goalkeeper having a blinder. We went all the way to Wembley and David conceded one goal, against Plymouth Argyle, in the fourth round. He was fantastic for us, time after time, and the best worker I have ever seen, an absolute perfectionist, fit as a fiddle – you had to drag him off the training field. He stayed behind for at least an hour every day – Portsmouth should have produced the next generation of great young goalkeepers with him as the inspiration. And, yes, David would make the odd mistake, but he would also make saves that nobody else could reach. He pulled one off like that at Preston, late on. Take that away and we wouldn't have made it to Wembley.

Kanu was another who proved brilliant value. Despite our summer signings, when the 2006–07 season was about to start we had a striker crisis. Benjani was struggling with injury and so was Svetoslav Todorov. I was going through my contacts book, frantic, when I thought of Kanu. He had been playing for West Brom, who had got relegated the season before. Tony Adams wasn't impressed. 'You can't take him,' he said. 'He was finished three years ago. I've spoken to the medical people at Arsenal – they say no way.' But he didn't look finished to me on the odd occasions I had seen him play. He looked as if he had more talent in his big toe than half the strikers in the Premier League have in both feet. I phoned Bryan Robson, the West Brom manager. 'How was he, Bryan?' I asked.

'Different class,' Bryan said. 'He was just unlucky he couldn't keep us up, and now we've had to let him go. But he was brilliant for us.'

I decided to ignore Tony and eventually tracked Kanu down.

'How are you doing, what are you doing?'

'Nothing, boss.'

'Have you been training, have you kept fit?'

'I went over the park for a run, you know.'

'How often?'

'Yesterday.'

It wasn't a promising start. He'd had one run all summer – and I wasn't convinced he'd had that. But we weren't in a position to be picky.

'Do you want to play this season?'

He said he did. So he came down to train with us. The very first day, he arrived with his agent to sign a contract. I told him we couldn't do a deal without seeing him in a match first, so I put him in the reserves against Cardiff City. He scored an absolute world-class goal, bent into the top corner, exactly as he aimed it, but after

60 minutes he was finished. Exhausted. Had to come off. Still, we could work on that. We did the contract the next day.

Our first game of the season was on the following Saturday, against Blackburn Rovers. It took Kanu three days to properly recover from the Cardiff match, he had a light session on the Friday, and I named him as sub. The doctor said Todorov could last 45 minutes, tops, so I had Kanu earmarked for half-time. As it was Todorov kept going on for nearly an hour and put us 1–0 up. Then Kanu came on. He was a revelation. We won 3–0 and he scored two and missed a penalty for what would have been a thirty-minute hat-trick. We went to Manchester City midweek, drew 0–0 and he just about lasted 90 minutes, and then it was to Middlesbrough away, live on television, Monday night. He was stunning. We won 4–0, he scored twice again, messed the defenders about as if they were babies, and for his goal in the second half he went on a zigzag run from the halfway line, made as if to shoot with his great big left foot, let the goalkeeper dive and then deftly went round him, putting the ball into an empty net. Bryan Robson was right. He was a different class.

We couldn't fly into Southampton Airport after the game, so we came back to Bournemouth, which was where I found Kanu, slumped on the seats by the luggage carousel. By now he had earned his own nickname at the club. 'You all right, King?' I asked.

'Gaffer, I can't move,' he said.

I thought he was joking. 'Right, get your bags,' I told him. 'We've got to go.'

'I told you,' he said. 'I can't move.'

Our doctor reckoned his body had gone into mild shock with the exhaustion. We had to lift him up – it took a few of us – put him in a wheelchair and get him out to his car that way. Then we hoisted him into the passenger seat and our masseur drove him home. He was one of those players that had to be handled differently. He used to ring me at 11.30 p.m. every Sunday, because he knew I'd be in bed, and leave a message on my answering machine. 'Hello, Gaffer, it's the King. I won't be training tomorrow ...' and there would follow that week's excuse. He had an upset tummy, his knee was hurting, he just don't feel good, his calves have tightened up. Every week, without fail. It was fair to say he didn't like Mondays.

He still lived in London and, basically, he wasn't going to schlep to Portsmouth just for a warm-down. We would see him the next day, when training got serious. Some players are like that. You have to apply different rules. Paul Merson was another that needed kidding, so was Sol Campbell. Sol liked a massage rather than training some days, but I could live with that – providing the player was doing it on Saturday. They knew, if they put it in, they could get a little special treatment. I didn't have a problem with it. Never have. With some players it will always be about the Saturday. Merson, or Kanu, couldn't be bothered through the week, but they would come in on Saturday and win the game. Do that, and I won't care if you feel a bit stiff and cry off on Tuesday – and I think most managers are the same. I am quite certain that if Ryan Giggs tells David Moyes he would rather have a rub down than train, he will be cut a little slack. Those players have been around. The manager knows they are not trying to dodge training. It is about peaking at the right time, and Giggs will know how to get the best out of his body by now. Saturday is when you keep your job in football. If you can't get Saturday right, it doesn't matter whether Monday to Friday was fantastic – you are going to be out of work. A manager has to know his players. It is about getting the best out of them in matches – and the different methods you use to achieve that are really immaterial. Kanu was probably the greatest example of a player that needed to be nurtured in a unique way. He would mope around all week, and then have a day when he blew the opposition away on his own. And for a player who was finished in 2003 according to Arsenal, he was still turning out for Portsmouth in the 2011–12 season. Kanu was another who was instrumental in our FA Cup win, scoring the only goal of the game in the semi-final and the final.

So we got good value, at first, for very little expenditure. I remember Sacha even joking with me about it. 'Everyone tells me you like to spend money,' he said, 'but you don't. Why? What is the matter? Are you not well?' I think he was impatient for some big-name arrivals, but I wanted value. Glen Johnson eventually cost us £4 million – but we did have him for the first year on loan. And we sold him to Liverpool for £17.5 million.

That is what I truly do not understand about Portsmouth's financial plight. Yes, we did invest in the team – but the money we made on those players by comparison was enormous. Lassana Diarra cost us £5.5 million in January 2008 and we sold him to Real Madrid less than a year later for £18.8 million. I've heard we paid big wages. Well, I've got my doubts about that, too, but even if we did, we didn't pay £13.3 million in one year. Diarra would need to be earning in the region of £300,000 per week for him to have cost us a penny. It doesn't make sense. Sulley Muntari was £7.1 million, a club record, when we took him in 2007, but he was sold to Inter Milan for £13.6 million two years on. I bought Jermain Defoe for £6 million from Tottenham and then took him back there later for £15.75 million. From Portsmouth's point of view that was brilliant business. I cannot comprehend how they ended up in so much debt. The wages were decent, yes, but not crazy. I think Glen Johnson earned three times as much at Liverpool as he ever did with us. The only deal I recall losing money on was John Utaka. I went to Rennes a few times to watch him and he cost £7 million – but he never really hit the same form for us. I think he went to Montpellier for roughly £3.5 million after I left – but it still wasn't the sort of loss to bankrupt a club. Every manager makes the odd mistake – buying players isn't an exact science.

One of my best deals was getting Sylvain Distin out of Manchester City on a free transfer – although how that did not end up in the newspapers, I will never know. He was going to be out of contract in the summer of 2007, but I rated him very highly and wanted to get the deal done before the others got a sniff. It was the dead of winter and Peter Storrie and I arranged to meet him at a hotel in Manchester. We were paranoid about the news leaking out, so I sneaked in the back way, slipped up to a room we had booked under another name and began talking to him about coming to Portsmouth. At which point, all the fire alarms went off. 'Don't worry about that, Sylvain,' I told him. 'It's probably a drill, or some kids messing about.' But it wouldn't stop. The next thing we knew, there were hotel staff banging on the doors. 'Everybody out, everybody out – this isn't a drill!' Now we had to go. I wanted to keep our meeting secret, but it wasn't worth having to jump from a blazing building to do so. So that's where we had our hush-hush talks – in the hotel car park surrounded by about eight hundred people, some of whom at least must have been wondering what Portsmouth's manager was doing with Manchester City's centre-half. We stole a march on everybody that day, though – we took Sylvain on a free and later sold him to Everton for £5 million. He's still a great player, as quick as lightning, and his partnership with Sol Campbell was exceptional for us.

And the owners were right behind all of it, all the way. Sacha even helped with one of our biggest transfers. We got Diarra from Arsenal because Sacha's sister was going out with his agent. 'Mr Redknapp, we can get Diarra,' he said. 'Do you like him?' 'He's a fantastic player, Mr Gaydamak,' I said, 'but we'll never get him. Why would he come to Portsmouth from Arsenal? No chance.' The next I knew, there he was. Sacha just went out and did the deal.

People might think I was in his ear all day asking for players, but it was quite the opposite. Sacha wanted to be successful and build a team every bit as much as I did. As far as I knew, we were going to have a new stadium, a new team and the best training ground in the country. I remember attending a big launch in London, a huge presentation, all very secret, about the future of the club. The architects unveiled their model and there were gasps in the room. It was a floating island stadium in the docklands area, all lit up like a spaceship – and that was where Portsmouth were going to play. We were buying two hundred acres of land near Fareham for the new training facility – I had to attend that meeting, too. Sacha even selected a committee of six – players and coaches – to advise on what would be best for us. Of course, all this meant was that David James would turn up in a car made of wheat and you had to listen to him banging on for an hour about wind turbines and carbon footprints. By the end of it, we just agreed to whatever he said just to shut him up. He could have wanted to put the turbines in front of goal to blow the ball away for all I know. But everything was going to be the best – a better stadium than Arsenal, a better training ground than Tottenham. He bought all the land around Fratton Park, too. When people at the club told us about Gaydamak's background there was never any suggestion he would not carry forward this investment. It was a family business, and back in Israel the Gaydamaks owned the basketball team, the hockey team, and Ossie Ardiles managed their football club. They had property, they had oil interests, companies on several continents, we heard. I really don't know, as a silly old football manager, what I was supposed to do about clarifying these promises.

The critics say I should have been more cautious, seen through it all. But how would that have worked? If your owner comes to you and says he can get an outstanding player out of Arsenal, and then he gets that player, what are you supposed to do? Deny it has happened? Not play him, just in case? If you work for a company and they send you to do a job abroad, you don't ask to check the books to make sure they can cover the airfare. You take them at their word. I had absolutely no reason to believe Mr Gaydamak could not make good on his promises and ambitions, just as Arsène Wenger places his faith in the truthfulness of the board at Arsenal, and José Mourinho believes Roman Abramovich can afford to pay the wages. The manager does what the owner wishes. If he is asked to work within a limited budget, he does so; if he is required to spend more to achieve success, he does that, too. I did not spend a single penny at Portsmouth that I wasn't confident was covered. The crisis set in after I left when, as I understand it, the Gaydamaks' circumstances changed during the financial crisis and the banks started to call in their loans.

I believed in their project, though. And when I was offered a job at Newcastle United in January 2008, I turned it down. This was before we won the FA Cup, before we played in Europe, or made some of our biggest signings. I can't say I wasn't tempted – but in the end what we had going at Portsmouth seemed bigger than anything Newcastle could offer, and I decided it wasn't for me.

It was after Sam Allardyce had left, and I was contacted by Paul Kemsley, a former director of Tottenham who is a friend of Mike Ashley, the Newcastle owner. He asked to meet me about the vacancy, and I went to his office, where he spoke to me along with Tony Jimenez, another of Mike's friends. Mike thought if he contacted me directly he would contravene Football Association rules, but I told Portsmouth about the Newcastle offer anyway. I asked for a couple of days to think about it. Don't get me wrong, I think Newcastle is a great club – but I couldn't see myself moving the entire family up there, and I thought Portsmouth were matching them step for step in terms of ambition. I had a good team, a good life – all I would benefit from was an improved contract. I didn't think it was worth it. We had played Newcastle away two months earlier and demolished them, 4–1. I didn't see them as a big club, the way I could see the potential in Tottenham some years later (although I nearly turned that move down, too). I spoke to Peter Storrie at the training ground on the Saturday morning and told him I was staying.

Would it have made a difference had I talked to Mike directly? Maybe. The owner of a club can sell you his ambitions more passionately. Paul and Tony did their best, but although the money was good it wasn't life-changing – not like living in Newcastle would have been for me. I appreciated it was a big challenge, reviving one of England's great clubs, and when I called Paul on the same Saturday I could tell by his voice that he had several thousand reasons to want me to be Newcastle manager. He likes a bet, Paul, and I got the impression he was very confident I would be taking the job. 'Fucking hell, Harry,' he said. 'Don't do this to me.' 'Sorry, Paul,' I insisted. 'I just don't want to go.' 'But, Harry, I've done my bollocks here ...' I couldn't help that. And I don't regret my decision for one instant.

That was the season we won the FA Cup, beating Cardiff City 1–0. I know on my CV this stands as the highlight of my career but, believe me, I'm as proud, if not prouder, of other achievements: keeping Portsmouth in the Premier League, winning promotion with Bournemouth, getting Tottenham into the Champions League. I think these are every bit as special as my big day at Wembley, and success in the lottery of a cup competition.

Not that it wasn't wonderful. The elite clubs are so powerful now that very few managers get a chance to win one of the big prizes, so to do that was obviously very special. Beating Manchester United away in the quarter-finals was a memorable day, too. They had a good team out – Cristiano Ronaldo, Paul Scholes, Wayne Rooney, Carlos Tevez – but we deserved our win, from a penalty by Sulley Muntari. It meant I had knocked Manchester United out of the FA Cup with three clubs – Bournemouth, West Ham United and Portsmouth. I'm proud of that, too.

We beat West Brom in the semi-final on 5 April, and then it was back to Wembley the following month to play Cardiff, the first Welsh team to reach the final since they were last there, in 1927. The players were nervous. We had some big-match experience in the side – Kanu had won the Champions League, UEFA Cup,

Premier League and FA Cup – but for many of the others this was the game of their lives. On the night before, to ease the tension, I took the players to a little Italian restaurant in Henley. I booked it out and ordered in a karaoke machine for later. I'll never forget Hermann Hreidarsson, our Icelandic left-back, turning up in a full Elvis Presley outfit and bringing the house down. He did the greatest impression. I'd asked Kenny Lynch, an old mate, to do a few gags for the boys later and, after watching Hermann, he turned to me and said, 'How am I meant to follow that?' Hermann had the lot – the Elvis wig, the white suit, the gold chains, the glasses, the moves – the only trouble was his voice was horrendous, but that just made it even funnier. Hermann used to live near me in Poole and, when him and his wife had their friends over from Iceland, they would always start a sing-song in our local restaurant. They were great fun.

Sometimes preparation is about more than just a tactics board. That karaoke night completely relaxed us and, despite the slender scoreline, we were well worth our victory the next day.

So, even without my friend Milan, I had a wonderful run at Portsmouth the second time around. In fact, the only sour note concerned events happening off the field. By 2007 I was the subject of a criminal investigation, but a year earlier, the BBC news programme *Panorama* had linked my name to an investigation into corruption in football. What a load of rubbish it was. I was accused of tapping up Andy Todd of Blackburn Rovers, and they suggested that Kevin Bond was taking backhanders to make certain transfers happen. It was an absolute farce. I wanted to sue the BBC when the programme was broadcast, but those things only end up dragging on and becoming a lot of time, money and hassle, so eventually I let it go. I know Sir Alex Ferguson didn't speak to the BBC for years when they made damaging accusations about his son, but that's not my style. I couldn't blame the sports guys for something *Panorama* did – but that doesn't mean I wasn't upset by it.

Again, I got dragged in because I was trying to do somebody a favour. Kevin called me and said that Peter Harrison, a football agent he knew, wanted to come down to meet me. He had a guy who was buying his business for millions and he wanted to show him that he had contacts in football. I didn't know Peter all that well, but Kevin spoke for him, so I didn't see the problem. Kevin said Peter and his investor had arranged a meeting with Mark Hughes, the Blackburn Rovers manager, because we were playing on the Saturday, and wanted to set up one with me for the same Friday, 7 April 2006. I said Friday was out of the question. We had training, then the usual press conferences, and I had to plan for the match. It was my busiest day of the week. Kevin came back on and said the guy sounded really desperate. He only wanted five minutes of my time. We arranged that Kevin would take the meeting and I would just pop by. How much harm could that do? Plenty, as it turned out. Harrison came in and Kevin had a meeting with him, and his business partner Knut auf dem Berge, who we now know was an undercover reporter working for *Panorama*, and the architect of the whole thing. They sat in the canteen in full view of where the players go after training – so that's how underhand and furtive it was. I came over and Peter started talking to me about going to watch some of the matches at the 2006 World Cup. They were going to fly some managers over, and would I be interested? I was nodding along, yeah, sure, not even listening, really. And then he asked me what I thought of Andy Todd. I said he wasn't bad. If he was a free transfer he could be worth pursuing. And that was it. I had no more to do with Harrison or Auf dem Berge. He wasn't asking for payment, there was no suggestion I wanted anything out of the deal. I got up and left and went on with my business, never giving it a second thought. And then, some weeks later, I got a letter saying that I was on *Panorama*, that I was being filmed and that what I said about Todd constituted an illegal approach. What, telling an agent that I thought his player was OK? If that's illegal, half of football should be banned. Conversations like that happen all the time.

It was Kevin who ended up the real loser. After I left they started talking to him about doing all our business through them. Kevin said they could come to some arrangement, but if you listen it is the people from *Panorama* making all the running.

Kevin had left Portsmouth and was a coach at Newcastle United at the time the programme aired, and it ended up costing him his job. Yet if I thought for one second that he was taking bungs, he wouldn't have worked with me again. What I saw on that programme was Harrison and Auf dem Berge making proposals, and Kevin being too nice to tell them where to go. Not because he's a crook, but because Peter Harrison had kidded him that this guy was going to buy his business for millions, and Kevin did not want to spoil that by making a scene. Kevin said he knew there was something fishy but didn't want to be confrontational. He said it was like when you meet someone on holiday and say you're happy to stay in touch but have no intention of seeing them again. I have known Kevin since he was a schoolboy. He's the sort of guy that doesn't want to offend, doesn't want to rock the boat and is happy with a quiet life. He'll say his piece in staff meetings, and he's a damn good coach, but he's not the sort for confrontation. He's just a lovely, family man – and as straight as they come.

I used to argue with people about Bobby Moore and the alleged stolen bracelet in 1970, because I knew the real man. Steal a bracelet from a jeweller's in Colombia? Bobby? Our World Cup-winning captain? Are you sure? If someone put a £1000 watch in front of him and said he could have it for £1, he wouldn't take it if he thought it was crooked. People were always coming around the training ground at West Ham with hooky gear. One week it would be Slazenger jumpers, the next Italian shoes, and all the lads would buy them – but not Bobby. Kevin's the same. He was too naïve to see the set-up, and too polite to tell this stranger where to go. As he said, it was like one of those occasions when you meet people on holiday and they want to stay in touch. Maybe they're not your cup of tea. But you don't say that: you exchange phone numbers and smile and are very polite, and then forget it. Why cause offence? Yes, Kevin could just have told the pair of them to get stuffed – but he thought that might have ruined Peter's business and they would only have tried to convince him otherwise. He wanted them gone. So he played along, waved them goodbye and did not follow it up. That is the key for me. If Kevin had really been after a bung, he would have made contact again, tried to pursue the relationship. Yet his contact with Harrison and Auf dem Berge ends that day. He actually wasn't interested at all.

I felt terrible for Kevin that he had to leave Newcastle. He was assistant manager to Glenn Roeder, and the club simply did not stand by him. I was luckier with the backing I received at Portsmouth. The people at the club knew the reality, and I think most people in football did, too. I have never had a problem employing Kevin since, and he went with me to Tottenham and Queens Park Rangers.

As for bungs, generally, I have heard a lot of chatter in my career but very little evidence. I do not believe the practice has ever been widespread in football. Not now, not at any time. Put it like this: I'm married, I've got a lovely wife, a lovely family, a lovely house; I've got seven grandchildren, one son has been a professional footballer, the other is also very successful, so why would I risk all of that, even for £200,000? If I was caught, if the news leaked out, I would be finished – my professional life would be finished, my family life would be finished – I could go to prison. Why would I risk that when I don't need the money anyway? I've had good jobs, I've been well rewarded, I'm not greedy. If I was motivated solely by money, I would have taken some of the bigger jobs that I have been offered – I would be the manager of Ukraine now.

How could I take a bung knowing that, in one phone call, a person could ruin me and put every aspect of my life at risk? I would have to be mad. I don't understand what my motivation would be. I think rumours get put around by jealous people, or agents who have got the hump that you aren't doing business with them, and then others, who haven't a clue how football works, pick up the gossip and spread it. The amount of people I've had poring through my financial records, if I had anything to hide it would have come out by now. Yet still the rumours persist. I've heard it said that there was a sinister reason I left West Ham, implying that I was taking a sneaky cut from transfers – but Lord Stevens looked at Rio Ferdinand's move to Leeds United, and every other transfer from that time, and there was never a case to answer.

My son Mark wanted to be a football agent and early on he had a couple of very high-profile young players – Steven Gerrard and Rio Ferdinand. Gerrard didn't concern me, but the first thing I said to him when I heard about Rio is that I wasn't doing any business with him at West Ham. 'I told you I didn't want you to do this,' I lectured, 'and there is no way I am sitting across from my own son discussing one of my players, or having you go into a meeting with the chairman at my club. It leaves me open to all kinds of accusations. It's not happening.' Mark ended up losing Rio, partly because I was adamant that I wouldn't enter any negotiations over the player while my son was his representative. Then Gérard Houllier recommended Steven Gerrard to another agent and, suddenly, Mark was out of business. I can't say I was unhappy; I couldn't leave myself vulnerable to criticism like that.

That's how I feel about bungs. How could I live, waking up each morning wondering whether this was the day my secret was going to come out? How could I walk into the dressing room and try to command the respect of the players, if I knew an agent could tell his client that I siphoned money from a deal? No manager could cope with that. He would be at risk of blackmail. Do it once and where would it end? You wouldn't be able to select the best team because your whole life would be spent trying to avoid getting found out. 'Pick my player or I'll go to the papers about what we paid you.' How could you live like that? How could you carry on knowing that if an agent was skint, or down on his luck, he could make a fortune by selling a story about you?

Do I speak to agents? Of course I speak to agents. Do I use agents? All the time. But not just one. I'm not loyal. I'll use anybody that can bring me a player, set up a deal and help me improve my team. I find some agents just take; others are grafters. They come up with a name you might not have thought possible, or show you talent you didn't know existed. I watch football whenever I can, but I can't be across every match in every league. So if an agent has a player who is worth a look, I don't care who he is, I'll listen to him. Yet, once I've had that conversation, I pass the deal on to the executives at the club. As I mentioned earlier, anyone who thinks the manager has control of the money these days is mistaken. If an agent did want to do a deal on the sly, he would be more likely to go to the chairman or the chief executive – they do the business now, not us.

I remember signing Patrik Berger for Portsmouth in 2003 after we had been promoted to the Premier League. Milan and Peter Storrie went off with his agent, Patrik and I went to have pizza – for four hours. We got into the restaurant at 1 p.m. and it was 5 p.m. when Peter came through the door and announced the deal was done. That is the way with modern transfers. He could just as easily have arrived and told us it was all off – it is out of the manager's hands these days. I can't remember the last time I told a player we had signed him – he gets the news from his agent, and I get mine from the chief executive. The only time I was ever involved in transfer negotiations was when I was first at Bournemouth. I did the deals with our secretary – I was earning £80 per week and I would argue over whether a player was worth £70. I remember those early contracts: big money was a £1,000 signing-on fee, spread over instalments of £250 over four years. But even then, once Brian Tiler came in as chief executive, the procedure changed. From Brian to Peter Storrie, to Daniel Levy and now Phil Beard at QPR, it is the club that controls the purse strings these days.

That is not to say I never get involved – more that, in my experience, if I'm needed it usually means something has gone very wrong. Take Amdy Faye. He was a Willie McKay player that I bought during my first spell at Portsmouth in 2003. He was with Auxerre in France when I saw them against Arsenal the season before. I made Faye their best player by a long way, so was delighted when Willie called and said he was available. He had a year on his contract but had fallen out hugely with the manager, Guy Roux. They were arguing all the time, but the club were still reluctant to get rid of him because it was very close to the start of the season. I said I would need to see him in training first. 'You're mad, he's in dispute with the club, he's not a free agent,' said Willie. 'He belongs to Auxerre, he's still under contract – he can't just go training with Portsmouth.' 'I'm not interested then,' I told him. He got the message and said he would see what he could do.

Willie is one of those grafting agents, so he came up with a plan. Faye was suspended for the first game of the new season, so he informed Auxerre he was ill and brought him over to us. We were pre-season training in Scotland when Faye arrived. After one session Teddy Sheringham came over to me. 'Who's that?' he asked. 'He's different class.' And he was. An imposing, tall midfield player; aggressive, a good passer, never gave the ball away. Everyone could see in an instant that he was a talent. He did two sessions and then we had a friendly with Kilmarnock. I decided to play him. Some of the staff were worried in case he was spotted, but by then I knew he was for us, and wanted to see how he fitted in with the rest of the team. Willie being Willie he immediately phoned up just about every club in the country to get them along to watch him, just in case there was a better deal going. I had Amdy down on the team-sheet as 'Andy Henri', but it made no difference. The world and his wife were there. By half-time we were leading 5–0 and Amdy was our Rolls-Royce. All my instincts confirmed, I took him off, but it was too late. Now the word was out. The following day at the hotel we were knee deep in faxes from other clubs – Middlesbrough were particularly persistent. I read one, sent directly to Amdy. It promised to top whatever Portsmouth were offering. Meanwhile, our negotiations were dragging on because Auxerre were asking for £3 million. I got hold of the girl at the hotel reception, I spoke to the manager: 'No more faxes for Mr Faye. He needs his rest and is not to be disturbed with any more messages.'

We had another friendly on the Saturday, but I was not going to chance him again in that. I flew back to Bournemouth and left Jim Smith and Andy Awford, our chief scout, in charge of Amdy. By now, we had moved him to a hotel on the south coast. 'Just watch him,' I said. 'Go and see him lunchtime, spend the day with him, make sure he's OK. We just need to keep him under wraps for two more days.' That Sunday I went to Tottenham to watch Jamie play a friendly. Sandra came, too. We were all going back to Jamie and Louise's house for a barbecue. It was a lovely warm summer day, absolutely perfect. About ten minutes before the end of the match, Andy Awford called: 'Harry, he's disappeared. I've just been round the hotel and he's not there. They think he's gone to Heathrow to get a plane back to France.'

'He's not going to France,' I said. 'He's going to fucking Middlesbrough!' I told Sandra the barbecue was off. We were leaving.

'Where are we going?' she asked.

'Heathrow Airport,' I told her. It was like a scene from a film – and a pretty far-fetched film at that.

We arrived at the airport, dumped the car on a double yellow line outside, and ran into terminal number one. I was frantic. I wasn't even convinced Amdy had got the right airport and, even if he had, finding him was a million-to-one shot. 'What does he look like?' asked Sandra. 'He's a very tall black boy,' I said. 'Is that him?' she asked, pointing to a middle-aged Rastafarian with a woolly hat on his head. I told you she doesn't know much about football. After five minutes of searching, I turned a corner – and there was Amdy Faye. His English wasn't the best.

'Where are you going?' I asked him.

'I go home,' he said.

'No, Amdy, you can't go home,' I insisted. 'You have to sign for Portsmouth first. Come with me. You come with me.'

So we left the airport and I put him in our car. 'Tomorrow, we sign,' I told him. The moment we pulled up at our house, our dogs started barking and Amdy froze.

'Dogs – I no like dogs,' he said.

'They're not dogs, Amdy,' I assured him. 'They're bulldogs. They're more vicious than dogs. Half-dog, half-bull. If you try to escape, they bite your balls off.'

The barbecue at Jamie's was well and truly off now, so Sandra cooked Amdy dinner and he went upstairs to bed. We made sure he knew that the dogs were left downstairs at night. The next day Auxerre caved and we agreed a fee of £1.5 million. So managers do get involved in transfers sometimes – just not always in the way you might think. A bit like bulldogs.

CHAPTER THIRTEEN

THE RISE

I joined Tottenham Hotspur in October 2008. When Daniel rang, Tottenham were bottom of the league and the fans were desperate for a new manager; Portsmouth wanted the £5 million compensation and had my replacement already lined up. It was a deal that suited all parties.

I felt sorry for Tony Adams' predicament after I left, but I accept no responsibility for it. I brought him to the club when other managers wouldn't take that chance – not even Arsène Wenger at Arsenal. I like to mix it up with the backroom staff from time to time – a fresh voice, fresh ideas – and Tony was a man I had admired so much as a player. I didn't know him, but I knew of him, from Jamie and so many others that I had spoken to, who said he was the greatest captain during the 1996 European Championships. Maybe I saw a little of Bobby Moore in him, too – a player who had been a great leader for his country, who just needed a break. He clearly wasn't going to get it from Arsenal, just as Bobby didn't from West Ham United, so I called Tony out of the blue and asked him if he fancied a role at Portsmouth. He jumped at it.

Tony was good for us, except he was a lot quieter than I had imagined. He used to be a heavy drinker; now he was a heavy thinker – and quite introverted. Maybe the boozing gave him the courage to be that other person, I don't know. He was a lovely man, though, and forthright in his opinions, which is what I wanted. When I left, I thought they might make Joe Jordan manager, but they gave it to Tony instead – and he only lasted sixteen games. He has struggled to get back on the ladder since then, and ended up taking a completely unsuitable job in Azerbaijan. I imagine he was as out of place as Bobby Moore and me at Oxford City. It is such a shame that clubs do not give young managers more of a chance; sixteen games is no time at all. I am very grateful for the patience that Bournemouth showed with me many years ago. As for Tony, I just find it strange they have no role for him at the club he captained so wonderfully, Arsenal. He was such a great player for them, and a great leader, surely there is something the club can do. I have always believed that John Lyall feared being overshadowed by Bobby Moore at West Ham, but that cannot be true of Arsène Wenger and Tony. Wenger has done so much for Arsenal, nobody could put him in the shade.

Of course, leaving Portsmouth meant I had to endure the standard volley of abuse – even though it was the club themselves that were pushing the deal through – and I had one final obstacle to overcome. The Tuesday after I left I was due back in the city to receive the Freedom of Portsmouth, in front of a large crowd at the Guildhall. I knew exactly what to expect. The reaction, it is fair to say, was mixed. There were plenty of boos as I entered and chants of 'Tony, Tony' for the new manager. Gerald Vernon-Jackson, the council leader, then began his speech. 'Harry Redknapp has had a huge impact on this city,' he said. 'I was thinking, what do I call him? Is it Mr Redknapp or Mr Harry Redknapp?' But, before he had a chance to deliver his punchline – 'No, to everyone here he's just Harry,' – some bloke in the crowd shouted out 'Judas'. Lovely. I had to give a speech and, to be fair, that went down well. There was a lot of applause at the end and a woman even shouted out, 'We love you, Harry.' I suppose it was just another piece of bad timing on my part. I'm used to it by now. I know some of the fans still blame me for spending big during my time there, but I know the truth. I didn't force anyone's hand in the transfer market, the overwhelming majority of buys were good investments, and it is not my fault that the Gaydamaks' business concerns meant their priorities as owners changed. I left Portsmouth with my conscience clear – and went on to the biggest job of my career.

Everyone in football knew why Juande Ramos had got the sack. The club had replaced Martin Jol with Ramos, the manager of Sevilla, but he was a disaster. I have no idea why it didn't work for him at Tottenham, because his record at his last club was outstanding, but when I arrived Tottenham were bottom of the league, with two points from eight games. Ramos had gone and so, too, the director of football, Damien Comolli. I was appointed on the Saturday and the following day, Tottenham were at home to Bolton, in a match that was already being termed crucial. No observing from the directors' box – I had to get straight to work.

Clive Allen had been in charge since Ramos's sacking and, as he had been with the players all week, I decided to go with the team that he had picked, with one small alteration. I moved Luka Modrić into a more advanced role. What I had seen of Tottenham under Ramos, Modrić was often being swamped in a conventional role in a midfield four. He needed more protection, and to play further forward where he could genuinely hurt the opposition. There was no point slotting him in deep, where he had to do a lot of defensive work and had huge traffic between him and the opponent's goal. I knew Luka from the European Championships and Croatia's victories over England in qualifying: this was a top midfield player, one of the best in Europe. We needed to take the shackles off. It was a small change, but it made a big difference.

I was right about the timing, for once, too. Had I come to Tottenham at a different time the fans may have been harder to win over, and an unpopular manager only puts extra pressure on the players. Now, bottom of the league, those same fans demanded change, and we were 'Harry Redknapp's blue-and-white army' from the start. That may sound trivial but, believe me, it takes so much stress off the players when the fans are united behind the team. The atmosphere lifted and we won 2–0, the first league victory of the season. I came down to the touchline during the game, made a few switches, bringing on Darren Bent, who scored our second goal – it was precisely the impact Daniel Levy hoped I would make.

I received a lot of praise for my first season at Tottenham but, believe me, any fool could have taken that club out of the bottom three. What was Ramos doing? One look at the squad told me there was no way we were going down. On my first day in the job, the starting line-up included Modrić, Ledley King and Roman Pavlyuchenko, with Bent and Aaron Lennon on the bench. The following week, away at Arsenal, the first team I picked included Gareth Bale and Jonathan Woodgate. Yes, improvements could be made – any manager will tell you, improvements can always be made, and this Tottenham squad lacked depth – but it was a good group of players and there was no way they should have been bottom. I can remember Clive Allen introducing me to the squad. I was looking around at all these big names and famous faces thinking, 'How are you lot in trouble?'

And it wasn't just the stars you might be thinking of. Often the heartbeat of the club is an unsung hero – in the case of Tottenham it was Michael Dawson. I don't think any English football club can succeed without a player like that at the centre. Brave as a lion, heading the ball off the line one minute, up for a corner and putting his head where it hurts the next – he was a guy that led by example. Off the field, too. If there was a hospital visit or a charity function, Michael was always the first to put his hand up. There will always be players with more ability than Michael – the goalscorers, the match-winners – but every manager will know what I mean when I say there was no individual more important to the club.

Sometimes the role of the manager gets exaggerated. Any decent coach could have kept Tottenham up that season – just as even Sir Alex Ferguson would have struggled to turn Queens Park Rangers around in 2012–13. If you haven't got the players, there is only a certain amount you can do, but I knew straight away that Tottenham were a mid-table team, at least. With a little investment, we could be right up there – and so it proved. I am not saying that, on my first day, I knew we would be in the quarter-finals of the Champions League, playing Real Madrid in two and a half years – or that just any manager could have got Tottenham to the Bernabéu – but I knew from day one that there was no way we were going down. I didn't pull off any tactical masterstrokes that season. We got organised, we released Modrić, played him in the middle rather than wide, and in the transfer window I brought in a few players who greatly improved our squad – two strikers, Jermain Defoe and Robbie Keane, a reserve goalkeeper, Carlo Cudicini, plus Wilson Palacios and Pascal Chimbonda. Keane, Chimbonda and Defoe had all been sold by Ramos, so I already knew that they would fit in with the existing group. They were all good players, and I couldn't understand why he had let them go.

It was easy, at first, managing Tottenham. The club had fallen so low that climbing the league was a reasonably straightforward mission – and it certainly wasn't hard going to training and watching Bale hit shot after shot into the top corner, or Modrić mess the ball around while some of his teammates watched in awe. We had a group that could rip teams up on the counter-attack, the beginning of a team that would do the same to Inter Milan in the Champions League. When you have got good players, managing is a pleasure, and there was no pressure in that first year. We were not expected to finish in the top four, or overtake Arsenal – the board were just happy that we were no longer getting beat. Just getting the basics right at last was enough to impress them. If we could stop the defence conceding, and get out of the relegation hole, that was success; but we managed to play some fantastic football, too. We knocked it around with a lot of freedom, and had a lot of fun as we turned the campaign on its head. Every new regime needs a fillip to get it going, and mine came early with a fantastic comeback against our north London rivals Arsenal. We were 4–2 down with two minutes remaining, but goals from Jermaine Jenas and Aaron Lennon gave us a 4–4 draw. It was the impetus we needed. The following Saturday we played Liverpool and got absolutely murdered, until Pavlyuchenko scored another injury-time winner to give us three points. Any manager will tell you the little breaks are so important, and we kicked on from there.

Roman Pavlyuchenko was a fans' favourite and had tons of ability, but I always thought he was a different player away from home. He was a great family man and he seemed to be uneasy with any time he spent away. He could be unplayable at White Hart Lane one week and then anonymous on the road the next, yet the supporters never seemed to see it, and that became a problem for us. In the end, if he wasn't in the team, I was almost reluctant to name him among the substitutes because after ten minutes, if the game wasn't going well, the fans would begin to chant his name and that would make the other strikers on the field even more nervous. Supporters are entitled to their opinions, obviously, but I don't think they realise that, sometimes, something that seems harmless can have a very real and damaging effect.

We ended up beating Liverpool and Manchester City twice that season, plus Chelsea once. I remember in that game I was quite concerned about Modrić. Chelsea had such a hard-running and physically imposing central midfield – Frank Lampard, Michael Essien and Michael Ballack – that I thought we might get swamped. I played Wilson Palacios and Jermaine Jenas for extra protection, but I was worried about how Modrić would handle the sheer brute force of the game. I needn't have fretted. He just got on the ball and made us play, even scored the winning goal. Essien was taken off because Chelsea were chasing – and we battered them. Luka was just an exceptional talent. He could cope with any amount of physicality, and I never worried about letting him go up against a powerhouse midfield again. I know when Ramos signed him a few people, including Wenger, thought he was a big risk. Wenger believed he was too slight for English football, but that match against Chelsea taught me a lot. Luka was absolutely vital for us throughout my time at Tottenham, and that was why we fought so hard to keep him. There was one summer when Chelsea came in for him and we turned them down. Then the season Manchester United lost the title to Manchester City, Sir Alex Ferguson called me that night, asking me to name my price for Modrić. I went on holiday to Sardinia, and he called me every day out there, too.

Yet such worries were a long way off in my first season, and my only regret is that we didn't land a trophy, having reached the Carling Cup final. We were unlucky to lose to Manchester United on penalties – it was a rotten result, and undeserved, but I was very proud of my players that day. We played three games in seven days going into that match but, apart from a bit of cramp late on, it never showed. I thought United's goalkeeper, Ben Foster, had more saves to make – but penalties are a lottery, and United's numbers came up. We did practise shoot-outs after training that week but, I must admit, I was hardly filled with confidence. We weren't the best and, when you add the pressure of the occasion, as we gathered on the Wembley pitch at the end of extra-time I feared the worst. It is at that moment a manager often loses one of his five choices as a player suffers a crisis of confidence. It may surprise you but it is often the best, the most assured, penalty-taker that suddenly loses his nerve. I remember Modrić didn't fancy it, which surprised me. I didn't hold it against him, though – I would rather a player be honest about the way he feels than put on a fake front and blast one over the bar. I was happy with my five but, sadly, we didn't get beyond three. Jamie O'Hara had been one of our best penalty-takers in training, with a lovely left foot, but he went first and missed. Vedran Ćorluka scored our second but David Bentley struck a terrible effort for our third and Anderson gave United the trophy. Their first three penalty-takers had been Ryan Giggs, Carlos Tevez and Cristiano Ronaldo and, unsurprisingly, all three scored. They beat us 4–1 from the spot. I felt very sorry for David. He was getting a lot of stick from the fans at the time, and missing the key penalty in a final made it ten times worse.

One of the questions I am most frequently asked is whether dumping a bucket of water on my head cost David Bentley his career at Tottenham. The answer is no; but that doesn't mean I was happy about it. The incident happened after our win at Manchester City to qualify for the Champions League, when I was giving an interview to Sky. I was talking, proudly, about the quality of my backroom staff – Joe Jordan, Kevin Bond and the rest – when Bentley invaded the screen with a crowd of jeering players and dumped a full, large container of water all over me. On camera, I had to laugh it off, but privately I was furious. I thought it was disrespectful, frankly, and totally out of keeping with our relationship.

However I may sound to the viewers at home, I am not one of those bosses who wants to be one of the boys. I am not an ogre, I'm not a schoolteacher, but I'm certainly not Dave Bassett at Wimbledon, either. Dave was as much a part of the Crazy Gang as the players sometimes, and they all thrived on it. I'm different. I didn't mix socially with the team, I took an interest in them, but I would never think of myself as a mate. I thought Bentley and the other players – all the ones who couldn't get in the team, incidentally – took a liberty. Would Bentley have dumped a bucket of water on Sir Alex, had he been a player at Manchester United? He wouldn't have lasted long if he did.

It didn't just make me look bad, it made the club look bad too – it undermined us when we had just taken a giant step to join the elite. The only good news was that we auctioned the ruined suit for a leukaemia charity on radio and fetched £2,000.

And no, David didn't exactly thrive at Tottenham, but it was nothing to do with the events that night. Had he been performing he would have found no manager more forgiving than me.

Having said that, I'm not sure his Tottenham career ever recovered from that penalty miss, to be honest. From my perspective, it was a hard defeat to take, but I couldn't feel too angry about losing in this way. All you ever hope is that your players rise to the occasion, and we did. Lennon was the best player on the field and ran Patrice Evra ragged. And unlike a lot of League Cup finalists, we didn't let up, despite the defeat, and ended up coming eighth in the Premier League, missing out on European football to Fulham by two points.

What people also remember about that season, though, is a throwaway line I came out with on 18 January 2009 – inadvertently catapulting Sandra on to the back pages. We were playing Portsmouth – always a tense one for me – and the score was tied 1–1 when, with ten minutes to go, Bentley crossed and Darren Bent missed an absolute sitter at the far post. All strikers miss, but this was abusing the privilege. Asked about it afterwards, I couldn't contain my disappointment. 'David James had given up on it,' I said. 'He had turned his back and was getting ready to pick the ball out of the net. My missus could have scored that.' As far as I was concerned, I was speaking honestly. I said what 30,000 people in White Hart Lane were thinking. What supporter hasn't turned to a mate at one time in his life and said my missus/

my mum/my nan/Sheila down the local could have scored that? Well, I'm no different. I think about football, just as you do – and react to it, sometimes, the same way. The next thing I knew, Darren Bent's agent was on the telephone to Daniel Levy, saying his client was very unhappy and wanted a transfer. All because of a little joke. Well, I'm sorry, Darren, but I stand by it, even today. It was a shocking miss, one of the worst I have seen. And I could have been ruder. I could have said that for £60,000 a week, or a £16.5 million transfer fee, we expected a bit more – which also would be the truth. As it was, I accepted that Darren didn't do it on purpose, and I took the mickey rather than rant and rave. I think it is a shame that people are too precious to laugh at themselves these days. I've made some rickets in my life, and I'm the first one to find that funny. Football, and footballers, are too serious these days. Asking for a transfer because his feelings were hurt? He would have been better off spending another hour each night on the training pitch, to make sure it never happened again.

The one positive in following Juande Ramos was that it gave me the freedom to select my own backroom staff. I like to give people a chance, so I kept Clive on, because I thought it was important to have somebody who was familiar with the club. I know some managers come into a place looking to sack everybody that was part of the previous regime, but that has never been my style. If I can find a way to work with somebody, I will, certainly a good lad like Clive. I can remember being coached by his dad at school all those years ago, and he had played for me at West Ham. He wasn't a stranger. The only real change I made was getting rid of Ramos's goalkeeping coach, Hans Leitert, who had a very scientific approach, which wasn't my style. I brought in

Tony Parks, who did a great job, and has been retained by André Villas-Boas.

The one area in which I think a British passport makes a difference is that of goalkeeping coach. I brought Tony Parks in at Tottenham because I think the demands of the English game are totally different to the rest of Europe and it needs a man who can convey that and make preparations for a very different physical contest. It doesn't matter where the goalkeeper comes from – he has to learn that England is a game apart in the six yard box. And a Brazilian being taught by another Brazilian will simply not understand that. How can a guy that has never played in England know that, up against a team managed by Sam Allardyce, you are going to get four guys around you at corners, Kevin Nolan backing in, the referee turning a blind eye, and you'll have to be ready to deal with this? It has never mattered to me what nationality my goalkeeper is – providing the coach taking him for training knows English football inside out, every little trick and stroke that is going to be pulled.

Tony was, of course, a Tottenham man, and I added Tim Sherwood and Les Ferdinand to the coaching staff for much the same reason. I wanted young, fresh voices to work with the junior players – but also people who knew Tottenham and its culture of good football. I thought it was important to get back to that, and I believe during my time there the fans enjoyed our open, attacking style, with lots of width, and Modrić pulling the strings in the middle.

My favourite member of staff, though, was the legendary Northern Ireland goalkeeper Pat Jennings. He wasn't involved with the first team, but would come in a few times each week to work with our young goalkeepers. I really looked forward to those days. What a lovely, gentle man. One of the best guys I have ever met through football: so much wisdom, so much common sense, a real asset to the club. It was a pleasure to talk football with Pat each day. Every club should have a Pat Jennings, and it amazes me how many discard these characters, the fantastic club servants, without a second thought. Just his presence and influence around the place was worth its weight in gold. You could talk to Pat about anything, ask his advice on players, and his opinion was always worth hearing.

I wasn't always having to go to the transfer market at Tottenham, though, because the squad was basically strong. I've been at clubs where after two weeks I have thought we needed nine players, and that is a scary feeling. Tottenham could not have been more different. People say I didn't buy because Daniel Levy wouldn't sanction the transfers, but the truth is we didn't really need much. We bought, of course we did, and Daniel does drive a hard bargain – but some of the answers were under our noses, not least the one that ended up transforming my second season. That was the year Gareth Bale came of age, and helped propel us to the Champions League late in the day.

There is some right old rubbish talked about Gareth's time with me at Tottenham, so I would like the opportunity to correct it now. Was I ever going to sell Bale? No. Was I going to loan him? No. I've heard talk – everyone from Richard Keys to Alex McLeish – making it sound as if what happened to Bale's career was a fluke and that I never fancied him. I would say in response that whatever faults I may have, I do know a player, and if you go right back to the first team I ever picked as Tottenham manager, against Arsenal on 29 October 2008, Bale was in it. In fact, he played for me a further nineteen times that season – in all four competitions: Premier League, FA Cup, Carling Cup and UEFA Cup. The problem was, he rarely won. There is a lot of false information bandied around about Bale's losing run at Tottenham, too. It isn't true that he didn't win a game for close to three years. He started when we beat Liverpool 4–2 in the Carling Cup, again when we beat Wigan Athletic in the FA Cup, Burnley in the Carling Cup semi-final, and when we defeated Dinamo Zagreb and NEC Nijmegen in Europe. He just couldn't get a win in the league. It was an anomaly, and one I was determined to break in my second season. I put him on against Burnley on 26 September 2009, when we were 4–0 up with five minutes to go. There was no way we were going to fail to win from there – in fact, Robbie Keane got his fourth goal of the game and we won 5–0 – and the next time Bale played in the league, nobody could say he was a bad luck omen for Tottenham.

It is funny, because I had been speaking to Sir Alex Ferguson about him a couple of weeks earlier, telling him about the problem with his winless streak, and Alex revealed a superstitious side. He said he didn't think he could select a player that had gone twenty-five league games without winning, no matter how good he was. He feared that the rest of the players would see his presence as a curse and that it could harm them psychologically. I'm glad I never took his counsel on that one.

With Gareth, it was all about building up his confidence. I brought him on late against Manchester City and West Ham around Christmas, when we were in control of both games, and I played him in matches when I fancied our chances – Peterborough in the FA Cup, or away at Leeds United. The idea that I was prepared to let Gareth go is, frankly, ridiculous. I had watched him emerge as a youngster at Southampton, and as manager of Portsmouth I'd see one of his early games for Tottenham, against Fulham. He scored the goal that put Tottenham 3–1 up – they ended up drawing 3–3 – and I raved about Bale to Joe Jordan all the way home. When I joined Tottenham, one of the players I was most excited about working with was Gareth. I really fancied my chances at getting the best out of him – he struck me as an exceptional talent: strong, quick, with a superb shot. It upsets me that people believe I was ready to ditch him – although the story has been told so many times now that maybe even Gareth thinks it is true. Alex McLeish says I was going to loan him to Birmingham City but, although I remember the conversation, it never got beyond the wait and see stage, and would only have happened had I thought Bale couldn't get enough matches with us. Nottingham Forest wanted him on loan, too, with a view to a permanent transfer, but I did not entertain that for a second. I would never sell Gareth. All he needed was toughening up.

We had to tease that combative streak out of him because, at that time, he was regarded as a left-back and was up against Benoît Assou-Ekotto, one of the best in the Premier League. Gareth seemed too soft to be a defender, so we decided to try him further forward. He drove me mad in training. Technically, he was outstanding, but he always seemed to be playing with his hair. It was never right. He'd be flicking the fringe, or wiping it out of his eyes and I would be going quietly mad, just watching. 'Gareth, leave your barnet alone! Gareth! Stop touching your hair!' He was always getting a little knock in training, too. He'd go down, then limp off, and I always thought the physios made too much fuss of him. It was the same pattern every morning: Gareth would tumble and stay there, and they'd all go running over. In the end, I told them just to leave him alone. 'Don't worry,' I said, 'he'll be fine in two minutes. If it is anything urgent, we'll soon know.' That's what they did and, as predicted, Gareth got up, got on with it, and got better and better. He was beginning to show his true potential. We shifted him to wide left, and moved Modrić inside, so they would link up. Now we were beginning to hurt teams. That Tottenham side had a nice balance, and Gareth began showing the form we saw on the training ground. At the crucial closing stages of the season he scored the goals that proved to be the difference in victories over Arsenal and Chelsea.

Those matches set us up for a sprint to the finish line and in the end it came down to a match away at Manchester City on 5 May 2010. Whoever won was going to claim that last Champions League place – and most of football had no doubt it was going to be the home team. They were managed by Roberto Mancini and had spent an absolute fortune on players. When I look at their team that night – Emmanuel Adebayor, Carlos Tevez and Craig Bellamy up front; Roque Santa Cruz on the bench – I'm still not sure how we pulled it off in such style.

I think that is one of my defining matches as a manager, because of the way we played. I decided that it did not matter that we were the away team, this was a Cup final, a one-off, and we were going to go for it. We played a very attacking team – Peter Crouch and Jermain Defoe up front; Bale, Modrić and Lennon in midfield, with Tom Huddlestone holding. It was said that it looked as if Tottenham were at home, and I'm happy with that. Without wishing to stereotype, maybe Mancini's Italian nature got the better of him. Serie A teams often tend to be quite cautious, and perhaps he did not feel comfortable taking the risk we did. He certainly seemed a different animal the following season. I was getting a lot of advice from my coaches that week, and all of it seemed to be that we should shut up shop and try to nick a win on the break – but I thought our midfield had the beating of City and couldn't see the point in putting the handbrake on. I wanted to occupy their defenders with two forward options, and when everyone was telling me to play 4–5–1, I disagreed. I thought we could get at them – particularly down the flanks. Lennon was half-fit, but he came through for us that night, and Bale was immense. The midfield worked like stink, none more than Modrić, and with eight minutes to go Crouch scored a thoroughly deserved winner.

That was a huge game for us, to win at their place, and everyone at the club recognised it. It set us up for Champions League football in a way, because being able to get a result in a one-off match stood us in great stead the following season. We knew that, in Gareth Bale, we had a world-class player who was only going to improve. He was finally scoring the same goals in matches that we saw from him in training; he was stronger and had developed a fantastic physique. He had pace, he could dribble, shoot and was great in the air. Finally, the full package. I predicted he would be our Cristiano Ronaldo that next season, and that's just what he was.

I had always felt there was more to Gareth Bale than left-back, or even left-wing. Don't get me wrong, if he wanted to be a left-back, he could be the best in the world, another Roberto Carlos. Even if he had stayed in that role his whole career, he would still be an extraordinary player. He can rip a team to pieces from deep or further forward on the left, but there is so much more to his game. Gareth is a player capable of going free through the centre of the pitch, either as a forward or just floating and arriving anywhere he fancies. I had talked with our coaches for a number of months about using Gareth this way because teams were crowding him out on the left flank, putting so much traffic in his way that it was just getting harder and harder. At least through the middle he would have three options: left, right or dead straight. On the flank he was beginning to run out of pitch.

The match I remember the new plan coming together was against Norwich City on 27 December 2011. He was magnificent that day and scored twice as we won 2–0. Unfortunately, Gareth's switch then coincided with a few dicky results for us and a few people, looking for easy answers, put two and two together and ran out of fingers. They would chant, 'Gareth Bale – he plays on the left' as if this little innovation through the middle was the cause of all our problems. Of course, a year later when he was scoring for fun in that position in André Villas-Boas's team, it was hailed as a genius move. The bottom line is that Gareth can play anywhere.

I think Carlo Ancelotti, his coach at Real Madrid, will view him the same way as me – a free spirit, not tied to any one position. His biggest test will be to step out of the shadow of Cristiano Ronaldo with confidence. That won't be easy. Ronaldo is a huge star at Madrid and will probably want to take nine out of ten free-kicks – at least. Gareth will have to assert himself and that will require a strong mind. He has to think, 'I'm an £86 million player' and act like it, taking responsibility, claiming the ball when he fancies his chances. And yet at the same time he cannot dwell on his fee and what it means too much, because that would put him under immense pressure. It is a tricky balancing act. He will have to be ready for the matches when he goes it alone, has a shot, misses and

Ronaldo starts throwing his arms up in the air. He cannot, at that point, go into his shell and become this timid little creature. But it is not natural for Gareth to behave in an assertive way.

Don't get me wrong, he knows he is good. The fee is crazy, amazing money, but he wouldn't have fought so hard to get the deal done if he didn't fancy his chances of living up to expectations in Madrid. Yet, equally, Gareth is a quiet lad, who spends time with his girlfriend and family, and I'm not sure being in the same bracket as Ronaldo and Lionel Messi will suit him. I saw the photographs of him on his first day in Madrid, surrounded by relatives, and wondered how that young man will fare with a paparazzi camera being pushed into his face wherever he goes. His relationship with Ronaldo is the key to it all, because if the football is going well, then all the added stresses are a minor irritation, and nothing more. If the football is a struggle, the other aggravations appear ten times worse. Not many major British players go abroad and those that do are as likely to fail as succeed. If Ronaldo feels threatened by Gareth's arrival, Madrid could be a lonely place to be, so he will need to lean a lot on Ancelotti, his coach, who speaks good English, and Paul Clement, Carlo's assistant, who is English. Luka Modrić is another old friend who could help him settle in.

The one thing the club cannot provide for Gareth and Cristiano is a ball each – so they will need to work hard on that partnership because they are such similar players. They are freaks, really. They can both shoot, both are good headers of the ball, they can both make 50-yard runs and stand over six feet tall. Madrid must guard against Gareth falling into the role of support act. He had a little trouble adjusting to the bigger environment of Tottenham after leaving Southampton, and this is ten times as great as that move.

If I have a worry it is that I remember the days when Gareth's confidence was draining fast at Spurs, and there were genuine fears he might not make it. He wasn't the strongest of characters back then and he cannot be allowed to fall into that same negative state of mind. If it doesn't start like fireworks for him, he will need Carlo and the backroom staff to make sure he does not become isolated, left alone with his thoughts. He won't like the attention a difficult start brings either. Gareth is a very private person and he won't enjoy having every move scrutinised.

The positive is that Gareth has grown a lot since his earliest days as White Hart Lane. His performances improved, but so did his attitude. He wasn't flash, or cocky – never the sort to be up the West End with a bottle of champagne – but he was more assured. He has to take that maturity to Madrid, though, or it will be hard.

CHAPTER FOURTEEN

AND FALL

Managing in the Champions League was one of the greatest experiences of my professional life. Winning against AC Milan in the San Siro stadium, battering Inter Milan at White Hart Lane – so many great nights, so much drama. Yet our adventure against the elite of Europe was almost over before it had begun. At 3–0 down in the first leg of our qualifying game, understandably, I feared the worst.

The fourth-placed Premier League team has to pre-qualify for the Champions League group stage, and we had sent Clive Allen over to scout our opponents, a Swiss team called Young Boys, from Berne. 'Bang average,' he reported back. His write-up made it sound as if we would have no problem at all. Yet the minute we arrived at their ground, I had a bad feeling. It was an artificial pitch. The players kept coming off to change their boots, trying other ones on – didn't like them, back to change again. Nobody looked comfortable. There was a little group that were planning to go to a sports shop the next morning because, they said, nothing felt right. I didn't like the sound of that at all. I had played on AstroTurf in America all those years ago, and I knew the problems. The ball runs differently, bounces differently – it takes a while to get used to it, and we had one light session, the night before the game. I knew there would be issues – we were all over the show, and I can remember going to sleep that night with a real sense of foreboding. Sure enough, within 28 minutes we were three behind.

Everything I was afraid of happened. We couldn't get into our game at all. Already leading 3–0, Young Boys got a free-kick on the edge of our box and hit the post. I'm not sure we would have come back from that had it gone in, but three minutes before half-time our luck changed. Sébastien Bassong got a goal back for us. Frankly, if we could have shaken hands there and then, I would have taken it. On that pitch, 3–1 didn't seem the worst score to me, and I fancied our chances on grass at our place. As it was, with seven minutes to go, Roman Pavlyuchenko made it 3–2. We nearly lost another goal before the whistle went, but I was delighted to get away with a narrow defeat. I knew the return leg would be different and, in many ways, those matches set the tone for our campaign in Europe.

The return leg, we annihilated them. We were a goal up after five minutes, two clear before half-time, and ended up winning 4–0. Peter Crouch scored a hat-trick, because they simply couldn't handle him. It was like that in the group games, too. We drew 2–2 away at Werder Bremen, but beat them 3–0 at home; we drew 3–3 with FC Twente, having beaten them 4–1 at our place. In our two qualifiers and six Champions League group games we scored twenty-five goals, more than three per game. We played fantastic, open football, and took the game to our opponents wherever we went. Manchester City struggled in the Champions League in their first two seasons, and people said it was a lack of experience, but that was our first season, too, and we played with absolutely no fear. We ran teams ragged most nights, and showed fantastic spirit if the match was going against us. Of course, the two games everyone remembers were against Inter Milan.

Those were the nights that Gareth Bale truly arrived on the world stage. We all knew how good he was, obviously, but I don't think the major European clubs had yet taken notice. They soon did. I don't think I have ever seen one player terrify a team so completely as Bale did Inter Milan. They did not know what had hit them. Not that we made it easy for ourselves.

To manage a team in the Champions League at the magnificent San Siro stadium was obviously a highlight for me. José Mourinho may be blasé about it, but my career has not been spent in and around the great clubs of the European game. I still get a buzz from playing at Old Trafford. The feeling as we came out and saw those famous blue and black colours flying everywhere, with our fans corralled in a little pocket on the top tier, was just incredible. Not that I had much chance to enjoy it. Javier Zanetti scored for them after two minutes. Then, six minutes later, our goalkeeper Heurelho Gomes got sent off. I had no option but to replace a forward player with a substitute goalkeeper – so off came Luka Modrić, and on went Carlo Cudicini. This was now about damage limitation. It wasn't going to be Luka's night. Three minutes after that, Samuel Eto'o scored. Another three minutes, a third goal from Dejan Stanković. By 35 minutes, we were 4–0 down and playing with ten tired men. It was humiliating – and, frankly, it could have been worse. Carlo had pulled off some decent saves, too.

At half-time I went into a little side room to gather my thoughts before speaking to the players. We were in big trouble, and I didn't know where we were going in this game. Down to ten men, what could we do? How could we get out of it? Tim Sherwood came in to speak to me. He didn't have any grand ideas, either. So, backs to the wall, I decided there was only one thing for it – shoot our way out, Western-style. 'You know, Tim,' I said, 'this isn't the knock-out stage. It's a group game. We've got three other matches after this – win those and we'll go through. It doesn't make any difference to us what happens here. Fuck it – we'll have a go at them. See what they're made of.' That was the message I relayed to the players – and that's what we did. And, do you know, I think if that second-half had gone on for five minutes longer we wouldn't even have got beat. We came back from 4–0 to 4–3, and Bale scored a hat-trick. They were hanging on the ropes like a punch-drunk boxer by the end. They were gone. I think in Italy when a team goes 4–0 down, it is game over. It took them a while to realise that we didn't think we were beaten, and by then the impetus was with us. They couldn't handle Gareth at all. From a point where I genuinely feared we could have lost by eight or nine, we came off feeling almost as if we had won. It was shaping up like a manager's worst nightmare, yet we left for home celebrating. We knew we could have Inter Milan at our place – and that is exactly what happened.

'Tactically naïve.' I have heard that plenty of times in my career. It washes over me now. I know I wouldn't have lasted as long as this in the game if I didn't know how to set up and organise a team, and improve players. People make out it is all down to motivation, as if all I've got by on throughout my life is the gift of the gab. If that is what they want to believe, fair enough, but players soon see through a smooth talker. I have principles, I have my own style. I like teams with width, I like my defenders to play out, and I believe in putting the best players in the position where they can do most damage, a favourite position, where they feel at home. Bale is a lightning-quick, left-footed player, so I used him on the left throughout that season. The fashion was for left-footed players on the right at the time, like Ashley Young, so they could cut inside and get to goal – but I saw in Gareth a player that needed to build confidence. He was best playing in his natural position, at first. As I mentioned, once he felt at home, and defenders began doubling up on him, that was when we looked at switching flanks, or using him down the middle. I only mention this again because Inter Milan's manager at that time was Rafael Benítez, who is widely acclaimed as one of the game's great tactical thinkers. And if I had done what he did in the second leg at White Hart Lane I'd have been absolutely slaughtered. Naïve wouldn't have been the half of it.

Despite his thirty-eight-minute hat-trick in the first match, Rafa made absolutely no extra provision for Bale at all in the return. I find that so strange. When the game began, we couldn't believe our luck. We had been working all week on how to counteract what Inter would do to Gareth and, when it came to it, Rafa left him, one on one, with Maicon. I felt sorry for the lad. It was embarrassing. By the end of it the fans were singing, 'Taxi for Maicon', and I don't think his career has ever recovered. He left Inter and went to Manchester City, but he didn't break into the team with any regularity there, either, and left the following summer. He started that night at White Hart Lane as the best right-back in the world, and ended it the punchline of a joke. I know what would have been said about the tactics had he been one of my players.

I noticed in the first game that Inter didn't really operate with a wide right midfield player offering extra protection, but I felt certain this would change at White Hart Lane. I told Gareth that they would double up on him – instead Maicon was hung out to dry. I think people make presumptions about foreign coaches sometimes. They regard them as so advanced tactically and forget they can make mistakes like the rest of us. Maybe Rafa thought the first game was a fluke. Maybe he thought Gareth just had one great half of football, nice and relaxed because the game was already lost, and he would be different under pressure at home. That aside, I can't understand his thinking. Anyone in their right mind could see what a threat Bale was in that first game – and how important he was to Tottenham.

I was so pleased for Gareth that he was finally getting the acclaim he deserved because he is, basically, just a really nice kid. I know he gets a lot of stick about diving, but the boy I knew was always very honest – from arriving on time and training well to the way he played the game. I simply think that he's going at such pace and he changes direction so quickly that, as he's trying to avoid outstretched legs, with that amount of speed and body movement, his momentum sometimes takes him over. I wouldn't say he has never dived – I don't think these days that any footballer has never dived – but I don't think he looks for it. He might think someone is about to kick him, and anticipates it, but running like that I defy anyone not to at least flinch at the prospect of impact. To me, he's a model professional. No problem, low maintenance. I was lucky with that Tottenham team because most of them were the same.

Modrić, Pavlyuchenko, Defoe, Crouch – they were all good lads and did not give me any hassle.

We had taken Rafael van der Vaart that summer, and he made a huge difference to us in Europe. He was one of Daniel's signings. The chairman asked me if I wanted to take him on loan, and I said, 'Of course.' Then he came back and said we couldn't arrange a loan but he could do an unbelievably cheap permanent transfer. Would I still be happy? It sounded a fantastic opportunity and I jumped at it. Rafael was another one who said I wasn't much for the tactics board, but what did he think would happen? That I would get him in the team and tell him how to play? I put Van der Vaart in a position I thought would suit him best, and let him dictate the game. The better the player, the more advice should be kept to a minimum. Of course we had moves and tactical plans, but you have to walk players through at Bournemouth a lot more than you do at Tottenham.

People think Daniel and I were always clashing over players, but it wasn't like that. Yes, he had his own views, but we never made a signing that wasn't run by me first – and even though I knew he didn't fancy some of my choices, I got most of them. Daniel was unsure about Younès Kaboul and Scott Parker for reasons of injury and age but ended up trusting me, so we went for them.

The difference now, of course, is that Tottenham have a director of football, Franco Baldini, in place. But that is not my way, though. I'm old school, like Arsène Wenger and Sir Alex Ferguson. I pick the team, I choose the players. If I carry the can, then why should I have to work with another man's choices? I've never heard the fans chanting for a director of football to be sacked – well, not until Joe Kinnear went to Newcastle United, anyway. It just shows the way football is changing. The foreign coaches seem to insist on having someone in that role, certainly André Villas-Boas welcomed Baldini's arrival at Tottenham. Looking back, maybe on occasions I've paid the price for not bending with the times. I must confess though that I hear about this brave new world, sometimes, and it makes me laugh. Liverpool's owners are supposed to have this new way of assessing player value, based on *Moneyball* philosophies taken from baseball – yet Brendan Rodgers has spent a huge amount of time trying to offload signings that were bought at vastly inflated prices. I think any of the new philosophies will be hit and miss, just like the old way of allowing the manager to make his mind up.

Sometimes it's good to move with the times, but sometimes old school is still the best way. My relationship with Sir Alex Ferguson was always a little different to that of other managers. I can remember one match when I was manager of Tottenham when the club officials had to come and knock at his office door, to remind us that the match was due to start, because we had got lost in conversation. He had to give his team talk, I had to give mine, and we were keeping the players waiting. It was always different when you went to Old Trafford. Before the game is the worst time, I find. You put in your team, see the other starting XI and begin refreshing your plans if there are any little surprises. Maybe Nemanja Vidić isn't playing, so you have to reconfigure the set pieces, working out who will mark who, and who is United's danger man at free-kicks now. Once that is done, however, and the team leaves to warm up, the manager is left hanging, twiddling his thumbs, waiting for play to start. It is dead time, and then the nerves begin to set in – that is why I always looked forward to the welcome I would receive from Alex. 'Coming in for a cup of tea,

Harry?' he would ask, and he would close the door to his office behind me and we'd talk.

The racing was always on the TV in the corner, or maybe the pre-match build-up on Sky and over a cup of tea and biscuits we'd set the world to rights. Players we had seen, teams we had played, who was on form, who was struggling, a bit of football gossip, how his son Darren was doing at Peterborough, and then it would be time for the 2.40 at Sandown Park. Alex is like me, he knows what is going on across all four divisions, not just the Premier League. If there was a good kid at Rochdale, he'd be on his radar and despite the quality of the opposition, I often felt more relaxed before matches at Old Trafford than at any other ground. The time just flew.

I've heard people say that the foreign coaches aren't the same, but it isn't black and white like that. They are not rude, they just come from a different culture. I've never had a cross word with Arsène Wenger at Arsenal, for instance, but I can count on the fingers of one hand the times I've seen him after a game. Even if you pop into his office, in all likelihood he won't be there. And I've never seen him just watching a match, either, even when we've played Arsenal's youth team. He's either got the best disguise in the world, or he trusts a network of scouts and analysts to give him the information. I think some foreign coaches just have a different way of working – I didn't see Rafa Benítez at too many matches either, whereas David Moyes is everywhere.

I do miss the get-togethers after matches, though. When Jim Smith was at Derby County, there were always a few old faces about, like Dave Mackay, and it was great to catch up. Jim would open a bottle of red, or two, and soon enough you would find yourself laughing, even if you had just lost and had come in with a sore head, at war with the world. Howard Kendall at Everton was a personal favourite. He'd always pop in for a glass of wine after the game, and sometimes before, too. Of the modern foreign coaches, I find José Mourinho as welcoming as anybody. Even when he was under pressure in his final season at Real Madrid, he always found time to send me a text wishing me well at Queens Park Rangers. One contained an extremely strong hope that I would beat a particular Premier League manager who is clearly in José's bad books – I'll leave you to guess who.

The fissures of my final season seemed a long way off on Tuesday 15 February 2011, when I returned to the San Siro for the second time that season, this time to play AC Milan in the Champions League knockout stage. This battle-plan certainly wasn't going to be gung-ho – in fact, it couldn't have been more different to our previous visit. We had no Bale, but I filled out the midfield with Wilson Palacios and Sandro, and left Modrić half-fit on the bench, with Peter Crouch on his own up front. We played really well, worked so hard, and then hit them on the break with ten minutes to go and Crouch scored. It was a classic counter-attacking goal – a real Italian job – but it didn't win us too many friends locally. After the game I said the Premier League was better than Serie A, and the top Italian team might not even make the Champions League places in our league, and they hated that – but I stand by it. In fact, they were lucky. We should have had a penalty early on, and Mathieu Flamini should have been sent off for a quite scandalous tackle on Vedran Ćorluka that could have broken his leg. Gennaro Gattuso, a legendary hard man at Milan, was going mad, on the pitch and off it, and even made the mistake of squaring up to Joe Jordan. Joe was 60 next birthday, but I know who my money was on – Joe every time. I'll admit, I couldn't understand a word of their row, but it sounded as if Joe gave as good as he got. Joe was a player in Italy, and his daughter teaches English over there, so he speaks the language very well. I think Gattuso's married to a Scottish girl, so they probably understood each other. Joe was giving Gattuso plenty of it. He's a quiet man, Joe, but anyone who knows him will tell you he's not the sort to mess about. He's as fit as a fiddle and strong, and I think he was about to introduce Gattuso to a good old Glasgow kiss – and not the sort he'd get from his missus – when they were pulled apart. All in all, a great night to get a result.

It was a tough game at home, too. Milan dominated large parts of the match but we kept a clean sheet. It was strange, but there was a lot of praise for my tactics that night – far more so than when we were averaging three goals a game in Europe. Why do goalless draws impress people so much? We can all set a team up to bore the opposition to death – I even managed it a few times with Queens Park Rangers. We drew with Manchester City and Tottenham, kept a clean sheet against Chelsea – it is not that hard, but it always seems to count for more than winning with style. I don't understand it, really. It's as if you've got to draw 0–0 to be acclaimed as a tactical genius. Yet I've been watching and playing football since I was five – if I don't understand it now, I never will. I don't think there are a huge amount of tactical geniuses, not even Sir Alex Ferguson. We were very patient against Milan, they had some great players, but we kept it tight. It was a great result, but not my favourite game.

We drew Real Madrid in the quarter-finals, but that match was over almost before it had begun. We lost an early goal, to Emmanuel Adebayor, and then Crouch got sent off after fifteen minutes. He made a silly foul and picked up a booking, did the same thing a minute later, and was gone. Madrid won 4–0 and this time there was no way back. They came to White Hart Lane, did a job on us, and Cristiano Ronaldo scored the only goal of the game. It was over.

The Champions League run was fantastic, but it took its toll. We came fifth and failed to qualify for the competition the following season. We had the odd flirtation with fourth place and even rose to third, once, but for the majority of the season we were trapped outside that top band, and ended up six points shy of Arsenal. I felt sure we would be back, though, and better for the experience. If we could get a few top quality players in, I was certain we could do even better next time. I had no idea that 2011–12 was to be my final season at Tottenham.

You always remember the little bits of bad luck that go against you. When we went to Old Trafford in October we played well, but left with nothing to show for it. We were losing 1–0 but were right in the game until six minutes from time, when Nani scored an absolute scandalous second for Manchester United. It is one of those that will keep turning up in the 'What Happened Next?' round on *A Question of Sport* for years. Nani went through and thought he was fouled by Younès Kaboul. He went to ground and even put a hand on the ball to stop play, but Mark Clattenburg, the referee, gave nothing. Thinking the free-kick had gone our way for Nani's handball, Gomes picked the ball up, threw it on the ground in the penalty area and prepared to take a long kick to restart. Yet Nani had spotted what none of us had – that Clattenburg had not given a free-kick to either side and the ball was still live. He stepped up and kicked it into our net and Clattenburg gave the goal – despite the linesman holding his flag to indicate where the free-kick should be taken. He thought it had been given too! I was raging. At 2–0 down with six minutes to play, now there was no way back. I was incensed. Nani had deliberately handled the ball. Now he gets to be the hero? It made no sense. I know Alex blamed our goalkeeper, but I thought the referee made a real hash of it for us that day, and Nani showed poor sportsmanship.

So what went wrong in that last season? I wish I knew for sure. We were right up there in the league and with the addition of one or two top quality players I do believe we were capable of winning the title. Instead, injuries caught up with us. On just about the final day of the window we bought Louis Saha on a free transfer from Everton – to be serious about winning the title I thought we had to act more decisively and boldly than that.

I know the conventional wisdom is that I was distracted by talk of the England job, and that is a sexier story than having too many injuries, but sometimes the simple explanation is the genuine one. We lost Lennon, who was key to us, and age was finally catching up with Ledley King. I was partly to blame for that. We were short of central defenders and I probably gave Ledley a few games too many. He was struggling and, as much as he was saying to me he wanted to play, he really wasn't fit. Towards the end there were a couple of games where we really struggled and so did Ledley, and I am sorry I put him in that position. He was such a great boy and, when he was fit, a fantastic player. What I didn't know at the time was that Ledley's contract was based around him playing a certain amount of games – quite a big number, actually – so he was motivated to play even when he shouldn't. He would say he was fit and I wanted him to be fit because I didn't have too many choices; it wasn't a healthy situation. When I found out that not playing cost him money, it just made it worse. I think he retired five games short of what he needed that season. 'I don't want you to think that I'm not playing you because I'm trying to find the club the money, Ledley,' I said. 'I'd rather you got the money. Whatever you are earning, you deserve it.' But he knew by then that he couldn't play on. His knee would blow up after every match and take six days to go down again. He couldn't train, he was losing his mobility. In the end, his knees just went. In the last four games of the season, when we had Kaboul and William Gallas fit again, we won three and drew one.

It still wasn't enough because of the miracle of Munich. How Chelsea won the Champions League that season I will never know, but they did, and because of that took the spot of the fourth-placed English team – which was us. I made one of the biggest mistakes of my life that night – I went to the match. Jamie invited me over – he said Sky had a box at the game and I should go as his guest. In any other circumstances it would have been a great night – Chelsea winning, with my nephew Frank Lampard captain of the team. But for me it was just horrendous. I won't lie – for all that Frank and his dad have meant to me, I was desperate for Chelsea to lose. If they won, we were out of the Champions League, despite finishing two places and five points clear of them. Jamie felt the same, I could tell. Meanwhile, Ruud Gullit, who I had tremendous respect for as a player, was carrying on right in front of me like a lunatic. He had nothing riding on the game – Chelsea had sacked him, for heaven's sake – but he didn't care. And what a way for Tottenham to lose out. When the season started had we been offered two places clear of Chelsea we would have jumped at it. Now, it wasn't even good enough for the Champions League.

You all know what happened. Chelsea were outplayed – as they had been by Barcelona, and by Napoli, in the previous rounds – Bayern Munich missed a last-minute penalty, conceded a late equaliser and then lost the penalty shoot-out. I was distraught. I felt like crying. All the while, Ruud was jumping around, cheering, singing, banging on the windows to draw the attention of the Chelsea players – and, when they looked up, in the background was me, feeling probably at my lowest as a football manager. In the end, I think Jamie got quite upset on my behalf. 'Ruud, do us a favour, they sacked you, didn't they?' he said to him. 'Ah, yes, but that was different people,' said Ruud, and then carried on oblivious. I felt embarrassed being there, really, as if I was spoiling the party, but I still think his behaviour was over the top. Put it like this – I wouldn't have done it to him, had the roles been reversed. He could see how I felt and, yes, I knew he was happy for Chelsea, but it was non-stop, and in the end it just pissed me off. There was one final humiliation to go. I had to walk past the Chelsea fans to get out of the stadium to where our car was parked to take us back to the hotel. They had all been kept behind and when they saw me they started singing, 'Thursday night, Channel 5,' – which is the time the Europa League matches are shown. Chelsea fans have always been great with me – I think because I'm Frank's uncle – but that was difficult. I remembered it when I saw them all on the box a year later deliriously happy to be celebrating victory in … the Europa League final. We got back to the hotel and I went straight to bed. Next morning we headed home. 'Get a top-class front man in for next season,' I thought, 'and the sky's the limit for us.' Little did I know I had twenty-five days left as Tottenham manager.

We had been through a lot together that year. There were people from Tottenham in the crown court every day during my trial, and our season had gone so well until the injuries intervened. Even taking away Chelsea's Champions League win, we were close, just a point in it between us and Arsenal in third place. On the last day of the season Arsenal went to West Bromwich Albion who were missing their first-choice goalkeeper, Ben Foster, and the reserve, Márton Fülöp, had a complete nightmare. He was at fault for Arsenal's first goal, and their third, and he could have done better with the second. Arsenal won 3–2. I'm not blaming Fülöp for Tottenham missing out on the Champions League – we had plenty of chances to secure the points ourselves – but it seemed that everything that could go wrong went wrong for us in the closing months of the season.

Yet I won't let that cloud my time at Tottenham. We did well and I loved every minute of it. And I am proud of my record there. They had never seen Champions League football until I arrived – and haven't since – and it's not as if they were a top-four Premier League team in the recent past, either. They had finished behind West Ham three years on the spin when I was at Upton Park – so I think some people have short memories. Looking back, would I have survived even had Bayern Munich won the Champions League final? I just don't know. I have no problem with Daniel Levy. He was the first person to ring me up to wish me luck when I took over at Queens Park Rangers, and even on the night I left Tottenham, the car phone rang and it was Daniel. 'Harry, let's keep in touch,' he said. 'I hope we can still be friends.' I thought, 'He's got some front. He's just sacked me and now he wants to be mates.' But we have stayed in touch. I'm not one for grudges.

My departure wasn't straightforward by any means. It certainly wasn't a case of walking in and being sacked. In fact, we had previously been talking about extending my contract. I had a year left on my deal and had met Daniel, requesting a little more security. I had done a good job and didn't think it right that I should enter the 2012–13 season with just a year left. Lose a few games and I'd be out of the door. I didn't think that would be fair after taking Tottenham into the top four, so I was looking for another year, to add to the one remaining. That wasn't unreasonable. Having had these discussions, I went to see Daniel again. 'What's happening, Daniel?' I asked.

He seemed very unsure. 'I don't know, really,' he said. 'We can't give you another year. You've got a year left on your contract. Maybe when we've come to the end of that? I need to look at a few things first. Maybe, Harry, we've just come to the end.'

I wasn't happy, but I had to accept it.

If I looked back through the achievements in my career the job I did at Tottenham would be in the top three – beside winning promotion to the second tier with Bournemouth, and keeping Portsmouth in the Premier League. I got on fine with Daniel. I still do. He loaned me some of his players last season with Queens Park Rangers.

The season was over so I didn't even get a chance to say goodbye to the players, which was a shame. We were going forward together, and I am convinced I would have got them into the Champions League last season, when they came fifth. Jan Vertonghen was already on his way to the club and he was a huge player for them. He was at our final game of the season, against Fulham.

It was 4 a.m. by the time the details of our parting company had been agreed. I had a little walk to clear my head, and then jumped in a taxi. I felt choked. I had finished fourth with Tottenham but was still out of work. The voice that broke the spell was that of the taxi driver, a Tottenham fan. 'Harry!' he exclaimed. 'You're doing a great job at our place, mate.' What was I going to tell him? That I had just got the sack? When we pulled up at the hotel I asked him the fare. 'No, no, I couldn't take a fare off you, mate. Good luck next year. Great football we're playing, mate. I'm loving it – absolutely loving it.' I drove home and got back to my house at 7.30 a.m. The next day, I got up, had a round of golf and hoped the phone would ring.

CHAPTER FIFTEEN

PICK YOURSELF UP, DUST YOURSELF DOWN

For the first time since leaving West Ham United eleven years earlier, I was unemployed. It wasn't easy. I'm not really one to be sitting around reading a newspaper or filling in the crossword. I've got to be doing, I've got to be active, whether it is a football match or a game of golf. I was asked to give my opinions on the European Championship tournament in Poland and Ukraine, but that didn't feel right. If England did well, I could only sit there endorsing the Football Association's decision to chose Roy Hodgson over me; if they failed, any criticism I made would sound like sour grapes at not getting the job. I couldn't win. I went over to Abu Dhabi and did some television work there for the start of the Premier League season, and that felt different. It wasn't as if every word I said would be pulled apart to fuel a headline. Secretly, though, I was dreading the winter months. I was happy to play golf every day in the warmth of summer, but when the bad weather and darker nights came in, I knew I would be stuck without football. I didn't know what I was going to do.

Yet, in time, a strange thing happened. The longer I was out, the less bothered I became about getting back in. I was linked with loads of jobs, from Blackburn Rovers to coach of Russia, but none of it really interested me. I never thought I would feel that way about the game, but football had changed and so had my life. I was enjoying going about my day without the pressure; I was enjoying my freedom, not waking up every day with a weight on my shoulders. I went to New York with Sandra, because it was one place we always wanted to go together, and there was a further list of places we wanted to visit – Las Vegas and South Africa at the top – just cities and countries that had always been on our wish list, but football had got in the way. We had some nice breaks and were looking forward to more. Suddenly, I knew what guys like Joe Royle meant about enjoying retirement. Joe had been a manager the best part of twenty-five years – Oldham Athletic, Everton, Manchester City, Ipswich Town – but when I had bumped into him last he said he wasn't at all concerned about getting back into football again. 'The players don't bother now,' he said. 'They don't give a fuck. I couldn't go back to it, Harry, it would drive me mad. I used to enjoy it, but not any more.' There was a whole list of managers who didn't seem to be missing the game – Alan Curbishley, George Graham, Dave Bassett. I began to feel the same.

I had taken a very part-time role at Bournemouth as an adviser, and that suited me perfectly. I loved the club, and genuinely wanted to help them, but it wasn't a hands-on position. If anyone wanted my advice, I was there as a sounding board. Eddie Howe was the manager, who was one of my old players, and I said I would be as involved as he wanted me to be. I would have gone to Bournemouth's games anyway, just to watch a match, so it seemed a natural fit. They hadn't won all season, but the first match I attended in my new capacity was away at Yeovil Town on 8 September – Richard Hughes scored after 35 minutes and we held on for a 1–0 win. This felt great. I kept my interest in football, but could stay close to home and take time off as I wished. The perfect life. And then the telephone rang, and it seemed as if I might be off to Kiev.

It seems a contradiction to say that having begun to get used to life as an ex-manager, I was prepared to throw it all in to manage the Ukrainian national team, but it really had appeal. For a start, the financial package was tremendous – more than I had ever earned as a manager in the Premier League – and the terms were favourable, too. I wouldn't have to settle permanently in Ukraine. I could travel there for matches and stay some weekends when I would scout games. The rest of the time I would work from home in Bournemouth. They told me the flight times from London to Kiev and it really wasn't a worse commute than going from Dorset to Tottenham. There were two flights a day, about two hours in the air. I wouldn't be away from Sandra any more than I had been previously.

Paul Stretford, my agent, had been out there for two days talking to their people and came back with very positive reports. The deal was as good as done. They said I could have my own apartment in Kiev, or the best suite in a top hotel; they would give me a driver, credit cards, food and travel expenses and a salary of £5 million a year – net, plus bonuses. It was an amazing deal, the best I had ever heard. Jamie made me laugh. 'If all that comes out,' he said, 'it will look as if you are only going there for the money.' 'Well, it does help,' I told him.

'Why me?' you may think. The people at the Ukrainian Football Association explained the conundrum over dinner in London. Professionally, they wanted a man-motivator with experience to get their qualifying campaign back on track. Politically, they wanted an outsider. Somebody not at all connected to the Ukrainian football scene. As I understood it there had been a lot of infighting between their two main clubs, Dynamo Kyiv and Shakhtar Donetsk. Pick a man from Kyiv and he would exclude those from Donetsk, and vice versa. They wanted a coach with no club allegiance – in fact, I could even pick my own staff. It was my idea at the meeting to take someone like Andriy Shevchenko, who knew the country and could perhaps get the fans behind us. I was all for making a fresh start, but I thought I needed at least one person around familiar with the territory. I was really interested. I thought with a respected figure like Shevchenko onside we could make a difference.

Ukraine's squad has some outstanding players and I knew they were very unlucky not to have beaten England at the European Championships in 2012 and then again in a World Cup qualifier at Wembley. Ukraine were playing catch-up in Group H, but I didn't think their problems were insurmountable. Obviously, taking the job would have meant playing England – and for Ukraine to go to the World Cup, maybe England would have had to miss out, but I decided I could live with that. Remember what I said about club allegiances ending when a player signs professional terms? Well, the same applies. I love England, and nobody wants to see them do well more than me, but if I was manager of Ukraine I would feel very comfortable knocking them out – just as Fabio Capello would have gone all out to beat Italy. When it's your job, it is different. Nobody held it against Jack Charlton that time the Republic of

Ireland beat England at the European Championships in 1988. There are so many foreign managers working in other countries, as professional people we can't afford to think like that any more. Anyway, England did not want me – so why should I agonize about working for anybody else? I viewed it as a really interesting opportunity, new ground for me, and I was about a day away from agreeing the contract when Queens Park Rangers made contact.

Jamie was an influence there, too. 'You're a Premier League manager,' he said. 'That's where you want to be. This is your chance.' I sometimes wonder if I will one day regret not trying international football, but it was hard to resist working in the Premier League again. I did fancy having a last go at beating the likes of Manchester United and Liverpool – and with Rangers bottom of the league, I felt certain I could make a difference. Rangers arranged to meet me through Paul Stretford, and I went with him to the house of Phil Beard, the chief executive. Paul did the deal and I took over on 24 November 2012, with Rangers six points adrift of 17th place and safety, having taken four points from thirteen games. At that rate they were heading for 11 points all season – tying with Derby County for the lowest total in the history of the Premier League.

At Tottenham Hotspur I had found a good squad, and at Southampton a good club, but Rangers, unfortunately, had neither of those things. The training facilities at Tottenham were outstanding, but at Rangers they were nowhere near, and the squad was poorly balanced and short of confidence. The minute I saw that group together I knew it would be hard. The directors and owners were nice people, but they were naïve in football terms, and I think certain people they had trusted – agents and advisers – had let them down quite badly. They had probably never been around players, or indeed football before, did not know the market, and had spent unwisely on some very average foreign imports – some stars from bigger clubs, who did not have the attitude or the appetite for a relegation fight. They were getting some rude awakenings. They had players on astronomical wages, being watched by crowds of 18,000 at Loftus Road. It wasn't sustainable; it wasn't right. Still, once involved, I was as committed as I always have been. I shelved our trips to Vegas and South Africa and threw myself into the job at QPR. Every day on the training ground, every night at a match or on the telephone trying to sort out some new players. We certainly needed them.

George Graham's first rule of management was: never buy a player who is taking a step down to join you, because he will think he is doing you a favour. That is easy to say when you are manager of Arsenal and only a handful of clubs can be considered superior. Further down the league it isn't the same. To get Portsmouth out of trouble I had to take players like Paul Merson or Teddy Sheringham, who were most certainly taking a demotion. The trick was to correctly judge the good characters. Rangers had players like José Bosingwa, who just six months earlier had won the Champions League final with Chelsea but, unlike Teddy – who had scored in a winning Champions League final team – he wasn't going to give his all for the group. I soon found out the extent of the problems. We drew my first three games in charge and then won at home to Fulham on 15 December, but the day was marred by Bosingwa refusing to sit on the substitute's bench. I have had problem players in the past, but I thought his attitude was disgraceful. I decided to fine him two weeks' wages – and that was when I got the shock of my life when I found out how much he was on. Bosingwa's salary was ridiculous – certainly for the effort he was showing. The trouble that Rangers were in, anyone good was certain to get a start – I wasn't in a position to be picky. If Bosingwa was upset about being on the bench, he should have looked at his level of performance, not thrown a hissy fit. The problem was he wasn't the only one.

It was scary. Of course there were some good guys. Within weeks I had worked out that my best player was Ryan Nelsen, a 35-year-old New Zealand international central defender, whom I had taken on loan at Tottenham as cover during the previous January transfer window. Ryan, for one, was a terrific guy, but he had started only FA Cup matches against Stevenage Borough and Bolton Wanderers at Tottenham – now here he was, the captain and mainstay of my team. Even worse, I knew I didn't have him for much longer. He had an offer to coach at Toronto FC in Major League Soccer and was going to take it up a few weeks into the New Year. We really needed him but Ryan clearly couldn't wait to get out of QPR. 'You've got no chance,' he told me. 'Not a prayer. This is the worst dressing room I've ever been in in my life. You haven't got a hope with this lot. I don't know how you solve it – they are just so bad.'

'What do you think is wrong?' I asked him. 'Is it the team, the spirit … ?'

'It's everything,' he said. 'Everything is wrong. I wouldn't have one of this lot anywhere near my football club. It's not just that they've got a bad attitude – they're bad players.'

And then he started going through the group, individually, telling me their faults. He slaughtered them. I've never heard a battering like it. Maybe he was already thinking like a manager, wondering how he would handle such a group. He certainly wasn't going to be an arm-around-the-shoulder type, I can tell you that!

I can't vouch for Ryan's views because a manager isn't in the dressing room all the time, but a lot of what he said rang true, particularly when he told me about the players he thought simply didn't care. 'Those boys have ruined the spirit at this club,' he said. 'They're a disgrace and I have no time for any of them.' Ryan was a fantastic professional. I wouldn't say he was 100 per cent right about all of the group, but he wasn't far wrong about quite a few. If that was the captain's view, I knew I had a tough job on my hands.

Rob Hulse returned from loan at Charlton Athletic and said much the same thing. He was another player I could relate to, and his take was very similar to Ryan's. Charlton was Rob's seventh club. 'I've been around a lot,' he said, 'and this is the worst dressing room I've ever known.' He was right. The attitude stank. Attitude towards the game, attitude towards training. I can't remember a worse one – and behaviour like that cannot be altered overnight.

Bottom of the league, a new manager, the transfer window more than month away, you can't walk in and just start smashing people. You have to coax them along, try to take them with you. I tried to bring discipline in, with fines for lateness and poor behaviour, but the culture of decay was too ingrained. Part of the problem was that the owners hadn't actually spent serious money on transfers. They didn't buy players at the top of the tree, but they did pay big wages. So what they had was a squad full of very average footballers earning more money than they deserved. It made them very arrogant and contemptuous. They would rather come in late every day and just pay the fine than behave in a professional manner. When they were there they ran around and did what was necessary – but getting them in was daily aggravation. There were players who were late three, sometimes four, times each week – and the most we ever trained was five days. There was always an excuse. 'The traffic was bad.' Well, leave earlier, then. Whatever you said, whatever you did, it didn't seem to bother them. Not every lad – but the bad outweighed the good, and that made it very difficult.

One day I heard that one of our players had been out until 4.30 a.m. at a casino in London, when we were playing Manchester United at 3 p.m. the next day. When I called him into my office and confronted him with this information he seemed genuinely puzzled. 'Friday?' he said. 'I don't think it was Friday. Maybe it was Thursday.' That annoyed me even more. I was expecting him to be angry at the mere suggestion of it. A professional player out until the small hours, the night before a game? It is unheard of now. I was expecting a real row and to go back to my source with a load more questions. Instead, this idiot genuinely couldn't remember if he was out until dawn on the Thursday or the Friday – so clearly there was a chance he was out both nights. I thought he would go off his head, but instead of shouting and screaming at me for even daring to ask him, he sat there wondering. Not even an apology. Not even a thought that he had let the team down. I suppose that is what shocked me most, the lack of consideration for the rest of the group. I was brought up at a time when footballers were not the athletic specimens of today. Yes, we knew how to have a party – but we worked hard for each other, too. Yet some of these guys never seemed to give the team a thought. They would train all week, then have a mystery injury and cry off for the match on Saturday. Rarely would anyone play through a knock or a tweak. I don't know how they had the front to pick up their wages some weeks. I felt truly sorry for the guys like Clint Hill. Clint was not the greatest player, but he would run through a brick wall for QPR. You could tell he was disgusted with some of the attitudes he encountered. He didn't have the technical ability of those players, but if we had more like him we might have stayed up. It doesn't matter how good a player is technically – without heart, he is nothing.

The transfer window was looming but we had too much work to do. What was my plan? Ditch fifteen of them? No chance. I was probably being too open about my feelings, as well. After we lost at Everton, for instance, I said we were sloppy and undisciplined and had turned into Raggy Arse Rovers after half-time. It was the truth. We had been playing very well for the first forty-five minutes, easily a match for Everton, but their goal had taken a massive deflection off Clint Hill. We started feeling sorry for ourselves and had just faded from the game. I was fed up with it. You can't do that. We were meant to be fighting to the last breath, not chucking it in at the first sign of bad luck. Jamie was on the phone almost every week telling me stop having a go at the players. Really, by then, I didn't even know I was doing it. I'd get asked a straight question, and give a straight answer; I was too frustrated with too many of them to cover their backsides any more. If I could I would have booted half the team out in the January transfer window, but we couldn't have found that many replacements, and we just needed the bodies. Also, the players a manager gets offered in January are often a jump from the frying pan into the fire. I thought the agents and advisers that had dragged QPR into this mess had a duty to get them out of it – but the deals they came up with were rubbish, really. An agent would find a European club who would take Bosingwa – but only if we took a particular player of theirs on loan in return. I would search him out, and he would turn out to be another waster – just their equivalent of Bosingwa. You were just swapping one guy with a rotten attitude for another. What would be the point in that?

I looked around the dressing room wondering how many I could get out and in, but it was a doomed mission, really. There were too many who simply wouldn't get that sort of money elsewhere, and they knew it. Their agents knew it, too, and made life very hard. Any attempt to instil discipline was resisted. All we could do, in the January window, was try to buy our way out of trouble – adding to the squad in the hope of making a difference. I already had one name in mind.

Loïc Rémy, a striker with Olympique Marseille, had been a target during my time at Tottenham, and I was told he was still interested in coming to England. How interested he was in coming to QPR was another matter entirely. I flew to France to watch him play and had arranged to meet him after the game – but he wouldn't even see me. He sent a message saying he had met Mr Redknapp when he was manager of Tottenham and he was a nice man, but he didn't want to meet him now, because his team was bottom of the league and he didn't want to be rude by turning him down. Newcastle United were also in for him and had offered £9 million. I didn't think we had a hope of doing the deal. But Tony Fernandes, our owner, was fantastic. He took over the negotiations, and just when it looked as if Rémy was going to Newcastle he changed his mind and signed for us. People said I was frittering away the board's money again – but it was completely in Tony's hands. Despite only joining us in mid-January, and suffering rotten luck with injuries, Rémy was Rangers' top scorer during the season with six goals.

Christopher Samba was our other big signing in January, although he proved a terrible disappointment. With Nelsen leaving we needed a centre-half. I know Rangers had been interested in Michael Dawson at Tottenham, but that had come to nothing. I was talking to Tony Fernandes, who asked me who I thought were the best central defenders in the country. I told him there was no point in discussing the best – guys like Rio Ferdinand and John Terry were not about to come to Rangers. I said that I had always held Samba in high regard when he was at Blackburn, and he was meant to be unhappy at his new Russian club, Anzhi Makhachkala. I said an agent had called a few weeks back and had asked if I wanted Samba on loan. I was definitely interested but sceptical the deal could be done. 'He's here with me now,' Chris's man had said. 'You speak to him.'

Chris came on the line and we started talking. 'And you're available on loan, I hear?' I said.

'I don't know where's he's getting that from,' said Chris. 'It's rubbish – they'll never loan me.'

It wasn't the brightest start. I threw Christopher's hat in the ring with Tony, but I didn't think we stood a chance. A few days later, the owner came back. 'You'll never guess who I've got for you,' he said. 'It's a great signing, a brilliant player.' Tony had done the deal for Samba – and it wasn't a loan.

It was a shame that it didn't work out with Chris. I still think that when he is right and fit he is up there with any central defender in the Premier League, but he was unfit when he came to us and, after one very poor performance, his confidence completely fell apart. It was very strange. Chris had taken a few games to get up to Premier League speed again but against Southampton on

2 March he was outstanding in our 2–1 away win. That was a big result for the club, but also for me, personally. On the day of the game a newspaper report came out alleging all sorts about our winter training break in Dubai. It made it sound like a holiday camp, with players out drinking and no work being done. I knew that wasn't the case. I also had my suspicions about the source of the story – an agent looking to cause trouble.. There were players quoted, anonymously, too. The article stank. It seemed as if it had been planted deliberately to undermine me. Had we lost at Southampton, I could imagine the fallout on the back pages – but we won, Rémy scored, and Samba was magnificent. I really thought that night we might rise above all the negativity and turn it around. Yet just two games later we lost Samba for the rest of the season.

Not physically, but mentally. He still played, but his head was gone. He had a really poor game against Fulham and it seemed to affect him. He was at fault for two early goals and seemed so desperate to make amends that by the end of the game he had disobeyed all our instructions, and was playing as a centre-forward, looking for an equaliser. It was as if he had a brainstorm and he just lost his way after that. He wasn't as mentally strong as he appeared on the pitch. When I saw this big, imposing figure, I couldn't imagine that he would be mentally fragile – but he crumbled beneath the pressure of our fight against relegation. He didn't start in our final four games of the season and nobody could work out what was wrong with him. He went back to Anzhi Makhachkala at the end of the season, for the same money we paid. We might as well have got him on loan, after all.

We did some good business with Tottenham for loan signings, though, and Andros Townsend was excellent for us, but, overall, the team was short and we just didn't have the ability to stay up. As is usual with relegated clubs, goals were the main problem. The team had lost its two main goalscorers, Andy Johnson and Bobby Zamora, through injury, and never really caught up. The numbers say it all: Rémy was our top scorer with six goals: Aston Villa, who stayed up, got nineteen from Christian Benteke, nine from Gabriel Agbonlahor and seven from Andreas Weimann. Big difference.

On the football pitch, we were always finding ways to lose. It became our specialty. We went 1–0 ahead against Aston Villa away, and lost 3–2; we lost 3–2 against Fulham, when Rémy missed a penalty; we gave away a stupid free-kick in injury time against Wigan Athletic and Shaun Maloney scored to make it 1–1. Any way we could find to mess up, we would.

Indiscipline was also a huge frustration. Stéphane Mbia got booked every week, it seemed, so much so that I actually left him out against Everton, because I knew he would get a yellow card up against Marouane Fellaini and miss a game at home to Stoke City that was absolutely vital. It had been like that all season, even before I arrived. I saw Rangers play Arsenal on 27 October, they were doing really well, and then with eleven minutes to go Mbia made a stupid tackle, got sent off, and five minutes later Arsenal scored. It was as if there was a disease being spread – even affecting the reliable ones. I always found Bobby Zamora to be a sensible boy, the sort of lad you could talk to every day and he would always have an intelligent contribution. I liked him as a player, too. He was a good trainer, one of the few who wanted to play on even with injury, and when he was fit he was a handful. I can remember the night Fulham knocked Juventus out of the Europa League. He was terrific. Held the ball up, brought the other forwards into the play, he absolutely murdered Fabio Cannavaro. It was one of the best performances from a striker that I have ever seen. So what was he thinking when he got sent off against Wigan after 21 minutes, for a chest-high, studs-up tackle, defending a throw-in? It was madness, and so out of character. How many times did I have to impress on the group that season that we were going to need eleven on the pitch to stand a chance of winning?

As the weeks went by, the harsh reality was plain. Looking at the mentality of the players, the lack of goals and the general weakness of the squad I had inherited, we were going down. I don't think anyone could have kept them up, in all honesty. I don't think Mark Hughes would have turned it around had he stayed, I don't think José Mourinho would have made a difference had he come in – there was too much wrong and I had overestimated my ability to affect that. I can't have been much fun to live with over those months, either. A lot of managers say they are lousy to be with on a Saturday if they have lost, but I cannot imagine too many would be worse than me. It's sad. Pathetic, really. The day we lost at Everton, I couldn't even speak to Sandra when I got home. A couple of days later, when I can look back at it all rationally, I do think there is something wrong with me. Why am I like that? I get so low it is frightening.

Losing produces a weird reaction in me, no doubt about that. I surrender all sense of perspective. I don't want to talk to anyone, I don't want to go out; I don't want to mix, I can't bring myself to socialise. I just want to go home, and sit, and stew. It's just a horrible feeling. I know it's terrible, I know it's wrong, but I feel as if something really bad has happened in my life, as if someone has died. I know it is not like that, nothing is, but my emotions are just raw. I don't sleep all night: I lay in bed, with my head playing everything over again and again. It's ridiculous, really. All this over a football match.

We came back from Everton on the train and I found it hard to communicate with anyone at all. Normally, I might have tried to throw my thoughts forward, bounce fresh ideas off the other coaches, but I just felt so depressed. I was the same after the draw at home to Wigan. I'm not the sort of manager to throw plates of sandwiches around the dressing room in frustration, but that day I walked in my little office and I booted anything kickable up the air. I wrecked it. All the food that was laid out, the lot. It all went. There was no one in there but me and suddenly all my frustration came out. My head was exploding. I knew if I went in and started shouting at the players I might say something I would regret. When I had calmed down, I told them, 'Lads, you've got to learn how to win games. We can't give free-kicks away like that in the last minute. With a chance to keep the ball in the corner, we failed, and allowed them to score.' I stayed very calm, walked back to my room and felt the urge to start booting everything around again – unfortunately, there was nothing left that I hadn't already had a go at. Managing is hard when you feel that way. If I didn't care, I could go home and think, 'Well, I've got my wages, I'm not bothered.' A friend will say, 'Just keep taking the money,' but that's not what it's about. I didn't come back in just for the money. I could have got more money coaching Ukraine. In fact, the way my settlement with Tottenham worked, I wasn't earning much more at QPR than I was just sitting at home. And I would have given the lot back, my whole year's salary, to have kept them up. If I could have made a deal – work for nothing, but QPR survive –

I'd have taken it. Your pride wants to stay up, your pride demands that you are successful. There is nothing worse than being down there at the bottom; there is nothing worse than the crap feeling of being beaten. It's murder.

You would think, after all these years, I would have been able to adopt a more philosophical approach to it, but no. I remember, many years ago, meeting Ron Atkinson when he was manager of Sheffield Wednesday. He was working on television at one of the matches and his team had lost in the last minute the day before, maybe even against Manchester United. 'I bet you had a good night last night,' I said, sarcastically, thinking he was the same as me. I imagined him getting home with the raving hump, taking it out on the rest of the world, stomping off to bed, not saying a word. 'Yeah, we had a great night,' Ron said, all smiles. 'We got a karaoke in, had a Chinese, Gordon Strachan came over ...' and he continued telling me about this fantastic little party that he'd had, finishing up at about five in the morning. I thought then, 'I must be doing something wrong.' It must be lovely to be like that as a manager. I wish it could be me. I don't blame Ron. He had done his best at the match that day. His team had got beat. What can he do about that five hours after the final whistle? I'm the stupid one, not him.

If we have had a bad result, Jamie is about the only one who can get a civil word out of me once the game is over. After the draw with Wigan, he stayed up in town with me and insisted we went out to an Italian restaurant. I think he sees things right and is very supportive. I can talk to him; but even then it is hard when you are kicking every ball hours after the match has finished. I remember one crazy game when I was Portsmouth manager, in the 2007–08 season. Portsmouth 7–4 Reading – the highest scoring match in the history of the Premier League. It was incredible: 1–0, 2–0, 2–1, 2–2, 3–2, 4–2, 5–2, 5–3, 6–3, 7–3, 7–4. At one stage in the second half, Reading got a throw-in that had clearly come off one of their players. It happened right in front of us. I was giving the linesman plenty. Finally, I turned to Wally Downes, Reading's coach. 'Wally, you saw it,' I said. 'Wasn't that our throw in?' 'Harry,' he began patiently, 'I can't even remember what the fucking score is!'

But that's the way I am. I can feel that pressure mounting, usually in the second half, when the crucial part of the game is being played. That is when so many matches are won and lost and, because you know this, it becomes very hard to control your emotions.

I do worry about the effect it has on my health. I remember in the aftermath of the Everton game, I hadn't slept and I looked at myself in the mirror and I didn't look right, I didn't feel right. I was getting funny feelings, my body ached and my chest felt tight. I was really worried that I was going to give myself a heart attack, or a stroke. The stress levels that I must have put myself through that day were surely dangerous, and I have already had one heart scare. 'How much longer can I keep going on like this?' I thought. 'How much longer can I do this to myself?' I did worry that something serious was about to happen. My blood pressure must have been through the roof.

I'm not one for going to doctor's, though. I always think, 'Get a night's rest and you'll be fine tomorrow.' I know that's not a sensible attitude either. I've been due a full medical for two years, but keep putting it off. After my heart operation I was given tablets but, I'll admit, half the time I forget to take them. I carry them around in the car. Little triangular things – I don't know what they are, to be honest. It is always Sandra who will ask whether I've taken them, and I've usually forgotten, so she pads out to the bathroom, takes three out of the packet and puts them in my mouth with a glass of water. I don't look after myself properly, considering all the stress. I know that.

So the season with QPR in the Premier League was a real struggle. I improved the results from what they were at the start of the season, but it wasn't enough. We were doomed from a distance out, and on 28 April, four games before the season ended, we drew 0–0 away at Reading and both clubs went down. It was the direst match, a real stinker, and it wasn't hard to see why both teams were exiting the division. The headlines the following day were about Bosingwa, who was caught on camera laughing as he came off the pitch. Everyone said he was laughing about relegation. That just wasn't true. One of the Reading players, Daniel Carriço, is also Portuguese and an old friend of José's. He came up and made a remark in his native language, they shared a laugh, and put an arm around each other. Nothing wrong with that. There should be camaraderie in football; there should be a sense that it is only a game. We had just got relegated. What more was there to do? I made a joke to Nigel Adkins, the Reading manager, when the final whistle went, too. I had just sat through probably the worst ninety minutes I had seen in my life. I'm sure Nigel felt the same. As I held out my hand, I tried to lighten the moment for both of us. 'Don't worry, Nigel,' I said, 'it'll never replace football.' I didn't see any harm in that, or what Bosingwa did. He got away with a lot worse at QPR.

The last game of the season was away at Anfield. We lost – no surprise there – but I remember it for quite a different reason. It was the last time I saw my old mate Lee Topliss, a young jockey who has been riding for Richard Fahey at Musley Bank Stables since 2009. He is regarded as one of the best apprentices in the game. I was introduced to Lee at Les Ambassadeurs casino in London one night during my time as Tottenham manager. He seemed a nice kid. Wasn't dressed too well, looked like he could do with a few quid, but very open and chatty. We were talking about the season he was having, riding a few winners, regarded as a great prospect. 'I think I'll be champion apprentice next year, Harry,' he said. If you like a bet, he seemed a good man to know. Then the conversation turned to football. 'I love Tottenham, Harry,' he said. 'The only problem is, I can never get a ticket …' He left the sentence hanging. Muggins here finished it off. 'I'll get you a ticket, Lee,' I told him. 'Here's my phone number – just give me a call.' He took me up on that offer the following week. We were playing Arsenal, our biggest match of the season. He certainly wasn't shy. I left him a ticket and, as I was coming out of the dressing room after the game, a steward stopped me. 'There's a little Irish fella here to see you, Harry. Says his name's Lee.' So I sorted him out. Got him a pass to my office, and he was in there having a glass of wine and a sandwich with all the Arsenal staff, speaking to the players as they came out of the dressing room. Very busy. Suddenly, he was at near enough every home game. He'd ring me up, give me a few tips for horses – they usually got beat – and then arrange to come to the match at the weekend. Half the time I'd end up dropping him back to the station afterwards because I felt sorry for him. He looked a poor ha'porth, as we used to say in the East End.

He came everywhere. Directors' box at Manchester United and Arsenal, in a private box next to Roman Abramovich at Chelsea.

We all went out for dinner after the match that night – myself, Lee, Kevin Bond, Joe Jordan – and I've never forgotten the way he tucked into his food. I've never seen a jockey eat like it. He even had dessert. 'Are you sure you should be having all those calories, Lee?' I asked him. 'Oh, it's OK, Harry,' he assured me. 'I sweat it all out in the sauna in the morning.' What do I know? He went through the card and then I gave him £150 for a taxi back up to Newmarket. This went on for years. I have a box at Wembley and he was in there when Tottenham were beaten 5–1 by Chelsea in the FA Cup semi-final in 2012. If we had a big game, he was there. And then one day he said he had an offer to go to Dubai for a few weeks and ride for the Godolphin stable. 'It's a great opportunity, Harry,' he said, 'but I've got to pay my own way and I can't afford the air fare. I'll get prize money out there, but I can't collect it until the end of the month.' 'How much do you need, Lee?' I asked. 'About five hundred quid should do it,' he said. So I lent him £500. I never saw that again, prize money or not.

He was always talking about how unfortunate he was on this one, or what bad luck I'd had with that tip he'd given me. One day, a horse I part-owned was in one of his races and he said if it was going well, he'd ride to deliberately try to block off any challengers. That got beat as well. When I switched clubs, however, Lee's allegiance to Tottenham turned up not to be as strong as he made out. Now he was going everywhere with Queens Park Rangers. On the last day of the season, he came up to Liverpool as my guest, sat in the directors' box at Anfield and, at the end of the game, pleaded poverty again. 'I'm riding down at Newbury tomorrow, Harry, and I'm not sure I've got the train fare.' He even cadged a lift to the station out of me, which took me completely in the opposite direction to home. I just felt sorry for him. He was always on his own, and he obviously wasn't making much money, despite being a top apprentice. And then I got a phone call from Willie McKay.

'Do you still speak to Lee Topliss, Harry?' asked Willie.

'Yeah, I do,' I said. 'He's always calling me, more losers than winners, mind you, but, yeah, I speak to him two or three times a week. He says he's working with some two-year-olds that are going to be fantastic.'

'Right,' Willie continued. 'Well, I think I know why his information isn't so clever.'

'Why?'

'He's not Lee Topliss. He's a potman at a boozer in Newmarket. He picks up glasses – he's not a fucking jockey.'

Three years he'd had me. The best seat in the house, good restaurants, lifts here there and everywhere – and heaven knows what in hand-outs. And it was a sheer fluke that Willie found out the truth. Were it not for a chance meeting at Doncaster, he could still have been taking me for a ride. A while ago, 'Lee' had called me and said he had just ridden one beaten by a short head at Doncaster. Another hard-luck tale. We were chatting and I mentioned that Willie had a box there. I said I would ring him and see if he could invite Lee up. When Willie called, Lee said he was just leaving for Newmarket because he had to be up early on the gallops. There was one going that night, however, that was well fancied. He gave Willie the tip and, lo and behold, it won. The next time Willie was at Doncaster, he saw Lee Topliss's name on the card and wanted to thank him – but when he saw him ride around in the parade ring, it didn't look like Lee Topliss. Taller for a start. Willie put it down to the protective racing helmet he was wearing and thought no more of it. Then, a few races later, he saw Lee with his back to him in the paddock. Now was the chance to say something. He tapped him on the shoulder. 'Hello, Lee, I'm Willie, Harry's mate, thanks for the horse you gave me, good lad, it ran well,' he said. The jockey stared at Willie as if he was mad. 'I'm Harry Redknapp's friend,' Willie repeated. 'If you ever need anything, give me a ring.' Again, he was staring back at Willie as if he had landed from the moon. Then Willie began to study the lad's face. It wasn't the Lee Topliss he knew, the one he had met with me at Les Ambassadeurs. And then Willie started making enquiries.

I thought I was streetwise. This guy was a different class. I'm told when Istabraq won the Champion Hurdle, 'Lee Topliss' led the horse into the winner's enclosure waving the Irish tricolour. Everyone thought he was part of the trainer Aidan O'Brien's stable, but it turned out they didn't have a clue who he was either. He was a conman preying on the racing scene, and the little Irish rogue had us all. I'm told he was working the same racket with Glen Johnson, plus a couple of football agents and other managers. I can imagine him now, in his room full of signed shirts – Robbie Keane, Aaron Lennon, Gareth Bale, all collected through me. So I'd got sacked by Tottenham, relegated with QPR, my mate of three years turned out to be an Irish crook, and my last memory was of him disappearing off to Lime Street station with another £150 of my money. Oh yes, it was one hell of a year.

CHAPTER SIXTEEN

ALWAYS MANAGING

There is a story that, in many ways, encapsulates my thoughts on management. It was told to me by Graeme Souness. He was captain of Liverpool when they played the 1984 European Cup final against AS Roma in the Olympic Stadium, Rome. About ten days before the match, Graeme went to see Joe Fagan, the manager, with a message from the players. 'Joe,' he said. 'It's been a long season. The players feel washed out – they'd like to go away for a few days before the final, to recharge their batteries.' Joe didn't have a problem with it, so off they went to Ayia Napa in Cyprus. It was a real jolly boys' outing. Graeme said they were lying in the sun, on the booze all day, back to the hotel, quick change, then out every night, staggering home along the beach at all hours in the morning. David Fairclough, the pale-skinned, red-headed striker known as Super Sub, didn't put any sun scream on and got burnt to a crisp, so badly that he blistered. It was mayhem. They flew back on the Sunday, and the next day left for Rome, where AS Roma had been living at altitude, coming down only to train at precisely 8 p.m. each night, which was the time the match would kick-off.

Graeme said that when Liverpool arrived on that Monday it was pouring with rain, so they were ordered not to go anywhere near the stadium pitch. There was an alternate training facility, but Fagan thought it was too far away. 'Come on, we'll go to the park,' he said. They walked to an open space up the road from their hotel, put some training gear down as goalposts and played a nine-a-side game. By the end there were loads of fans watching them, because word had got around. Graeme said they all knew it was a crap practice session, but they didn't care. The following day, more rain, so it was back to the park again. Meanwhile, AS Roma were bobbing up and down the mountain, back and forth to their own training camp in order to be super-fit for the biggest match in the club's history. On the day of the game, Liverpool got to the stadium and went out to look at the pitch. Joe Fagan pulled Sammy Lee, their tigerish little midfield player, to one side. 'Sammy, Sammy, come here,' he said. 'I want you to do a man-for-man job on their playmaker.'

'What number is that, Joe?' asked Sammy.

'I don't know,' Joe replied. 'You'll see him when you're out there – he's the one that keeps getting the ball. Stick with him, son.'

Half the players were up in arms because they thought it was a negative idea, but Joe knew his football and was insistent. 'He's a good player, so Sammy should mark him.' All sorted. Right – Liverpool went out and beat AS Roma, at their own place, on penalties, to become champions of Europe. The moral to the story: if you've got good players who understand the game, managing can be easy. It's the rest of us that get driven mad by it.

As I said already, I had a heart scare a few years ago. It was towards the end of October, 2011, in my last season at Tottenham.

A very stressful time. My court case had been dragging on for years and, when I finally got a trial date, it was delayed. The case against Milan Mandaric and Peter Storrie was proceeding first, before mine, and they sat through five weeks of a six-week trial only for the judge to be taken ill. It was put back a week, and then two weeks, but the illness was serious and the trial was put off completely and had to start all over again. So my appearance was held back, also, and maybe all the worry and the drawn-out process got to me. It just seemed to be dragging on and on. Jamie came over to visit one morning and we went to Parkstone Golf Club to play a few holes. I walked the first and couldn't breathe, I was absolutely gone. I didn't feel good, and Jamie said I looked grey and was breathing in a peculiar way. 'Are you sure you're all right?' he asked. I wasn't – I was wiped out. We finished the hole and headed back in – Jamie carried my clubs all the way because I had no energy at all. He wanted me to go to a doctor's but I said to wait until the morning. We've got a treadmill at home which I often use for running, but after about five minutes the next day I had to stop that, too. I was knackered. I knew something was wrong. I saw our doctor at Tottenham and he took me straight to Whipps Cross hospital in Waltham Forest, east London. I saw a specialist and the diagnosis must have been quite dicey, because they took me in that night at the London Independent hospital for a coronary angioplasty. It isn't major heart surgery, but they have to put stents in to help unblock coronary arteries. After that, I was fine, but I don't think the stress helped – the court case more than the football. There was so much uncertainty about whether and when the trial would go ahead – in the end it just got to me.

I felt a lot better for the operation. I have to go back every six months and have a check-up, but I can't say I really think about it. As far as I'm concerned I'm OK now, I'm better. I might have been in trouble had I not been so active, but we caught the problem early and now I feel good. Even those times when I don't, I know I can't change my ways at my age. I can't tell myself, 'Don't get het up.' I couldn't do the job any other way. I went to see the specialist last season, when QPR were right in the doldrums, and he told me I was fine to carry on. He said if he was worried, he would tell me to stop – and I think if I can handle the aggravation with QPR last season, I can handle anything.

I'm not moaning. I know what a lot of the public think: 'Managers earn a lot of money, the country is in a recession, people like you wouldn't know what stress is.' I understand that, but I'm not talking about financial stress. I'm not comparing my life to a single mum trying to feed her kids, or low-income families living on the breadline. I didn't come from a wealthy household. I know what that stress is. This is a different type of pressure – I am representing people who love their team. There are the owners who are investing money, but also the fans, and, as a manager, you are in charge of their happiness. When you lose, it feels like you have let them down. So you take it all on your shoulders, and it isn't a lot of fun in a season that doesn't have too many good days. That's when you get low and I think it starts to affect your health. But you do it because you love it. Sam Allardyce, Sir Alex Ferguson, they've all had minor heart problems – but it didn't stop them.

Do I worry about the affect my lifestyle has on Sandra? Of course I do. She's very placid, very laid back; but, no, it isn't good for her to see me at a low ebb. Obviously, it concerns her. I'd love to be one of those guys who can get home after a hard day's work and go out to a nice restaurant with his wife, but Sandra knows it takes me a day or two to recover if we lose. She'll cook me a bit of pasta, maybe open a bottle of wine, but it isn't the same. My head's gone and I'm still buzzing. Sunday, I'm just about getting over it – and then Monday I'm back to work and it starts all over again.

Sandra sees the side of me that others don't. People have opinions about you, write books about you, presume all kinds of knowledge, speak to people about you that have never met you – there is a whole conversation going on when a person is in the public eye. Yet all of these people, these experts, they don't see how you live your life, who or what you care about, do they? But when you live with someone, they know.

Sandra's wonderful. She has never really put any pressure on me to stop, has always left it up to me. She knows I'd get bored, probably, once the summer golf season has ended. I've got nothing else to do, really. I'm useless round the house, I'm not a gardener. I love looking at the garden, love to see it looking nice, but I wouldn't know one flower from another. I suppose Sandra thinks, without football, I would just sit there and fade away. I'm not even one for going on the television and talking about the game, really. I did *Match of the Day* when I was out of work, after Tottenham, but it was a long slog. Getting up to Manchester, sitting around there all day in those new BBC buildings – very soulless compared to the old place. I thought I just wasted my time, really, and then I got back to Bournemouth at 4 a.m. It wasn't something I would look forward to doing again.

Pat, Sandra's sister, died on 24 April 2008, and that was a sad and sobering moment for all of us, not least me. I had known Pat almost as long as I had known Sandra, because of her relationship with Frank Lampard, my best friend at West Ham, and that probably changed how I viewed my life as a football manager. After that, I don't think there was ever really a chance of me taking a job that kept me away from Sandra all week. She would have moved anywhere at first, obviously, but that was many years ago, and now we are settled and like where we are. It's home for us. The grandkids are down here, so moving away and staying up north wouldn't work for me at all. If I can get home, I do. If that means getting up early to go back to work, I set the alarm. The number of clubs I have managed on the south coast gives something of a clue to the way I feel, and the swiftness of Pat Lampard's passing probably brought it home. The time I spend with Sandra is so precious. Pat died of pneumonia, ten days after she was admitted to hospital – it was so unexpected and sudden. One moment she was here, the next gone. It was terribly traumatic for Sandra. I don't think a day went by when she didn't speak to her sister. I think it brought home how much I relied on her, too. Seeing Frank without Pat made me think what I would be like on my own. Useless, really. She has waited on me hand and foot for years. I wouldn't have a clue what to do without her support. It is certainly not a dull life being the wife a football manager, yet she has ridden through it all – the grief, the abuse from the boatmen coming past our garden, the trial, the highs and the lows. And she's so quiet, so shy, I don't think I have any idea how difficult it must have been. How many times must she have thought, 'What have I got myself into here?' That's why I get home at every opportunity. I owe her. I owe them – my sons and their wives, and our lovely grandchildren. The little boys are just starting to play football now.

I hope I can be as much of a friend and a fan to them, as my dad was to Jamie throughout his career.

Looking back, it all started from Dad. He lived for football. Loved football. If there was a game – even a kid's game over the park – he would be there. He would go out on to the balcony of our old flats and stare over to the East London Stadium in Mile End, just waiting for the lights to come on. The minute they did, his face would light up too, like he had won the lottery – and that was it, coat on and off he'd go. He might ring me up later. 'Saw a right good player today, Harry. Cor blimey. Good kid playing for East London.' Half the kids I signed at West Ham already knew my dad from him standing in the rain on the touchline. I'd introduce him, and the lad would say, 'Oh, I know you – you used to watch my team play on a Sunday.' He never saw me win the FA Cup as a manager, but he saw Jamie play for England and captain Liverpool, and he absolutely loved that. His whole weekend was taken up watching Jamie play, and his week was taken up planning it. If Jamie was away at Newcastle at 4 p.m. on a Sunday, Dad would find a way of being there.

As for me, I think I'll always at least watch football, no matter what. Even when I've retired, I'd go to see Bournemouth every Saturday, whatever division they are in. We'll play them twice this coming season with Queens Park Rangers, and that will be a strange feeling. I've never played them in the league before, only in the FA Cup with West Ham. No matter what the future holds for me as a manager, I will always enjoy going to a match. I find it quite relaxing to watch a team that isn't my own – I enjoyed my brief time as an adviser at Bournemouth. I had the best of both worlds – I was involved, without the pressure.

And QPR? Nothing would give me more pleasure now than to turn it around at that club. I spent all summer trying to remedy our problems, shifting certain players out, getting others with the right attitude in. As I suspected, it wasn't easy. Clubs want to do everything through the loan system these days. Napoli wanted to take Júlio César, our Brazilian international goalkeeper, but only for a season. What use it that to us? They have him a year and then he returns to Rangers on the same astronomical wages. I wasn't standing for that – particularly as Napoli had just received £55 million for Edinson Cavani. It wasn't as if they were short of cash. They took Pepe Reina on loan instead – maybe Liverpool don't need the money as Rangers do.

The close season was a frustrating time for me as I spent most of it on crutches following a knee operation. With perfect timing, Adel Taarabt promptly got up to his old tricks. He turned up late for our training camp in Devon, so we sent him home. There were the usual excuses, but we're not standing for it any more. There has to be a different attitude if Rangers are to return to the Premier League. I know some of these players think they are better than this division, but I've been down there, and I know there are teams and players that will eat you alive if you are not fully committed. Our priority is to get rid of the troublemakers. Get rid of them, before they get rid of us. And we're doing it, slowly but surely.

Nothing would give me greater pleasure than to get QPR back into the Premier League. I've had more rows with chairmen than any manager in history, but my current employers are genuinely nice people, and they deserve to have more fun with their football club than they've had so far. The fans have been great, too. The biggest challenge at Rangers is finding and building a united squad, capable of winning promotion. I have enough faith in my ability to believe I can do that – and I'm realistic enough to acknowledge that if I do not, I probably won't get another season at QPR. Now I am starting life in the Championship, people think I might be bitter about the way it ended at Tottenham, but life is too short to think like that. Last season, I became caught up in what was interpreted as a row with my successor at Tottenham, André Villas-Boas, but I can assure you I feel no antipathy towards him at all.

It was just before we played Chelsea on 2 January, and I was asked about Rafael Benítez's prospects as interim manager at Stamford Bridge. 'You'd have to be a real dope to mess it up with that group of players,' I said. 'He has walked into a squad of Champions League winners – you've got to say he's got a chance.' The next day, the newspapers interpreted this as a dig at Villas-Boas, who had been sacked as Chelsea manager the previous season. Nothing could have been further from my mind. I was talking about the potential at a club like Chelsea, versus that at QPR. If you take over Chelsea's squad you've got a huge advantage – you would have to be pretty silly to get into trouble if you can call on Juan Mata, Eden Hazard and Frank Lampard. I wasn't even thinking about André at the time – and when we played Tottenham I made sure he knew that. Why should I hold a grudge against Villas-Boas? Did I think Tottenham were not going to replace me? All managers can only work with what they've got – that was my point. Taking over Tottenham, bottom of the table, and taking over QPR in the same position were totally different jobs for me, because of the quality of the players. There were easy solutions at Tottenham – and a permanent struggle at Rangers. I would have thought that was easy to understand.

I'm 66 now. I was 36 when I got my first job at Bournemouth. Looking back, what would I tell that young man now? What would I do differently? Certainly, I would counsel against being so hot-headed with chairmen. When I think back to how I used to speak to the business people who owned football clubs, I wince. I never saw it from their point of view, never appreciated that they were making a commitment to the club, too. I viewed every argument in simple terms, black and white, right and wrong; those who knew football versus the amateurs. If the boss said something daft, I was on him, and that wasn't helpful – to the club, or to me, really. Those guys have still got the power and will wait for the right moment to get their own back. Certainly at West Ham I was too confrontational, and it cost me in the end.

It's an idea to think before speaking to the press, too. Not because I've been stitched up, but because a flippant aside or a one-liner can sometimes cause more trouble than it is worth. The number of times I've seen something in headlines the next day and thought, 'Harry, son, what have you done?' I like to have a laugh, I like to make a joke, but sometimes that means people think I am not as serious about the game as others. I listen to some managers talking bullshit, but because they keep a straight face, they have a reputation as serious football men. I couldn't do that but maybe if I engaged the brain before speaking a few times, I wouldn't have so many rows.

Thinking it over, my management style hasn't really changed. I've had to adapt to deal with foreign players and different football cultures, but I'm the same person in the dressing room after a match. I wasn't one to rant and rave when I started out at Bournemouth, and I'm not now. I booted some sandwiches over Don Hutchison once, when I was West Ham manager, but that was about it. He didn't run with the left-back in the last minute and Southampton scored. I kicked this plate off the table and they all landed on his head. John Moncur got up to pick one off for a laugh, and I went for him, too. I ranted at him for about a minute before he could get a word in. 'Boss, what have I done?' he said. 'I was the sub. You didn't even put me on.' That's why I try not to lose my temper too much – you end up making no sense. (He was funny, John. He used to sit on the bench, desperate to get on to earn his appearance money. We'd be winning 3–0 at home, and there would be this constant chatter behind me. 'Come on, Harry. Put me on. I'm not earning the dough this lot are earning, am I? I need the money, come on, put me on.' I'd finally relent with about five minutes to go and, first tackle, wallop, booked. I think he played nine matches in a row for us once and got booked ten times.)

Fighting with the players has never been part of my make-up, really. I can't throw a decent punch, for a start, but screaming at them doesn't work, either. Those days have gone. I know Tony Pulis at Stoke City had a few old fashioned tear-ups, but you can't do it now. You'd lose the dressing room very quickly if you were too much that way. Jim Smith would tell me I was too laid back with the players, he thought I should lose my temper more. Compared to Jim, I'd say every manager is laid back. Some of the things he used to say to players came as a shock, even to me. He'd open with the C word and go from there – and you had to look lively or there would be a teacup on your nut.

There is a time for reading the riot act, but praise is important, too. Bobby Moore said something that stuck with me and has been a big help throughout my management career. We played a game one night and he was unbelievably good, absolutely outstanding, never put a foot wrong. And I told him so. He seemed really grateful, really pleased to hear it. 'Harry,' he said. 'You know in all the time I've been here, Ron Greenwood has never said, "Well done," to me. Not once. We all need to hear that.' He wasn't knocking Ron – Ron was a great coach and a nice man – but Ron just thought that Bobby was such a brilliant player, and his ability was so obvious, that he didn't need a pat on the back. He took him for granted because he was West Ham's captain and England's captain – but no matter who you are there is nothing like having someone put their arm around you and say, "Great job today." I have never forgotten that conversation.

So, one last Joe Fagan story, this one seen with my own eyes. I was managing at Bournemouth, and we were trying to sign Roger Brown, a big centre-half, from Fulham. I travelled up with Stuart Morgan, my assistant, to watch him play against Liverpool in a League Cup replay. We were sitting in the directors' box and Joe Fagan, the Liverpool manager, sat in front of us. I heard him tell people he didn't like the view from the dug-out at Craven Cottage, and he could see more from up there. Suddenly, a voice says, 'Hello, Joe,' and he turns around to see another chap sitting there, about the same age. 'Blimey! Hello, Billy!' says Joe, and it transpires from their conversation that they were in the army together, obviously big pals back then, but haven't met in years. They never stopped talking the whole game. 'Do you ever see Charlie?' 'No, he's dead. I saw Mickey last year, though.' 'Oh, how's Mickey? Remember when …' And out it all came, all these war stories. The sergeant did this, and this one did that, and in the meantime the game was going on with Gerry Peyton having to perform absolute heroics in the Fulham goal. (Liverpool got through eventually, Graeme Souness scored in extra-time.) The half-time whistle blew and that was Joe's queue to go to work. 'Anyway, Billy, it's been great to see you, keep in touch.' 'See you later, Joe, good luck with the game.' And off he went.

Stuart Morgan looked at me. We were both naïve young coaches. 'He hasn't watched a minute of that,' he said. 'What's he going to say to them?'

'He's the manager of Liverpool,' I said. 'Souness, Lawrenson, Hansen, Dalglish. He'll just tell them to keep going.'

And that's what I'll do. Keep going. Joe Fagan knew the score. His players were in another world, so the rest of us would just have to work that little harder. And keep managing.

PICTURE CREDITS

INDEX

(the initials HR refer to Harry Redknapp)

TOTTENHAM HOTSPUR v. WEST HAM UNITED

FOOTBALL LEAGUE, DIVISION I   **KICK-OFF 3 p.m.**

TODAY'S LINE-UP

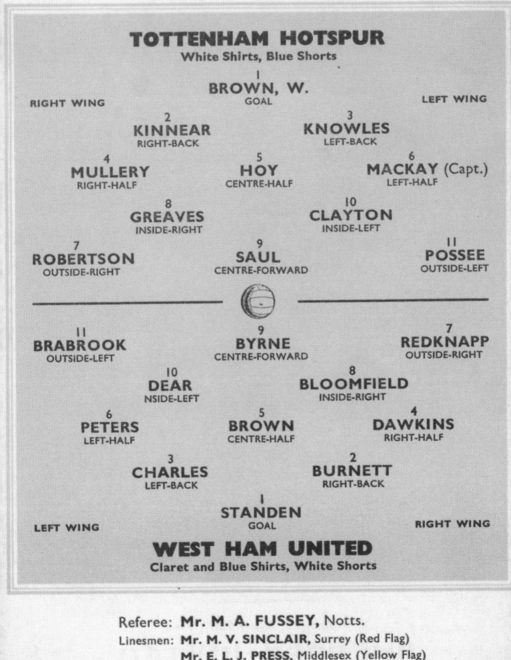

TOTTENHAM HOTSPUR
White Shirts, Blue Shorts

1
BROWN, W.
GOAL

RIGHT WING   LEFT WING

2
KINNEAR
RIGHT-BACK

3
KNOWLES
LEFT-BACK

4
MULLERY
RIGHT-HALF

5
HOY
CENTRE-HALF

6
MACKAY (Capt.)
LEFT-HALF

8
GREAVES
INSIDE-RIGHT

10
CLAYTON
INSIDE-LEFT

7
ROBERTSON
OUTSIDE-RIGHT

9
SAUL
CENTRE-FORWARD

11
POSSEE
OUTSIDE-LEFT

11
BRABROOK
OUTSIDE-LEFT

9
BYRNE
CENTRE-FORWARD

7
REDKNAPP
OUTSIDE-RIGHT

10
DEAR
NSIDE-LEFT

8
BLOOMFIELD
INSIDE-RIGHT

6
PETERS
LEFT-HALF

5
BROWN
CENTRE-HALF

4
DAWKINS
RIGHT-HALF

3
CHARLES
LEFT-BACK

2
BURNETT
RIGHT-BACK

1
STANDEN
GOAL

LEFT WING   RIGHT WING

WEST HAM UNITED
Claret and Blue Shirts, White Shorts

Referee: **Mr. M. A. FUSSEY**, Notts.
Linesmen: **Mr. M. V. SINCLAIR**, Surrey (Red Flag)
Mr. E. L. J. PRESS, Middlesex (Yellow Flag)

Substitutes: (*Home Club*).................................... (*Visiting Club*)...................................